Hardcore Punk in the
Age of Reagan

Hardcore Punk in the Age of Reagan

The Lyrical Lashing of an American Presidency

Robert Fitzgerald

The University of North Carolina Press CHAPEL HILL

This book was published with the assistance of the Authors Fund of The University of North Carolina Press.

© 2025 Robert Fitzgerald
All rights reserved
Set in Merope Basic by Westchester Publishing Services
Manufactured in the United States of America

Library of Congress Cataloging-in-Publication Data
Names: Fitzgerald, Robert (Robert James), author.
Title: Hardcore punk in the age of Reagan : the lyrical lashing of an American presidency / Robert Fitzgerald.
Description: Chapel Hill : University of North Carolina Press, [2025] | Includes bibliographical references and index.
Identifiers: LCCN 2024045136 | ISBN 9781469685441 (cloth) | ISBN 9781469685458 (paperback) | ISBN 9781469685465 (epub) | ISBN 9781469687599 (pdf)
Subjects: LCSH: Reagan, Ronald—Songs and music—History and criticism. | Punk rock music—United States—History and criticism. | Rock music—United States—1981–1990—History and criticism. | Punk culture—United States—History—20th century. | Punk rock music—Political aspects—United States. | Protest songs—United States—20th century—History and criticism. | United States—Politics and government—1981–1989. | BISAC: MUSIC / Ethnomusicology | SOCIAL SCIENCE / Popular Culture
Classification: LCC ML3534.3 .F575 2025 | DDC 782.42166—dc23/eng/20241015
LC record available at https://lccn.loc.gov/2024045136

Cover art: Ronald Reagan, 1982. Reagan White House Photographs, White House Photographic Collection, January 20, 1981–January 20, 1989. Courtesy of the National Archives via Wikimedia Commons.

For product safety concerns under the European Union's General Product Safety Regulation (EU GPSR), please contact gpsr@mare-nostrum.co.uk or write to The University of North Carolina Press and Mare Nostrum Group B.V., Mauritskade 21D, 1091 GC Amsterdam, The Netherlands.

For Teresa, Patrick, Delaney, and Devin

Contents

Introduction 1

CHAPTER ONE
Reagan's In 10

CHAPTER TWO
Only in America 36

CHAPTER THREE
Fuck Armageddon . . . This Is Hell 52

CHAPTER FOUR
Religious Vomit 75

CHAPTER FIVE
War Is Bad 106

CHAPTER SIX
Police Story 127

CHAPTER SEVEN
Guilty of Being White 146

Outro 168

Acknowledgments 183
Appendix 185
Notes 195
Bibliography 217
Index 227

A gallery of images begins on page 101.

Hardcore Punk in the Age of Reagan

Introduction

> Americans live in a Reaganized America.
> —GIL TROY

> [Hardcore] punk named Reagan as public enemy number one.
> —DEWAR MACLEOD

A Child of Light

On June 5, 2004, at his home in Bel Air, California, Ronald Wilson Reagan passed away. Diagnosed a decade earlier with Alzheimer's, he was ninety-three, making him the oldest president in the nation's history at the time of his death. In a public letter he said this day would come, and no one was to worry. All would be well. "When the Lord calls me home, whenever that may be," he wrote, "I will leave with the greatest love for this country of ours and eternal optimism for its future. . . . I know that for America there will always be bright days ahead." Reagan's faith in the nation was unwavering, his belief that the future always held something good in store unshakable even in the face of the degenerative disease that would plague him the last years of his life. He may have been dying, but his dream of America never would.[1]

After being displayed at the Ronald Reagan Presidential Library not far from his California home, his casket was flown to Washington, DC, on June 9, where he lay in state in the rotunda of the Capitol Building for two days of public viewing. He was the first in over fifteen years to be afforded the honor. Over 100,000 had visited him at his library. Another hundred thousand-plus did so in the rotunda. He was revered by many in life, and they came in droves to pay their respects now that he was gone, including four former presidents, many members of Congress, and an assortment of governors who attended the service held in his honor. Dignitaries or their representatives from across the globe came as well, including former Soviet President Mikhail Gorbachev, with whom he had forged a friendship, helping to bring an end to the Cold War, the capstone of his presidency. They were all there as extras in the final scene of a life that appeared to be as close to a Hollywood fairy tale as one could make it.

Of the eulogies given at the service, it was former UK Prime Minister Margaret Thatcher's that most reaffirmed the iconic stature of the man who served eight years in the White House during one of the world's most trying times. "Ronald Reagan knew his own mind," she remarked. "He had firm principles and, I believe, right ones. He expounded them clearly. He acted upon them decisively." It was Reagan, according to Thatcher, present but unable to speak live due to health issues, who through a candid discourse showed resolve in his dealings with the Soviet Union. He welcomed them to the table but on his terms, unyielding yet with compassion and understanding. His was a "large-hearted magnanimity" and American to the core. "With the lever of American patriotism, he lifted up the world," Thatcher praised. And now the world was watching in grief and with adoration, honoring him as the model of principled leadership all should look to for guidance.[2]

As the service concluded, one thing was clear, at least to those in attendance. To them, Reagan's apparent selflessness, dedication to service, and optimism were the source of his greatness. "If you have ever known a child of light, it was Ronald Reagan," former senator and presiding minister John Danforth remarked to close the ceremony. "He was aglow with it. He had no dark side, no scary, hidden agenda. What you saw, was what you got. And what you saw was the sure sign of inner light, the twinkle in the eye." With a final prayer the service was over, the casket removed to Andrews Air Force Base where it would depart for California and its final resting place at the Reagan Library.[3]

Punk's Not Dead, Reagan Is!

Not everyone shared the same feelings about Reagan's passing or the way his legacy was being framed. Of the critical responders, none matched the bitterness of those who, having railed against him while president, refused to let up now that he was dead. To them, Reagan was no sacrosanct idol to be posthumously lionized. In their youth, he had represented everything that was wrong with America. He had no inner light they could see, no twinkle in his eye they would recognize. Rather than joining the Reagan Revolution, they had started one of their own with him as the common enemy. Theirs began in the 1970s as Reagan emerged onto the national political scene; it gained serious momentum during the years of his first administration. They hated Reagan then, and they weren't going to engage in adulation now that he was dead. They were punks and their response to his passing was exactly what one could expect.

Less than twenty-four hours after Reagan's death, *Maximumrocknroll* (*MRR*), one of the leading punk rock zines first issued in the second year of his presidency, raged against Reagan with its weekly radio show. "The Yay He Is Dead . . . Reagan Special" featured a playlist of anti-Reagan songs by bands from the heyday of hardcore, an aggressive style of punk emerging simultaneously with his ascendancy, whose lyrics left little to the imagination in terms of what they thought about him. Beginning with 1983's "I Shot Reagan" by the Suicidal Tendencies, a band from Venice, California, who, according to punk lore, had changed the president's name to "the Devil" on the album sleeve after a visit from the FBI, the *MRR* show went through twenty-five songs, each with a special message for or about the former president. For many listeners, this was a clear reminder regarding their feelings for the fortieth occupant of the White House. For them, the two decades that had passed had done nothing to lessen their hatred, and the playlist that day made sure they hadn't forgot.[4]

"Fuck, Shit, I Hate Reagan," "Reagan Sux," and "Ronaldo Hitler" were just a few of the songs that *MRR* selected for the show, their point enunciated loud and clear. Ironically, the final one was "Kinky Sex Makes the World Go Around" by San Francisco's Dead Kennedys, a four-minute mock telephone conversation between the US secretary of war and the UK prime minister—sounding a lot like Margaret Thatcher—about staging a war to ensure corporate global dominance. It had been released in 1987, a year that saw the Iron Lady visit Reagan as a gesture of support during the Iran-Contra scandal, the lowest point in his presidency. While the twenty-five songs that made the cut appear to be a plentiful bunch, alone ample evidence of the disgust punk bands felt about Reagan, they are examples of only a few released during his time in office. If sheer volume is a barometer, then it is clear that punks in the '80s hated everything about Reagan, and *MRR* made sure the day following his death their listeners remembered.

Two months after the radio show, *MRR* released a special issue titled *Punk's Not Dead, Reagan Is*. Its black-and-white cover featured a collage of photos of a jovial Reagan appearing exuberant at the news of his own passing. Inside were statements by such seminal figures from the '80s punk scene as Jello Biafra of Dead Kennedys and Dave Dictor of M.D.C. (Millions of Dead Cops) on Reagan and the era that now bears his name. Angered by the constant commenting on TV surrounding his death, Biafra summed up his feelings with typical punk candor. "He was an old man, for Christ's sake, and while he was alive, he fucked over millions and millions of people deliberately." In case that wasn't enough of a reminder, guest columnist Mike Thorn added,

"Reagan died, and with him so did, seemingly, the knowledge of what a totally scum-sucking, sack of human garbage he was." He may have passed away, but MMR, long a standard source of insight for many in the punk scene, refused to let it happen without a proper invective.[5]

"The Great Unremembering" was what Eirck [sic] Lyle called Reagan's death in his contribution to the issue, the last hoorah in a post-presidency that seemed to whitewash anything and everything he had ever done. "[It] had seemed that as Reagan, the man, drifted towards complete senility," Lyle wrote, "the nation drifted with him into a casual fantasy world of his presidency." Fantasizing about being at the funeral procession, Lyle yearned to spit on Reagan's coffin, dragged away while yelling the names of punk legends like Will Shatter of Flipper and Minutemen's D. Boon, who died long before they should have, during Reagan's years in the White House. Like others, Lyle celebrated Reagan's death with some street art. "Fuck Reagan!," simple, callous, and yet ironically nostalgic, was the first of many tags graffitied on the walls of San Francisco that evening. "Punk's Not Dead, but Reagan Is!" found itself onto quite a few as well, a fitting punk rock requiem for a man who, although no longer living, still stirred up feelings of hatred and rage in many who had been in the scene during the 1980s.[6]

Fifteen years after leaving the White House and ten since being diagnosed with Alzheimer's, Reagan still brought out in some a level of disgust unmatched by opponents of all other presidents save maybe Donald Trump. To many who lived through and followed the punk bands of that decade, his death was no time to forget, to wax nostalgic about his years as president, but to recollect honestly about the nation he once led and shaped. As president, he embodied an America many at the time opted out of, rebelling against rather than uncritically accepting life within. How they remembered him would stay true to how they *actually* remembered him. Because for them, America in the '80s was a frustrating variation on the tale of two cities—the worst, rather than the best, of times. Much of the fault for this, in their opinion, fell squarely on the shoulders of the fortieth president and the revolution he brought with him into office.

While the ruthless but honest response from *MRR* to Reagan's passing might be shocking to some and downright mean-spirited to others, to those familiar with the punk scene of the 1980s this was par for the course. It was a decade that would not only be defined by his presidency, but also by the unique musical movement "fueled by young male anxieties about Reagan's victory," as cultural historian Kevin Mattson described it in his recent assessment of that time. During those years, punk bands in cities and towns across the country took aim at Reagan and the idea of America sold by his supporters. Small yet vibrant scenes emerged, challenging the communal norms and social values projected upon them by the popular media and consumer culture connected to the Reagan Revolution that many felt they just couldn't escape. They were loud and violent, evasive and independent, but also critical in terms of the message they pronounced. This could be witnessed in the clothes they wore and how they physically presented themselves, in the plethora of zines that bound the various cities and scenes together, in the shows they promoted and venues they gathered at, but most importantly in the music. In the last of these, particularly the lyrics, is evidence of a reaction to Reaganism that went unmatched at that time, written by those who refused to be seduced by the glitz, glamour, and grandeur that surrounded his coming into office, as well as the conservative, conformist, and consumerist culture that came to characterize his time as president. They were coarse yet candid, angry yet unique, and with a certain sense of authenticity that, although hard to explain, can be sensed by the listener. Left out of most written works on the era, especially those about Reagan, they deserve attention and inclusion as part of an important moment in the history of culture in the United States. Punk, to quote Mattson again, "expressed a hope for a world different from the decadence that Reagan . . . stood for." My hope is that this book turns more people to the music when they want to understand what life in America was like during his years in office.[7]

A Unique Legacy

Songs written by punk bands during Reagan's presidency tell an interesting story. Some expressed a dreary sense of disaffection with life in America. "I'm walking down a darkened street / Ignoring everyone I meet / Won't speak to me, they can't see me / In isolated apathy" and "Ain't got no job / My life's a drag / I'm just a waste / Put me in a bag" are from two of many that reflect this sentiment. Others were more personal, with lines like "Right here, all by myself / I ain't got no one else / The situation is bleeding me / There's no relief for a person like me," one of several statements of frustration and hopelessness from bands existing in a world where few felt a better tomorrow was possible. Although in 1984 Reagan would proclaim it was "Morning in America," the lyrics of too many punk songs like these suggested otherwise, and they should be used more often by historians to better understand how some young people in particular felt at that time. And while most presidents have witnessed some form of cultural backlash, Reagan is a special case due to the bands whose lyrics went straight for the jugular, musically haranguing him more than any other resident of the White House before or after. His name found its way into the titles and lyrics of songs by groups throughout the country and world, with lines like "We are the sons of Reagan, Heil!" and "You're fucked up Ronnie / You're not gonna last," common on albums released during the decade. Even his near-death experience at the hand of a deranged gunman was fair game, with more than the FBI-warned Suicidal Tendencies waxing musical about it. "He shot Reagan, he shot the pig, didn't he?" was from one of many songs that made the attempt on his life and actions of John Hinckley Jr., the would-be assassin, something to lyrically memorialize.[8]

"In the punk milieu," wrote Gerfried Ambrosch in his book on the poetics of punk, "the lyrics have a prominent status as a means of conveying messages and sharing ideas." While zines and show fliers across the country depicted Reagan in their own abusive way, the lyrics that made direct reference to him are uniquely revelatory. This book highlights those that saw Reagan as a dangerous conservative who would take the country down a dark path, and shows why they are important documents in our recent musical and political past. They show us the thoughts and feelings of artists reacting to their sociopolitical environment in real time, and, as the genre of punk prizes honesty and forthrightness, we get those essentially uncensored. What they tell us is how young adults—granted, most of them white men from middle-class, suburban backgrounds—reacted to one of the most influential and divisive leaders this country has ever seen, and how these seemingly simple lyrics sketch out a complex, musically inspired countermovement that is as canonical in the American songbook as the folk and rock protest music that preceded it. They have an invigorating essence that imagery just can't produce; they paint a picture through words that are strong and straightforward regarding the message about Reagan they aimed to send.[9]

Besides going directly after the president, punks during the 1980s took aim at other authority figures and wrote songs that served as meaningful testimonies about personal experiences. "Don't make a sound, we'll bash your teeth / You've got no rights, you're just a creep" is one of a plethora of lines that drew attention to the vicious treatment punks (and many others) received at the hands of law enforcement. Concerning the threat of constant war and the chance of being drafted, any one of a number of albums would have a lyric like "We don't want no fuckin' war / And we don't want to fight no more." Religion was also put in the crosshairs of punk bands as the Christian Right became more politically active around the election of 1980, prompting lines such as "God is broke / The well ran dry / So pay up while you can / Or you'll end up in hell." The church, the cops, the government . . . all found themselves targets of a punk lyrical assault that deserves more attention than has been given by those writing about the Reagan Era.[10]

America, as kids in punk scenes across the country saw it, was under attack in the 1980s, and it was the Reagan Revolution doing the pummeling. "I had a violent hatred of Reagan as a teenager," reflected punk chronicler George Hurchalla, "partly due to a teenager's overblown feelings about everything but mostly to do with a reaction to the insanity, the collective delusion, that he was the leading the country into." With limited agency (albeit with the white middle-class privilege to do so), those teenagers responded the only way they felt they could—through music. Their lyrics offer historians evidence of a unique legacy to consider when studying the Age of Reagan, particularly a backlash that has often been ignored in mainstream writings about the fortieth president. The attention they received was almost always negative, their music interpreted as the rantings of ignorant teenagers and dismissed as nothing more than an immature episode of angst and aggression. But there is so much more to them than that, and it is in their music where this can be best witnessed. While most Americans went about their lives uninterruptedly during Reagan's years in office, they refused to be subdued and silent. In song, they lamented lyrically about a world turned upside down and the man they thought was most responsible for this. This book suggests their words are insightful and worthy of attention.[11]

A Few Final Notes

The term *punk* can be problematic when describing a style of music. As Craig O'Hara stated in *The Philosophy of Punk*, "The major problem with trying to explain punk is that it is not something that fits neatly into a box or categories . . . [and] any project that tries to define punk or explain it must do so with very broad brush strokes." In the literature surrounding it readers come across so many variations it can be hard to keep track. Proto-punk, post-punk, hardcore, emocore, queercore, thrash . . . all are used to describe music that is at its most basic level opposition oriented. While these words might be used in the following pages, *punk* is the dominant descriptor. It won't be defined but rather explained as something that can be witnessed through lyrics, where its urgency and defiant tendencies are best experienced. For the reader still wanting to know exactly what punk is, it might be worth taking a page from former US Supreme Court Justice Potter Stewart, who in a case concerning hardcore pornography famously wrote, "I know it when I see it." Regarding punk, you know it when you hear it, and with the songs analyzed in the following pages, you really do.[12]

Punk scholar Kevin Dunn, describing its significance as an oppositional movement, once wrote that punk "represented not just a form of musical expression but a social and political disruption" and that punks "feel empowered to articulate" their frustrations in many forms, including music. The punk music considered in the chapters that follow, evidence of the empowerment described by Dunn, is that produced primarily by members of Generation X (the generation, not the band), the louder, faster, and more aggressive stuff from the 1980s that emerged in the wake of bands like the Bad Brains on the East Coast and Black Flag out west. It's often described as *hardcore*, but not all would have appreciated that moniker. Nor likely would all accept only being called punk. So be it. *Hardcore Punk in the Age of Reagan* recognizes that while the bands that recorded throughout the decade were stylistically different, lyrically they all were oppositional. They all were uncompromising in their lack of inhibition. They all were angry. They all were confrontational. In that regard, they were all punk.[13]

Punk music has loud guitars, a pulsating bass, furious drums, and bellowing vocals. Because these can tend to create an indecipherable mess, particularly to an untrained ear, the words often get left by the wayside. They shouldn't. The lyrics from punk songs offer us a rich repository of resources and should be used to make sense of the era in question rather than remain marginalized, as they often are, as the rantings of a few disturbed kids looking for something to do. We need to see their lyrics for what they are: primary source documents of a key cultural moment in the history of the United States and a first-responder, artist-based reaction to the Reagan Revolution. First-time listeners will likely not recognize this, their ability to judge meaning and importance clouded by the raucousness of the music, faster and more intense than any other they have likely listened to, the often inarticulate quality of the vocal tracks, screamed in ways that make deciphering nearly impossible, and the aggressive lyrics that speak truth to power concerning the hatred these kids had for Reagan, Reaganism, and life in Reaganland. Readers will hopefully be able to see through all of this and that my ruminations about these songs are not just rooted in my passion for them as a fan, but rather in my interpretation of them as a valuable part of the historical record. Punk music is the protest music of the 1980s. Punks are, to quote intellectual historian Jennifer Ratner-Rosenhagen, "interesting people we might not know otherwise but for the records of their minds they left behind." Their lyrics are a valuable part of a collection of "sources that can awaken us to all the ways Americans have constructed their realities and made meaning of their lives." To better understand the Reagan Revolution, we should listen to what they had to say.[14]

CHAPTER ONE

Reagan's In

> We must act today in order to preserve tomorrow.
> —RONALD REAGAN

> Reagan's in, we're going for good.
> —WASTED YOUTH

The Inevitable Decline (of Western Civilization)

On January 11, 1989, Ronald Reagan delivered his farewell address to the nation. For eight years he had been president and it was time to return to his California ranch in the Santa Ynez Mountains. Reflecting on his two terms, he clarified for posterity what exactly had transpired during his time in office. "They called it the Reagan revolution," he declared, "but for me it always seemed more like the great discovery, a rediscovery of our values and common sense." In that moment, according to Reagan biographer Lou Cannon, the president "spoke to the future of America with a compelling vision of the past." As Reagan proudly reminded listeners, "We meant to change a nation and instead, we changed the world." These changes were set in motion eight years earlier with his defeat of Jimmy Carter in the election of 1980, one of the most consequential in this nation's history. In many ways, the world would never be the same.[1]

While Reagan shellacked Carter in the electoral college, 489 to 98, one of the largest margins of victory ever, he received slightly less than 51 percent of the popular vote. Though this was far from being a mandate of the people, this didn't prevent Republicans from initiating the revolution their president would claim eight years later as having changed both America and the world for the better. "Reagan's mandate was illusory," according to historian Gil Troy, but that didn't matter to him or his followers. As the "Great Communicator" he became known as, he convinced himself and many Americans that the direction he would lead the country was back to a time when it was strong and when they had faith not only in their leaders, but more so in themselves.[2]

It was during his first inaugural address that Reagan attempted to reassure the people all was well. "We are not, as some would have us believe, doomed to inevitable decline," he told them. Faith, hope, confidence, heroic effort, and a sincere sense of patriotic duty, instead of relying on the government, would unleash a flood of creative energy and activity, exactly what the country needed to overturn the myriad failures of the previous decade. With a return to good old-fashioned American values like hard work, dedication, and pride in oneself, the greatness of the nation would be restored. "We must act today in order to save tomorrow," he told over 41 million people who viewed his inauguration. Such rhetoric, assertive yet optimistic, was the foundation upon which the Reagan Revolution would be constructed. Little did he know that across the nation a musical movement was gearing up, oppositional in its attitude, assertive but less hopeful, and intent on smashing the very thing he aimed to build.[3]

Hardcore Comes to Town

By the time Reagan was elected, punk, which had been around for a few years, according to Shayna Maskell in her work on the DC scene, started "to reek of mainstream respectability." What emerged was hardcore, a "rebellion against punk," but still punk. The seedlings of this more aggressive version had been sown with a number of groups releasing foundational albums as the decades changed. Those recorded were some of the first to draw attention to the political, social, and economic concerns elevated during Reagan's rise to power. Their processing of the coming revolution was impressive, and their songs served as prototypes for ones written in the years that followed. Although they didn't directly attack Reagan the way their successors did, they still took an aggressive lyrical stance in opposition to the America shaping up as he rose to power. In doing so they influenced kids across the country, with scenes emerging not only in the usual coastal cities, but in places like Boise, Akron, Lawrence, Rapid City, Tulsa, and Peoria. As Reagan was getting set to enter the White House, hardcore punk was entering spaces where kids were primed and ready to engage in the most forceful musical assault witnessed in American history.[4]

One of the early bands to lay this foundation was the Bad Brains, whose sociopolitical lyrics, according to Maskell, represented a continuation of the themes found in 1960s folk music—"alienation, antiauthoritarianism, class struggle, and the fight for marginalized voices to be heard"—which bands that followed would emulate. With their 1980 debut single "Pay to Cum," they are arguably the most significant of these groups, their music, style, and attitude influencing kids everywhere. Too many punk bands to count formed after seeing them play, their furious and breakneck speed becoming what many aimed to emulate. Henry Rollins, the future frontman for State of Alert (S.O.A.) and Black Flag, said after seeing the band in 1979, "['Pay to Cum'] was perhaps the most influential song of my life." While punk was primarily a youth movement led by white suburban kids like Rollins, the Bad Brains were an all–African American group whose frantic pace was described by one journalist as "lobotomy by jackhammer, like a whirlpool bath in a cement mixer, like orthodontic surgery by Black & Decker, like making love to a buzzsaw." Though they would eventually move to New York City, it was in Washington, DC, that they would hone their sound and become instrumental in helping shape the intense and aggressive musical style that Reagan-Era punk rock would be known for. The nation's capital would become a 1980s punk epicenter, and the Bad Brains had much to do with that.[5]

On the other side of the country, the year of Reagan's election saw bands in his home state of California put out some of the most important records in punk history. In San Francisco, Dead Kennedys, with leader singer Jello Biafra coming off an unsuccessful bid for the city's mayorship, released *Fresh Fruit for Rotting Vegetables*. Music journalist Alex Ogg described the album's significance as a transitional record, stating, "For many who believed that the movement was more than a showy outcrop of the unhindered continuum of rock 'n' roll, *Fresh Fruit* confirmed punk's potential to stand for something beyond the trappings of fashion and faux rebellion." With songs like "Kill the Poor," "California über Alles," and "Holiday in Cambodia," the album is a pioneering work in the annals of punk, its pugnaciousness more than present in Biafra's lyrics. While Reagan was yet to find himself in the band's crosshairs, he soon would be.[6]

A few hours away in Southern California, Los Angeles also saw groundbreaking records released in the year prior to Reagan's presidency. The seaside city of Hermosa Beach was where Black Flag had formed four years earlier, and in 1980 they released the 12" EP *Jealous Again*. With Ron Reyes on vocals, the second of four lead singers the band would have, the record included such punk anthems as the title track, "No Values," "Revenge," and "White Minority," one of only a few songs that took on the issue of race directly at that time (and which will be discussed in a later chapter). Featured in Penelope Spheeris's film *The Decline of Western Civilization*, Black Flag quickly became one of the leading bands of the emerging hardcore punk scene. Renowned for their grueling touring schedule and willingness to play anywhere for anyone, they would help bring punk across the country and into the lives of kids looking for a new way to make meaning of what many saw as a meaningless world.

Beyond the Bad Brains, Dead Kennedys, and Black Flag, plenty of other bands released records prior to 1981 that deserve recognition as foundational for the Reagan-Era punk scene. In the Bad Brains' backyard, the Teen Idles, a short-lived band that would include two future members of Minor Threat, released the *Minor Disturbance* EP, a crucial moment in a scene whose impact would be felt well beyond the nation's capital. Back across the country in San Francisco, bands such as the Penelope Houston–fronted Avengers (*We Are the One* and *Avengers*), Negative Trend (*Negative Trend*), and the Nuns (*The Nuns*) released records with a faster-paced style that would soon become the norm of punk. In L.A. bands like the Weirdos (*Destroy All Music* and *We Got the Neutron Bomb*), the Germs (*GI*), and Middle Class (*Out of Vogue*) would all make records bands would later recognize as critical to their formation. The last of these, released in 1979, is considered by many to be the first hardcore punk release, its rapidity unmatched among bands at that time. These and many others laid the foundation for a punk revolution that would certainly find a catalyst in Reagan's presidential ascendancy.

Hardcore in '81

The year that Ronald Reagan entered the White House saw an incredible artistic outpouring of angry, aggressive, at times absurd, often violent, and almost always disaffection-driven music. As *MRR* stated years later, "The explosion of hardcore in the USA in 1981 occurred at just the right time in socio-cultural context to recruit to its ranks a legion of incredibly talented and creative people." That year, a plethora of bands released albums, not just in one location but throughout the country. "Spread it did," Kevin Mattson iterated in the aptly titled chapter of his book, "It Can and Will Happen Anywhere," and punk became a national movement. What emerged was a musical backlash to what historian Rick Perlstein described as America's rightward turn to conservatism, culminating in the election of Reagan in 1980. To understand just how important Reagan was to the punk scene in the early '80s, one need only take a quick musical tour through the country to see his immediate influence. Lyrics to the songs recorded are important, but a brief look at the sheer number of bands, songs, and records that Reagan seemingly willed into being as his presidency began is warranted.[7]

There is no better album to begin an analysis of Reagan-inspired punk music than the first recorded by the Los Angeles quartet Wasted Youth. Not to be confused with the New York or London bands of the same name, the West Coast group released a ten-song, fifteen-minute fulmination in 1981 aptly titled *Reagan's In*. Its album cover, one of the most recognizable in the history of punk rock (and one of a few that appear in this book), included the face of Reagan with a Charles Manson–like carving on his forehead of the band's WY symbol. The black-and-white drawing by famed punk and heavy metal artist Pushead is an iconic image of punk's assault on the fortieth president, his blackened eyes menacingly looking down upon a mohawked youth with a can of spray paint in one hand and what appears to be a razor blade in the other. The youth's T-shirt has a bulls-eye on it, a reminder of the negative attention punks commonly received for their clothing and hairstyles. Visually, the album cover clearly indicates how the band felt about Reagan in the White House. Coupled with songs like the title track, "Born Deprived," "Problem Child," and "Fuck Authority," the last of which frustratingly professes, "Officials give us too much shit / No longer can I deal with it," and it makes for an insightful early example of the attention bands would give the Reagan presidency and its impact on the nation.[8]

On the other side of the country, and in the wake of the Bad Brains, a number of bands recorded albums in the months immediately surrounding Reagan's election. Washington, DC, the heart of American politics, was a fitting place for the burgeoning movement, and a group of kids from the suburbs came together to form one of the most important independent record labels ever. Dischord, founded by Ian MacKaye and Jeff Nelson of Minor Threat, would be critical in the early days of hardcore punk in helping get music to a wider audience through mail distribution and nationwide touring. In 1981, on the heels of the success of the Teen Idles' release, MacKaye and Nelson would record the *Minor Threat* and *In My Eyes* EPs by their band Minor Threat; *Legless Bull* by Government Issue; *No Policy* by the Henry Rollins–fronted State of Alert; *IQ32* by the Maumee, Ohio, band Necros; *Possible* by the DC-based Youth Brigade; and a compilation of other local artists titled *Flex Your Head*. Each was catalytic in the growth of hardcore punk in the first half of the 1980s. And although only a few included personal affronts to Reagan, evidence of what Maskell describes as "the contradictions that imbue DC as a national and local space," all included songs whose lyrics offer insight into the disaffection of youth during the earliest moments of his first term. As MacKaye would both encourage and warn on the anthemic title track of his second band's first release—"Take your time / Try not to forget / We never will / We're just a minor threat!"[9]

With the capital scene gaining momentum, back in California bands released EPs and albums on their own independent labels as well. Frontier Records put out *Dance with Me*, the first full-length work by T.S.O.L. (True Sounds of Liberty) as well as the self-titled debut by the Adolescents. Agent Orange, part of a trio of bands with the Adolescents and Social Distortion to come out of the Orange County city of Fullerton, released their debut album *Living in Darkness* on the Hollywood-based Posh Boy Records. Also on Posh Boy, Shattered Faith recorded their first work with the songs "I Love America" and "Reagan Country," fitting reflections for the year of their release. Not far away in Long Beach, SST Records, owned by Black Flag guitarist Greg Ginn, had two releases by the now Henry Rollins–fronted troupe, *Six Pack* and *Damaged*, as well as *The Punch Line* by San Pedro's Minutemen and *Paganicons* by Saccharine Trust. In true do-it-yourself punk fashion, D. Boon and Mike Watt of the Minutemen helped start New Alliance Records under SST Records and released Manhattan Beach's Descendents' first EP, *Fat*, that same year. These bands and the many others that formed in and around Los Angeles would make Southern California a punk rock mecca throughout the decade.

A few hours north, San Francisco would also witness its own remarkable year of releases. The Jello Biafra–owned Alternative Tentacles put out Dead Kennedys' *In God We Trust, Inc.*, described by one writer as "a stage post for the coming 'hardcore' generation." It also had one of the most important punk compilation albums ever. *Let Them Eat Jellybeans!*, subtitled "17 Extracts from America's Darker Side," poked fun at Reagan's affinity for sweet treats while juxtaposing his administration with the reign of deposed and beheaded Louis XVI and Marie Antoinette of revolutionary-era France. The three and a half tons of red, white, and blue jellybeans that had been shipped to Washington, DC, for the president's inauguration, just one example of the opulence of that evening, had clearly not gone unnoticed. With songs by Black Flag, Bad Brains, Circle Jerks, and Dead Kennedys, as well as a host of other lesser-known bands, *Jellybeans!* provided listeners a unique look into Reagan-Era punk starting to form into the nationwide phenomenon it would soon become.[10]

While attention concerning the early days of hardcore punk is often centered on the East and West coastal scenes, things started to gain momentum as well in Texas after Reagan's election. In Houston, Really Red, who had appeared on the *Jellybeans!* compilation, released *Teaching You the Fear*, one of the most underrated albums from the era. The band, according to lead singer

U-Ron Bondage, was doing what many in scenes across the country were, "trying to make high-energy rock that might be a small catalyst to inspire people to start thinking and to start standing up for social justice and political change." With songs like "Too Political?," "Bored with Apathy," and the title track, the album did exactly that. Less well known than the East and West Coast bands who often receive the credit for the musical surge of the early '80s, Really Red is widely respected within the scene and by punk enthusiasts. In 2020, C.I.A. Records, which put out their '81 debut, released a thirty-nine-song tribute album called *Teaching You the Fear . . . Again*, which included one song, "Let the Night Roar (with Us)," by the 2018-formed and perfectly named band, Reagan Era Rejects.[11]

Also in 1981 and not far away in Austin, the Randy "Biscuit" Turner-fronted Big Boys' full-length album *Where's My Towel/Industry Standard* was put out along with M.D.C.'s (Millions of Dead Cops) 7" single "John Wayne Was a Nazi," released on lead singer Dave Dictor's independent label, R Radical Records. Dictor would be a leading figure in the lyrical haranguing of Reagan and Reaganism, and the band's self-titled album released the following year would be one of the most critical pieces of art produced in the movement. He, along with Jello Biafra, would also be instrumental in coordinating the Rock against Reagan shows held in the months leading up to election of 1984. The Big Boys and M.D.C. would be part of a thriving Austin movement that would also include bands like the Dicks, D.R.I. (Dirty Rotten Imbeciles), and Butthole Surfers. As one author noted about the city's early '80s scene, it "was a collection of artists looking for creative ways to express angst and disaffection toward mainstream culture." Even in Texas, life in Reaganland appeared to afford ample encouragement for punks to use music as an instrument of expression and an outlet for their frustrations.[12]

Up in New York, 1981 witnessed the formation of bands like Agnostic Front and the Cro-Mags, both instrumental in an important musical crossover movement: thrash, a hyper, sped-up, and even more intense form of punk that would gain a number of groups metal-label album deals by mid-decade. Others like New Jersey's Adrenalin O.D., Murphy's Law, The Undead, Urban Waste, and The Young and the Useless would release records shortly after forming that year. The last of these would include a young Adam Horovitz, future member of the Beastie Boys, a group that also formed in New York City around this time as a punk outfit. While most would not release material until the following year, one that did in '81 was Heart Attack, with its three-song 7" *God Is Dead*, a subject that would draw the attention of many bands, particularly in light of the public voice given to Christian

Right groups like the Moral Majority during Reagan's rise to power. Of all the New York bands formed at that time, the one with the best name was Queens' Reagan Youth, who would eventually record their 1984 classic album, *Youth Anthem for the New Order*. In true punk fashion, they would last only during Reagan's eight years as president, disbanding soon after the end of his second term.

The Northeast also saw punk grow around Boston in early '81, led by bands like Cape Cod's the Freeze, who had been part of Massachusetts' late-1970s scene, and new arrivals the F.U.'s, Gang Green, Jerry's Kids, and the Proletariat, all of which formed the year of Reagan's election. Each contributed songs to the critical compilation albums *This Is Boston, Not L.A.*, and *Unsafe at Any Speed*, both released the following year. Not long after, the F.U.'s would release *Kill for Christ*, while the Proletariat would record the *Distortion* EP on their Non-U Records label. Soon after came Jerry's Kids' *Is This My World?* as well as *Land of the Lost* by the Freeze, with a photo collage cover including the head of Reagan on a muscled body, all smiles, with what appears to be the Four Horsemen of the Apocalypse trampling over a barren wasteland. Like so much album artwork from the era, it offered a disconcerting visual interpretation of what was perhaps to come under Reagan's reign. On these albums would be songs like "Religion Is the Opium of the Masses," "Me Generation," "Build Me a Bomb," and "Days of Desperation," marking the early scene in Boston as a vibrant contributor to the growing punk movement at that time.

In the Midwest, the Chicago scene was taking off also, with a critical live album highlighting various bands, recorded at Oz, one of the few clubs in the city that opened its doors for punks to play. Featuring songs by Naked Raygun, Strike Under, the Effigies, and others, 1981's *Busted at Oz* is one of the earliest looks into a Windy City scene gaining momentum in the early years of the Reagan Era. With songs like "State of the Union" and "March Forth" by the Subverts, "Fucking Uniforms" and "Anarchy Song" by Strike Under, and "Bomb Shelter" by Naked Raygun, the album represents a strong collection of concerns by groups from a scene that tends to get overlooked in terms of musical contribution and importance. Nearly all on the record would put out albums in the months following Reagan's inauguration. That same year would see the formation of Articles of Faith, formed after frontman Vic Bondi had seen the Bad Brains play live in DC. By the end of the next year they would record their *What We Want Is Free* EP, described in *MRR* as full of "highly intelligent blasts . . . the music fast yet tight, the songs infectious." Interviewed in the first minutes of the documentary *American*

Hardcore, it was Bondi who set the tone for the film, describing the musical movement of the early 1980s as a direct reaction to the "Ronald Reagan white man order" his election aimed to restore in the country. Articles of Faith and their fellow Chicago bands were as much a part of this reaction as any others.[13]

Beyond Chicago, towns across the Midwest saw bands get into recording studios while Reagan was entering the White House. In Ohio, Dayton's Toxic Reasons put out the EP *Ghost Town* with its five-minute title track, an eternity for a punk song, expressing concern about living in a post-apocalyptic world, a feeling of dismay most groups sang about. Maumee's Necros released their *Sex Drive* EP, a four-song, four-and-a-half-minute, 7" record that included swift and stinging critiques of American culture such as "Police Brutality" and "Caste System." Not far away, Touch and Go Records, which grew out of the East Lansing fanzine by the same name, released the *Process of Elimination* EP highlighting Michigan bands like Negative Approach, Youth Patrol, Meatmen, Violent Apathy, and the Fix. Members of the first two had even started out a few months earlier under the name the Dead Reagans. Though not released until years later, the 1981 recordings of Detroit's Bored Youth were arguably some of the best from the state's scene. Songs such as "Bored Youth," "They Don't Have the Right," "No Chance," "Misfit," and "Outcast" are anthemic statements of ennui and angst that help explain the reasons why so many kids got into punk in the first place. Coupled with their Ohio and Illinois neighbors (as well as those that would form in Indiana, Minnesota, and Wisconsin, all of which had vibrant scenes), Michigan bands made the year of Reagan's election as meaningful a moment in the Midwest as did their coastal counterparts.

A few albums instrumental in the punk rock takeoff of 1981 were released by groups from Canada whose impact was felt beyond its border. Formed two years earlier in Vancouver, the Dayglo Abortions' debut album *Out of the Womb* came out with songs like "Scared of People," "Idiot," and "I Am My Own God." Most directed at the Reagan Revolution was "R.B.F.'s" or "Religious Bumfuck's," a verbal tirade against fundamentalism connecting the president to the rise of the Christian Right. Their second album, *Feed Us a Fetus*, included on its cover drawn likenesses of Reagan and the First Lady smiling over a plate with a late-term aborted fetus, sprinkled with jellybeans, flanked by a fork and knife. It stands as a grotesque and shocking depiction, a common approach on album artwork across scenes. Also from Vancouver was D.O.A., whose album *Hardcore '81* was released in April that year. Like their American counterparts, they didn't mince words when it came to lyrical expressions of disaffection and disappointment. With songs like "I Don't Give a Shit," "001 Loser's Club," and "Smash the State," the album was characteristic of the style of punk music its title helped name and shape. In the last of these, singer Joey Shithead expressed the frustrations felt by many youths, suggesting they "Smash the state" because of "the fascist rape" happening at that hands of Reagan, Canada's Pierre Trudeau, and Margaret Thatcher. In the song's final moments, he boldly announced a recourse for all their wrongdoing—"kill them all"—an exhortation specifically about Reagan a number of American bands would make as well.[14]

Reagan's In

Reagan and his conservative policies for sure ignited a musical movement in cities and towns across the United States. While presidents since have attracted attention, even from old guard groups still around like D.O.A., M.D.C., and Dead Kennedys' Jello Biafra, it remains Ronald Reagan, more than any other president, who captured the imaginations and intellectual ire of disaffected kids. He found himself in the crosshairs of punk bands, often with many mentioning him either by name in the title or somewhere in their lyrics. From critiquing specific aspects of his administration to rejoicing in the attempt made on his life, these songs cover a broad area of concern shared by many. The lyrics of Reagan-oriented releases are more than rage-filled rantings of kids. Rather, they are insightful statements of concern expressed through a musical style that was aggressive and violent, and through words that were often profane and macabre, at times witty and riddled with sarcasm, but always honest in terms of the anger and concern felt by those who wrote them. If punk was really about making the world a better place, the '80s version of it could not avoid the one person many felt was making it worse. To them, Reagan was the problem, and they made sure to let anyone listening know.

The punk lyrical haranguing of the fortieth president began almost immediately. With the release of its fifteen-minute classic, Wasted Youth helped make targeting the president a punk pastime for bands across the country. Beginning with the line "Reagan's in, we're going for good," the title track drew attention to the militarism of the Reaganites and the chance that young men, such as those in the band, would be drafted and sent off to war. Reagan had campaigned on a promise to end Selective Service, comparing it to what had been done in Nazi Germany. When he changed his mind after the election, punk bands, most of which included members of age to serve, took notice and quickly began labeling him a Nazi, likening him to Hitler, and characterizing his administration as fascist. (Songs concerning the draft are discussed in more detail in chapter 5.) The lyrics to "Reagan's In" warned listeners that "Reagan don't care, he won't fight / He'll try to send us with all his might," and one of the first, Wasted Youth, would not be the only band to enunciate this concern in song. Although there would be so many written about Reagan that it became a topic for some bands to parody (such as Chronic Sick with their 1983 track "Reagan Bands"), those from his years in the White House illuminate a certain anxiety surrounding his presidency as well as a sense of unity among punks that came with making him the primary target of their angst. As the enduring band NOFX later wrote, "Guess what, nostalgia sucks / But I miss songs about Reagan sucks." There would be plenty of those to go around.[15]

Along with Wasted Youth, another of Southern California's earliest bands recognized in Reagan's election a cause to write about. Self-described as one of the bands from that era that "live hard and fast, challenged authority, played loud, and ultimately defined the SoCal punk scene," their slower tempos and more melodic, yet darker, music offered a stark contrast to most punk groups emerging at that time. Their first release included "Reagan in '81," sometimes called "Reagan Country," with a far less aggressive tone than others, but still insightful in terms of concerns punks had about the incoming president. Beginning with the line "I close my eyes and yesterday he was finally here / Year one of the eighties is gone and the future is so clear," the song illuminates the anxiety surrounding Reagan's ascendancy and uncertainty as to what his first term had in store for the country, something felt not just by punk kids but by many Americans in the months following his inauguration. Although there was apparent clarity in terms of the immediate future, according to the band, "we'll just have to see" whether or not the "radical changes" brought in by our "American president, Hollywood star" will "bring our country back," a statement that rang far less critical than the message relayed by the many other bands attacking Reagan at that time.[16]

While most lyrically lambasted the president with a violent and hate-filled tone, Shattered Faith's effort is a pensive reflection about the changes they perceived were coming at the time of Reagan's election. While the song ends with the continuous chant of "Ronald/Reagan," compared to the other anti-Reagan anthems of that time it is a relatively benign critique. It was the other song on their release, "I Love America," that harshly assaulted the president, his "regime" described as a modern Babylon ruled by "capitalist pigs" that would eventually witness "havoc and destruction" due to its devolving nature. Lyrics such as these, aimed not only at Reagan but also at the America emerging after his election, became the norm during the 1980s. What follows is an analysis of just a few of the many songs about this, as well as an attempt to show consistency of thought across scenes. These are legitimate and enlightening primary sources of a unique countercultural response to the Reagan Revolution. These are the protest songs of his presidency.[17]

Reagan der Fuhrer

In terms of themes across the lyrics, one that stands out consistently and powerfully is the association of the president with Hitler and the Nazis. Punk bands alluded to Nazism often in their music and used the horrors associated with it to make listeners aware of their perceived similarities between America in the early 1980s and Germany of the 1930s. Punks had a strange affinity for Nazism, using its imagery as a shock mechanism in song, dress, and promotional materials. Though a white power subgenre within punk would embrace and use Nazi rhetoric and symbology for an entirely different purpose (and bands like Dead Kennedys and the lesser-known Hypnotics, among others, would rhetorically rebuke them with songs like "Nazi Punks Fuck Off!" and "Nazi Snotzy"), songs juxtaposing Reagan with Hitler expressed a more-than-serious concern about the incoming president and his alleged fascist tendencies.

One of the most controversial moments during Reagan's first term that sparked a Nazi-oriented response beyond even punk concerned his visiting a place many felt was inappropriate for an American president to visit. One June 6, 1984, he attended a ceremony in Normandy, France, to commemorate D-Day alongside other world leaders, minus Helmut Kohl, the chancellor of West Germany, who was not invited. Feeling slighted, Kohl invited Reagan the following year during an economic summit in Bonn to visit a German cemetery near the town of Bitburg. The two would lay wreaths during a ceremony intended to show the strengthening bond between the two countries. Reagan accepted and during preparation for the trip, members of his staff failed to investigate the location, unaware of the forty-nine Nazi SS soldiers buried there. Knowledge of this soon became public, and the Reagan team tried to quell the storm by adding a visit to the Bergen-Belsen concentration camp. This did little to assuage the feelings of the fifty-three senators and leading members of the American Jewish community who vehemently opposed the visit, including Elie Wiesel, who, the day after the senators announced their opposition, was awarded the Congressional Gold Medal by Reagan. In punk-like fashion, he would use his acceptance speech as a public opportunity to chide the president for his Bitburg plans.

Reagan proceeded with the visit and on May 5 delivered a heartfelt speech at Bergen-Belsen that, according to one biographer, "alleviated the ignominy of Bitburg" but ultimately could not heal the scars left by the controversy. The stubbornness of the president and his team's willingness to go through with the visit did not go unnoticed, and the Ramones, with two Jewish members, wrote and released a month later the single "Bonzo Goes to Bitburg" as a response. With a cover including a photo of the president delivering his Bergen-Belsen speech superimposed on one of the rows of tombstones at the cemetery, the song was a fitting response to Reagan's decision making and the Bitburg visit. Poking fun at the president's acting career (he had costarred with a chimpanzee in the 1951 film *Bedtime for Bonzo*), it was a melodic narration of the serious lack of historic and symbolic awareness informing his visit. A plea from the band to Reagan to "pick up the pieces" and "sort your trash better," the lyrics characterized the concerns among punks that he was, to quote the title of an EP by the New York anarcho-punk group A.P.P.L.E., a sensitive fascist. Their record, released a few years after the Ramones', would use a collage of ridiculous Reagan faces for its cover.[18]

Ironically, the song would be on the band's next album *Animal Boy* but listed as "My Brain Is Hanging Upside Down," the first line sung in the chorus, with the "Bonzo" title added parenthetically. The change was apparently made to appease guitarist Johnny, a Republican and admirer of President Reagan who never wanted the Ramones to become a political band. Lead singer Joey, one of song's writers, explained in an interview why he wrote it anyway. "Reagan going to the SS cemetery . . . I thought that it was really fucked up," he told *East Coast Rocker*. "[And] I was outraged enough to write the song." Mirroring the confusion many felt concerning the president's visit, Joey poignantly asked in the same interview, "How can you fuckin' forgive the Holocaust?" This sentiment was reflected in many of the lyrics contained in the song, most notably, "You're a politician / Don't become one of Hitler's children," the concluding lines of the first verse. There is a candid sense of frustration expressed throughout it, particularly in the opening of the chorus, where the lines "My brain is hanging upside down / I need something to slow me down" are repeated, a clear expression of the challenge many felt in trying to understand why Reagan was doing what he did. As the Ramones were never as politically charged as other bands, "Bonzo" is evidence of the extent to which Reagan did inspire punks to illuminate their frustrations concerning his presidency in song.[19]

Associating Reagan and the Republicans with Hitler and the Nazis was a recurring theme in punk at that time, and a number of groups pushed the connection well beyond the rather subdued assessment of the Ramones. One was Reagan Youth, also from New York City, that had formed before Reagan had won the election in response to the possibility of his even becoming president. An obvious play on the World War II–era Nazi indoctrination youth groups, the band's name and lyrics took aim at the mindlessness of young people getting caught up in the Reagan Revolution and what they perceived to be the fascist leanings of the Republican Party. Although the group formed in 1980, the first record would not be released for another four years, just in time for Reagan's reelection campaign. *Youth Anthems for a New Order* was a seven-track, parodic assault upon the Reaganites with album artwork alone that leaves little to the imagination. Connecting those that supported Reagan with the Ku Klux Klan through its imagery, a common technique by punk bands, the opening song, "New Aryans," spelled things out succinctly, with lyrics like "Be proud that you're a white American / Blonde hair, blue eyes, a fine new Aryan." This is followed by "Reagan Youth," announcing, "We are the sons of Reagan, heil" for each of the song's three verses. Even more emphatic were its chants of "Reagan Youth, heil, heil, heil," capped off with an emphatic "Sieg heil" each time. Through lyrics such as these, the band worked to do what the tagline of its webpage states it had set out to do from its inception—"to expose the evils of society through punk music, especially the evil ones known as Ronald Reagan, the Religious Right, and the Republicans, and Racists."[20]

On the other side of the country, where punk had begun to really take off, the clearest connection between Reagan and Hitler came from the Fullerton, California, band D.I. One of those that emerged in Orange County along with groups like the Vandals, T.S.O.L., Adolescents, Social Distortion, and Agent Orange, they made that area a hotbed for punk in the years surrounding Reagan's election. Released in 1983, its self-titled EP included "Reagan der Fuhrer," the most obvious song title of the era on the subject. In it, Reagan represented an America distorting reality and distracting people from what is actually going on around them. After asking listeners "When will you open your eyes?," the last half repeats "Reagan's our Fuhrer, we need someone newer," only to end with singer Casey Rower emphatically declaring, "If I had my way, I'd hang him on a skewer." Beyond the Nazi association, Rower's capstone comment did what a number of punk songs bravingly did: threaten the life of the president of the United States.[21]

I Shot Reagan

Ronald Reagan clearly engendered a special kind of dislike among punks. The malicious songs about the attempt on his life and those that suggest harm prove this emphatically. It was a little more than two months after being sworn in that Reagan was shot outside the Washington Hilton Hotel, hit by a .22-caliber bullet that had ricocheted off the side of his limousine. Also hit were a police officer, a Secret Service agent, and White House Press Secretary James Brady, who suffered permanent disability. Although no one died and Reagan would be released from the hospital in less than two weeks, most Americans were dismayed as they watched the news stations repeatedly play the video that had captured the chaos of the moment. Reagan's popularity, which had been waning, improved dramatically after the failed attempt, with his approval ratings shooting up over 70 percent. Punks, far less likely than the average American to empathize with the injured president, thought differently, and the lyrics they wrote made this very clear.

The man who intended to kill Reagan that day was John Hinckley Jr., a songwriter hoping to gain the attention of Jodie Foster, an actress in the movie *Taxi Driver* with whom he had become infatuated. In the film, she played a child prostitute who befriends a deranged Vietnam veteran planning to assassinate a presidential candidate. In the days immediately following the attempt on Reagan's life, her name would be adopted by a newly formed group from Phoenix, Arizona. Born in that moment was Jodie Foster's Army (JFA), who like many would make the circumstances surrounding the president's brush with death a topic for lyrical consideration. JFA, as the band became more commonly known, released their first EP *Blatant Localism* with the song "JFA," written before they had considered adopting Foster's name as their moniker. Beginning with "He shot Reagan, he shot the pig, didn't he / He shot the secretary in the head, didn't he," the nearly inaudible first verse luridly concludes with the lines, "Between the eyes, in the chest, .22s are the best / For your dear, for your honey kill the prez, leave the rest." With its continuous chanting chorus of "We're Jodie Foster's Army," it was one of the first of many songs that openly made the attempt on Reagan's life lyrical fair game.[22]

With the memory of Kennedy's assassination fresh in the minds of most Americans, the thought of another president being gunned down was harrowing. Yet, while most rallied around Reagan and prayed for his recovery, it was bands like JFA who challenged the near-fallen hero narrative with a candor and level of insensitivity rarely heard in song. In many ways, those like "JFA" came to characterize what punk in the '80s was truly about—an unabashed critique of Reaganland, regardless of the president's near-death experience. When it came to the music, nothing seemed sacred surrounding Reagan, his life included. In many ways, JFA's name and lyrics characterized the honesty that came with it, and like them, the band Ism thought the failed assassination worth singing about, particularly the Hinckley/Foster situation, which they covered in the inquisitively titled track "John Hinckley Jr. (What Has Jodie Foster Done to You?)." Formed in Queens in 1980, the group was one of the earliest in the New York scene and plenty controversial due to their overtly offensive lyrics and imagery. Originally included on the '82 compilation *The Big Apple—Rotten to the Core*, it was also on their first full-length album put out the next year, *A Diet for the Worms*. While primarily about Hinckley's mental health issues, it references Reagan early, coupling him to the successful attempts on the lives of other presidents. "First Lincoln, then Kennedy, but Reagan got away!" opens the song before frontman Jism (Josef Ismach) recounts the story of the Hinckley trial and his insanity verdict. The track has a carnival-like feel with the question, "John Hinckley Jr., what has Jodie done to you?" repeated over a carousel-sounding organ riff. Although more about Hinckley than Reagan, it enunciates the contempt for the latter that punks held, as singing about anything surrounding the attempt on his life would have been perceived to be in poor taste by most Americans, an effect few punks, including Ism, would likely not have cared much about.[23]

Lansing, Michigan's Crucifucks would add to the work of Ism and JFA with "Hinkley Had a Vision," released in 1984 on their self-titled LP. Though mostly about the rise of the Christian Right and their increasing influence during Reagan's first term (songs specifically concerning this are addressed in chapter 4), it has frontman Doc Dart's high-pitched and creepy voice repeating the line "Hinkley had a vision" after brazenly expressing a desire to kill the president himself. Concluding with the eerily repeated question "Should I?," the song goes the furthest of any in making a verbal threat against the president, something that contributed to the band's status as "one of the most extreme bands in a musical scene that was already pretty extreme to being with." At the point where the music drops out, Dart loudly whines, "I wanna take the president, chop off his head, and mail it to them in a garbage bag," a repugnant lyric that would have been offensive to even the president's harshest critics, save possibly punks. It as well as the other songs that make similar suggestions are critical artifacts of the absurdist tendency in punk, something that often deflects attention from its more serious side. Though more distasteful, it is important they be included in the greater history of protest music in America, regardless of their gross insensitivity and gratuitously violent suggestiveness.[24]

Not nearly as extreme but still threatening in its tone was Tongue Avulsion's "Libyan Hit Squad," included on the 1982 *Not So Quiet on the Western Front* compilation. Affirming that "Mo Khadafy is our boss," the band, projecting itself lyrically as the title, vowed in the first verse, "We're gonna kill Ronnie Reagan and his whole administration." The threat is made three more times, emphasized by the chorus "We're here to kill / We're here to kill / We're here to kill." Although it appears that the band is intent on assassinating the president, the song was likely influenced by unconfirmed reports of a plot to actually kill Reagan and other officials close to him by hitmen from Libya who had supposedly entered the country sometime in 1981. Described by Libyan officials as a product from "the CIA fantasy farm," it was taken seriously enough by the administration to have security heightened around those thought to be under threat. The only other person mentioned in the song as a target along with Reagan was James Watt, the controversial secretary of the interior and Christian fundamentalist who had banned the Beach Boys from playing at the 1983 Independence Day concert in DC. Angering Reagan, his reasoning had been that they were less "wholesome" than the act he preferred, Wayne Newton. Ironically, Watt would be forced to resign only a few months later for a derogatory comment about the diversity of his department. Never known to let such an opportunity pass by, punks got to it as one band, DC's Mission for Christ, would title their 1983 demo cassette *2 Jews, a Black, a Woman and a Cripple*, the exact quote that got Watt removed.[25]

Included with the Tongue Avulsion track on the *Western Front* compilation was "Assassination Attempt" by the band Demented Youth, one of the more bemusing songs from the album as there appears to be no lyrical content on the recording, but rather a few screams and some inaudible blabbering after a quick "Mr. President" attention-getter starts things off. (The group would also include another lyrically indecipherable track titled "Reagan's War" on their 1982 demo cassette. With no lyric sheet available, all that can be heard on that one is a harshly pronounced "Guess what, Reagan? We all hate you!") Coupled with the title, it's clear the song is intended to be about the attempt on Reagan's life, as the lyric sheet included in the album booklet confirms. Beginning the first verse with "Ronald Reagan, you make me sick / Ronald

Reagan, you're a fucking dick," the band let loose swiftly just what they thought of the fortieth president. The chorus, which is completely indecipherable when heard, spells things out even more clearly with "Assassination attempt, this time we missed / Don't worry Reagan, you're still on the list / Ronald Reagan you lived . . . / We're gonna run you over with Greyhound bus." Like the Crucifucks, Demented Youth took their lyrics to the extreme in terms of violent suggestiveness surrounding Reagan and the failed plot to kill him.[26]

The most interesting story surrounding lyrics connected to the attempt on Reagan's life concerned the Suicidal Tendencies (ST) track mentioned earlier. The third song from the first side of their eponymously titled debut record was listed as "I Shot the Devil," allegedly changed from "I Shot Reagan" due to pressure placed on the band's recording company by the FBI. On the liner notes inside the sleeve, unviewable without purchasing the album, the song is listed with the "Reagan" rather than "Devil" title, while on the openly visible back cover it is the opposite. Whether or not this actually happened seems to bear little importance as the story is still retold as legend and the track listing disparity offers more than enough encouragement for those doing the telling. In terms of lyrical mention, the president's name appears early and often, beginning with the screaming admission, "I shot Reagan!" The opening verse also lists Anwar Sadat, John Lennon, and Pope John Paul II as the other targets of singer Mike Muir. All four had been victims of assassination attempts within a year of each other, with Sadat and Lennon both being killed. Continuing his haranguing of the president, Muir bluntly sings, "You're gonna rot in heaven . . . You're too bad for hell," the implication being that Reagan was so evil that he would preferably go to the latter and actually be forgiven there. And in case anyone was still not clear about the band's take on the attempt on his life, the song ends with one last "I shot Reagan" salvo followed by Muir waling, "I'll shoot him again and again and again!" to wrap things up.[27]

Like the others, the ST track uses orotund lyrics regarding the failed assassination to make listeners fully aware of just how much Reagan was despised by the band. While other presidents would draw the attention of artists whose work reflected a similar sense of disaffection and distrust, none witnessed the level of aggressiveness that Reagan did in songs that made the attempt on his life the subject of amusement and alleged disappointment. In many ways, they represent that side of punk music that deters persons not affiliated with the scene from taking it seriously. The absurdity and insensitivity of singing about/celebrating the near-death experience of a president, regardless of how one perceived their politics, as well as suggesting they should be disturbingly killed are causes enough to make those already less than enthusiastic about recognizing punk as a legitimate cultural movement even more dismissive than they already are. More songs would come, but few were as macabre in tone as these. This level of discourse, although still insightful, did not dominate the lyrical outpourings of the Reagan bands.

Hey Ronnie

While a lot of groups focused lyrical attention on more serious issues surrounding Reagan's presidency, others took a more satiric approach, mocking him with a comical tone in their songs. One of these was "Battle Hymn of Ronnie Reagan" by Seattle's humorously named The Fartz. Formed in 1981, their first EP, *Because This Fuckin' World Stinks . . .* , had on its cover a photograph of Reagan delivering a speech, his face with a Hitler toothbrush mustache, overcoat adorned with a swastika armband, and the SS symbol on his cuffs. Described as "crude, sloppy, pounding, heavy duty, hit your grandpa with a baseball bat when he's not looking type of music," it was recognized as one of the best punk releases of Reagan's first year as president. Included were songs like "Campaign Speech," "Con Game," and "Idiots Rule," all admonitions of the government and politicians as Reagan was coming into the White House. Also on it was "Waste No Time," which mentions Reagan as one of the global leaders punks should be confronting. Interestingly, the liner notes describe a canceled Rock against Reagan benefit in Washington because of the band's inclusion and the mayhem their involvement might cause. As the EP was released in 1981, this would make the nixed event earlier than the national tour of the same name that would begin two years later a momentous occasion in the history of punk that attempted to unseat the president in the next election.[28]

"Battle Hymn of Ronnie Reagan" was one of sixteen songs The Fartz recorded on the group's 1982 release *World Full of Hate*. With images of Reagan again on the cover as well as in the liner notes, and with phrases like "The World According to Reagan" and "The World's a Mess We Agree, So Now It's Up to You and Me," the album is an unabridged political and social commentary, an "all-purpose ass-kicker" according to an *MRR* review. Also in the notes are calls to action for listeners that express the band's social justice advocacy and support for ending the American plutocracy. "White, black, yellow, or red," it reads, "we are the people united in a fight to do away with the ruling classes [sic] control on the way we live and die." "Battle Hymn," using the tune from Julia Ward Howe's 1862 "Battle Hymn of the Republic," begins with a straightforward attack on the president's policies. "Mine eyes have seen the horror of the coming of the Lord / His name is Ronald Reagan and he's drafting all young boys," kicks off the minute-and-a-half presidential thumping, with singer Blaine's whining vocals letting the listener know that everything happening around them is only about keeping the Reaganites in power. Like many songs from the era, the message of "Battle Hymn" was pointed and easy to understand yet delivered in such a harsh and unfriendly way that few outside of the punk community could take it seriously, especially if they struggled getting past the childish hilarity of the group's name.[29]

While their name might have been a bit absurd, no one could doubt the seriousness of The Fartz' lyrics. Absent the immature moniker, the same could be said about Washington, DC's Government Issue (G.I.), one of the Dischord bands that had been part of their initial '81 wave of recordings. Formed in 1980, they would release a year later *Legless Bull*, a ten-song EP that included tracks like "Religious Ripoff," "Rock 'n' Roll Bullshit," "Bored to Death," and "No Rights." The record was, according to music historian Steven Blush, one of the best examples of "smartass suburban HC [hardcore]," which put the band up there with Minor Threat in terms of importance to the federal city's scene. Soon after the release of *Legless*, G.I. would have two songs included on the Dischord compilation album *Flex Your Head*, one of which was the benignly titled "Hey Ronnie." Nearly always on the lists compiled of "Reagan songs" from the era, its lyrics are not only mostly indecipherable, but they are also not included in the album's liner notes. As well, they apparently cannot be found with even a good amount of searching. Rather, in the booklet accompanying the compilation, which includes lyrics for nearly every other song on it, the band's listing for "Hey Ronnie" instructs listeners to "Figure them out for yourselves!!" What can be heard is a repetition of the lines "Hey Ronnie / You ain't no fun" in between indiscernible verses, making it a somewhat innocuous critique of Reagan. Besides this, the only other words sung by frontman John Stabb that can be made out are the "Hey, hey, hey, hey, hey Ronnie" chants repeated at the beginning and the creepily quavered "Ronnie" that wraps it up.[30]

While G.I.'s was rather mundane, absurdist lyrical harassment of Reagan reached another level on the *Western Front* compilation with an indecipherable song titled "Reagum," recorded by Lennonburger, a temporary band put together with Jeff Bale of *MRR* for the purpose of contributing to the release. Accompanied by liner notes with an image of Reagan wearing a swastika armband, picking his nose while talking about how the American flag gets him all fired up and how proud he is to run a country where young boys "help pay the price" by their willingness to go to war, the song seems utterly ridiculous in terms of its lyrical content. While beginning with an assessment of Reagan's faults, labeling him a "rightest pig" in particular, it takes on a farcical tone, with the president's bodily functions becoming the main theme. "Everybody knows he's doing it, doing it / He's picking his ass and chewing it, chewing it / Everybody knows he's doing it, doing it / He's picking his nose and chewing it," are the most absurd words strewn together by a punk band expressing displeasure with Reagan. Yet beneath the riotous veil of childlike stupidity rests a real critique of the Reagan Era, particularly the hypocrisy of the president's rhetoric concerning cuts in government spending and his wife's infamous spending habits. The last verse brings this to light with the line, "We know why Nancy spends so much / To give the White House her personnel [sic] touch / She had to wash the green and brown / That Ronnie spread all over her gown," a biting and satirical yet insightful critique of a first lady who was dubbed "Queen Nancy" by the media because of her taste for all things costly. The 1980s were an era of conspicuous consumption, and the Reagan White House reflected this. Lennonburger's appraisal, gross bodily fluids as well as a lack of personal hygiene aside, while definitely absurd, remains an astute assessment of this hypocritical aspect of the Reagan Revolution. Childish, yes. But still insightful.[31]

Reaganomics Is Killing You

Some of the more pointed punk critiques of Reagan went specifically after his economic policies. Reaganomics was grounded in a theory that growth would happen most when taxes were cut, government regulations minimized, and free trade allowed. In many ways it was the opposite of what the country had been doing since the New Deal, prophesizing that such a program would not only increase government revenue by decreasing taxes on the wealthiest Americans, but also improve the circumstances of everyone else through greater spending and investment. Reagan wholeheartedly embraced this, and his administration would see advocates of the theory placed in key positions and a legislation program passed in the months following his inauguration. A year later the country suffered a recession, with the unemployment rate up above 10 percent, the highest it had been since 1940. As one scholar wrote in 1988, sounding similar to the punk bands that criticized the program, "The awful truth was that Reaganomics was a fraud from the beginning." Just a few years earlier Dead Kennedys with their song "Dear

Abby" acknowledged this fraudulency with the rather harrowing advice given by Jello Biafra (serving as the advice columnist) to a disparaged and financially troubled coroner unable to feed his family—"DEAR REAGANOMICS VICTIM: Consult your clergyman. Make sure the body's blessed and everything should be fine."[32]

The hurtful impact of Reagan's program was felt by many Americans, especially those not part of the corporate elite that helped him get elected in 1980. Two books written in the first year of his administration reflected concerns about the impact Reaganomics had on average Americans. Arthur Rowse's *One Sweet Guy and What He Is Doing to You* and a volume of essays from *Social Policy* magazine titled *What Reagan Is Doing to Us* explained in detail these effects. According to Rowse, "For most business executives and owners, Reagan was a dream come true. . . . [He] made it crystal clear he was on the side of the corporations on every point of difference with the public and the government." Deregulating industry and undoing protections in place for decades concerning the health, safety, and welfare of the people, the Reaganites pushing his economic program appeared unmoved by the pain and suffering of millions of Americans. Punks, like the above authors, seemed moved to resoundingly share their interpretation of what Reaganomics was actually doing.[33]

As they did to him, bands across the country used the president's policy for the title of songs. One was "Reaganomics" by Houston's Dirty Rotten Imbeciles (D.R.I.), included on their 1985 album *Dealing with It!*, described in an *MRR* review as "25 songs as wickedly sharp as ever." Only forty-two seconds long, it is one of the simplest statements on the subject, with only the lines "Reaganomics is killing me / Reaganomics is killing me / Reaganomics is killing me / Reaganomics is killing you," repeated four times in as rapid a succession as a punk band could play. Released the same year and a bit more lyrically complex was Beefeater's "Reaganomix." One of the Dischord bands from Washington, DC, their cautionary critique was included on the LP *Plays for Lovers*. After a pretend-Reagan spoken-word intro, singer Tomas Squip (now Oman Emmet) delivered a harsh verbal assault on the president. "First four years were fun / No he's gonna fuck us again" is followed later in the opening verse with "Reaganomix, add the ingredients / One old asshole, an entire country / Reaganomix, stir up the batter / The poor get poorer, the rich get fatter." The notion that the economic policies of his presidency were hurting people, particularly the poor, while benefiting the wealthiest Americans was a common position taken not only by punks but by a number of academics as well. Like the authors mentioned above, but with a bit more punch, New York City's Cause for Alarm would reiterate this on 1983's "Time to Try" with the line "The price of things gets us annoyed / Cause some of us work but we're mostly unemployed." A few lines later they made sure listeners knew exactly who and what were the cause of this hardship—"Fuck Ronald Reagan and his fucking Reaganomics."[34]

Also using "Reaganomics" as titles were songs by the bands No Direction, Dog Killer, and the Accelerators. From Sioux Falls, South Dakota, No Direction was a trio who allegedly put out the first independent punk album in that town's history. Described as playing "earnest political protest numbers with a lot more spirit than technique," an apt description for many punk bands of that era, their 1984 self-titled release included not only "Reaganomics," but also disaffection-themed tracks like "Tear Gas Justice," "Radio Education," "Living in the '80s Depression," and "No Future No Past." The one aimed directly at the president's supply-side/trickle-down policies, with its refrain "Reaganomics, paint a pretty picture of it / Reaganomics, Reaganomics," lyrically painted a much different one for listeners with factory closings and unemployment exposed as the economic reality of Reaganism. Like many Americans, an individual described in the band's assessment is left "somewhere in the middle with nothing to do," an unfortunate but apparently acceptable side effect, as likely described by its proponents, of the Reagan Revolution. Prompting the band's response might have been the impact of Reagan's economic policies in their home state. In 1982, the year after his tax cut bill passed, South Dakota witnessed its highest rate of unemployment between 1976 and 2020.[35]

"Reaganomics" also found itself as the title of a song by Chico, California's Dog Killer on their 1986 demo cassette *Last Act of a Desperate Band*. Their only recording, which included other era-appropriate tunes like "No Reason to Live," "No More Tomorrows," "Superpowers," and an ironic critique of communism called "You Can't Eat Marx," it was described by a later reviewer as having "Superb guitars . . . snarky vocals and classic California attitude," all of which could be heard on "Reaganomics." As if written by Robert Lekachman himself, an economist, one of the staunchest opponents of the Reagan program, and author of two key critical books from the era, *Greed Is Not Enough: Reaganomics* and *Visions and Nightmares: America after Reagan*, it began with two questions many were pondering as Reagan's first term was leading into a second—"Are we really better off today . . . do you think that things are really all right?" Dog Killer took to task the complacency that characterized many Americans, their willingness to accept things as they were sold by the Reaganauts without thought. "DEFICIT SPENDING!," the song's concluding pronouncement, was what people should understand was really happening in the Reagan economic scheme. As Lekachman said in a 1988 review of the after-Reagan books starting to pop up, "the supply-siders left a legacy of massive federal and trade deficits which will require urgent attention by the next administration." Dog Killer not only recognized this, but also the apathetic tendencies of most Americans at the time to just sit and do nothing about it. Punks were not like most Americans, and those in bands like Dog Killer refused to sit on the sidelines while supply side was hurting so many people.[36]

On the opposite side of the country, a group from Union, New Jersey, called the Accelerators had its version of "Reaganomics" included on a 1984 compilation tape titled *I'm Buck Naked*, a fifty-six-song, multinational diatribe against anything and everything during the "Decade of Decadence," as one band on the tape labeled the 1980s. Coupled with the directive to "Fuck Off," the Accelerators' version, like D.R.I.'s, was as straight to the point as a band could make it. Frontman Ron Role, who described the twenty-five-second song as "sort of a joke," humorously expounded about the president's economic policies, four times to be exact, "Reaganomics, Reaganomics, Reaganomics Just Fuck Off!" The extent of its lyrical content, although less eloquent than Lekachman and other economists' critical comments concerning the president's fiscal policies, has essentially the same message. "The Reagan administration," Lekachman wrote in a 1982 contribution to the *What Reagan Is Doing to Us* collection, "will leave the American economy in far worse condition when it mercifully ends and becomes one of the nightmares of history." While it doesn't quite have the same emphatic tone of Role's lyrics, its assessment of the Reagan Revolution is more than similar. Role and the Accelerators also had a tune titled "Reaganland" long before Rick Perlstein's book by the same name was written. Its lyrics succinctly summed up what most bands singing about the president and his economic policies were saying: "Reaganland, it's my country / Reaganland where nothing's free / Reaganland, it's my country / Reaganland more poverty."[37]

Ronald Reagan Is a Wanker

While American punk bands dominated the musical discourse surrounding their president, he also became a large target for many outside of the United States. As was evident from the gathering at his funeral, Ronald Reagan was a global figure. With punk becoming a worldwide phenomenon during his tenure of office, non-American bands picked up on the Reagan-bashing vibe of their US counterparts and began to do some of their own. An extensive list of these as well as those by domestic groups not mentioned in this chapter are included as an appendix. And it is extensive. While the book is about the American punk rock assault on Reagan, a few from foreign bands are worth mentioning here as evidence of his extensive reach and the perception that his time in the White House was problematic not only for the country he reigned over, but also for the world.

In the Canadian punk scene, two already mentioned, D.O.A. and the Dayglo Abortions, torched Reagan in their lyrics as furiously as their southern counterparts. On the former's 1981 EP *Positively D.O.A. (No God No Country No Lies)*, the song "Fucked Up Ronnie" was included, one of the catchiest songs from the period haranguing Reagan. Assertive in its tone, it begins with the simple admonition, "You're fucked up, Ronnie" followed by the prediction "You're not gonna last," sung by frontman Joey Shithead with a clarity and conviction that often feels lost in the less audible and more obnoxious-sounding songs from the era. His fellow British Columbians took their turn with "Ronald McRaygun" on their *Feed Us a Fetus* LP. It ironically coupled the president with one of America's most recognizable exports, McDonald's, and playfully connected the "Mc" with nearly half of the words in the song. "I'm Ronald McRaygun, McDeath, McNuclear, McWar, McCommies, McFear, McMe, 'Cuz I'm McDangerously Crazy," while humorous as one of the more lighthearted punk beratings, insightfully situated Reagan at the top of the American consumer culture that brands like McDonald's were becoming increasingly representative of throughout the decade.[38]

While the Bitburg controversy wasn't for a few more years, the first years of his presidency saw several bands from West Germany join in the Reagan rankling, writing songs like "R. Reagan," "Hey Ronald," and "Ronald Reagan Nuklearer Cowboy." One cassette tape from 1982 was even titled *Zieh Leine Ronald!*, or *Get Out Ronald!*, with every song aimed directly at him. Plenty of others would follow during Reagan's White House years. Just north in Denmark, bands were as inquisitive as those in America on tracks like "What's Going on inside Ronald Reagan's Brain?!" In Belgium there were songs like "Mr Reagan No Future" and "Cowboy Ronnie." In the Netherlands, "Ronald Reagan Sucks" and "Ronnie Is Dead." In Finland, "Hullu [Crazy] Reagan" and "Ronald On Sika [Ronald Is a Pig]." And in Sweden, there was "Reagan Cowboy," "Ronnie Wants War," and "Ronnie Rotten," to name just a few. Brazil joined in with "Ronaldo Hitler," Australia with "The Jellybean Man," Spain with "Reagan Hijo de Puta," and Italy in "Isterismo di Reagan." These and many others are listed in the appendix and again are evidence that Reagan's reach in terms of punk attention and concern was extensive. American bands were clearly not alone in thinking things were not well, while the occupant of the White House, considered even then to be the most powerful person in the world, was the cowboy from California. One group from Sweden, The Past, stated succinctly in a 1983 song simply titled with the president's name what so many international bands seemed to think. "Ronald Reagan is a wanker."[39]

(Punk) Rock against Reagan

The punk assault on President Reagan formalized in the spring of 1983 when a group of bands came together for a Rock against Reagan tour. Led by M.D.C. with help from the Youth International Party (Yippies), the lineup would include some of punk's most legendary groups. Scheduled to play a series of initial shows from March through June were Dead Kennedys, Crucifucks, Dicks, D.R.I., and Reagan Youth, along with local bands that would join in the fun when the tour came through their town. It would culminate in the tour's arrival in Washington, DC, in July, just in time to perform near the same Independence Day concerts at which James Watt had attempted to ban the Beach Boys from playing. Their purpose was spelled out clearly in the *MRR* issue that spring. They were traveling across the country "to voice youth's concern about the state of the nation and the consequences of the policies of the US government with regard to the citizens of the USA, as well as the citizens of the world." Punks had definitely enough of Reagan after two years in office and were gearing up for a full frontal assault as the '84 election cycle was getting ready to start.[40]

Cutbacks in social services, the increased influence of the industrial military complex, support for violent regimes in underdeveloped countries, deleterious approaches to managing the environment, failed assistance programs for veterans of the Vietnam War—these and many more issues were what the Rock against Reagan bands and countless others across the country were hell-bent on singing about. Punk wasn't just loud, abrasive, and violent music, but rather an intellectually driven assault on a presidency many thought was disastrous, and not just punks. The rest of this book looks at lyrics as meaningful expressions of these concerns, beginning with those songs aimed directly at the nation Reagan reigned over during his eight years in the White House.

CHAPTER TWO

Only in America

> It's time for us to realize that we're too great a nation to limit ourselves to small dreams.
> —RONALD REAGAN

> It happens only in the U.S.A. / Only in America.
> —NAKED RAYGUN

Let's Make America Great Again

On March 31, 1976, Americans watching television had their programming interrupted for a political broadcast. What Reagan delivered that night became known as the "To Restore America" speech and was crucial, according to Mark LaVoie, in reviving a campaign and career that appeared to be dwindling. "That Reagan became the standard-bearer for the Republican party was a long time in the making," LaVoie wrote, "but 'To Restore America' helped Reagan flourish in the 1976 primaries, exciting conservatives about what a Reagan presidency could look like, and ultimately, facilitating his 1980 presidential victory." Whether it was unfairly high taxes, excessive government spending, or the increasing military superiority of the Soviet Union, America was in trouble and Reagan let viewers know that Gerald Ford was not the man to stop its slide. "Our nation is in danger, and the danger grows greater with each passing day," he told them. But while he convinced enough voters to win a few state primaries, he lost out to Ford at the Republican convention that summer. With head bloodied but unbowed, he began almost immediately to work toward 1980. Interestingly, less than a month after his address aired, four guys from New York's Lower East Side would see their debut album released, ushering in the birth of American punk rock. While Reagan was rekindling his political career in '76, the Ramones were kick-starting a musical movement that would soon turn him into the primary partisan for poetic pummeling.[1]

Four years after his failure to capture the nomination and Ford's defeat by Democrat Jimmy Carter, Reagan would be on stage in Detroit's Joe Louis Arena accepting his party's nod as candidate for president. He campaigned using a slogan Americans have since become quite familiar with, as red, white, and blue posters of a jovial Reagan and the words "Let's make America great again" spread his message of the need for renewal. "For those who have abandoned hope," he pledged, "we'll restore hope and we'll welcome them into a great national crusade to make America great again." The Carter administration had sapped the will of the country; it was time for it to pull together and restore confidence in itself and conviction for its principles. "The time is now, my fellow Americans, to recapture our destiny, to take it into our own hands," Reagan told those in attendance. His would be a presidency informed by an idea recently lost, that America was truly exceptional. The era of meekness and reluctancy was over. As journalist Stanley Hoffman wrote after his election, "The Reagan victory was a revenge of exceptionalist faith." America was great, Reagan was not afraid to let people know it, and many were ready to believe it again. But not everybody. Challenging this soon became central to the punk ethos of the 1980s, and the songs groups wrote about the nation expressed their concerns with clarity and conviction. One early band from Portland, Oregon, The Wipers, announced in 1981's "Youth of America" what many were feeling and would lyrically express throughout the decade. "The walls are coming down . . . It's time we rectify this now."[2]

Amerika Is Dying

Regarding America, many punk songs from the era used a variation of the nation's name in their titles, a clear and assertive counternarrative to Reagan's propagandizing about its greatness. Some took issue with certain national symbols and slogans used often by Reaganites to advance their American exceptionalist agenda and pro-patriotic policies. All provide interesting critical insight into what became known as the Reagan Revolution and its effect on the country as a whole, as well as offering a unique perspective into the punk counterculture of that decade and the anti-Americanism that informed much of it. Songs with titles including "America," "Amerika," and "Amerikkka" introduced listeners to lyrics critical of the United States and how things were shaping up under Reagan's leadership. These were many in number as bands in nearly every scene recorded one or more. "America songs" — ones that used Cs rather than Ks — were particularly abundant, with lyrics that served as warnings about the contemporary state of affairs. One early example came in Shattered Faith's "I Love America," included with "Reagan Country" on their 1981 Posh Boy release, drawing attention to the "Present state, Reagan's regime" and "Capitalist pigs" who seemed to be running things in the new American Babylon. A year later Tucson, Arizona's Conflict, fronted by K Nurse (Karen Allman), one of a handful of female punk singers among the Reagan bands, included on its first cassette "America's Right," which opened with the sarcastic declamation, "We're taking over and isn't it great!" Described thirty years later as "ahead of their time, definitely, and full of deliciously angst-ridden rage," their seven-song initial release was warmly reviewed in MRR by founder Tim Yohannan, who called it "ripping music that doesn't let up at all." As they had done to Reagan personally, ripping the country he was elected to lead became an essential aspect of punk as well.[3]

With the abundance of songs using "America" in the title, like those directly using Reagan's name, a few that share a consistent strain of thought provide enough insight to support the claim that punks used lyrics to express a profound dislike of and distrust for the country as much as for the president who ruled over it. One theme that appeared in these often concerned its possible demise, which some bands seemed to wish for. From New York City, a group called Money Dogs recorded an eight-song cassette in 1983 including an example of this. "America Is Falling," both song and cassette title, was a quick stab at the country, its expiration due particularly to "too many people [having] their finger on the trigger." Described musically as "disjointed trash" in MRR, their "uncompromising lyrics" about the downfall ("America is falling down, falling down, right now") were also heard in songs like "Peace Moscow" ("It's America that's got me shaking in my knees / 'Cause America's got the power / America's got the bombs / America's got the assholes") and "Your Town (X-Town)," which brought Reagan directly into the picture with lines like "Ronnie ain't no cowboy / He's a corporate president / Ronnie ain't no cowboy / He's a sick motherfucker." Money Dogs would put the first two of these on a demo tape released the same year that also included "Sick Society," "Dumb Fucker," and "Stop It," each lyrically uncompromising in terms of messaging. Its title, hand-scribbled in black marker on the included insert, was a bit more forceful than its '83 co-release: *Salute to America (Let's Blow This Fucker Up)*.[4]

Adding to the idea that the country was in a downward spiral under Reagan was the work of bands like Palo Alto's Whipping Boy and Buena Park's Pig Children, both of which went further than the fall, with lyrics expressing the need for a more ultimate ending. The adroitly named Whipping Boy, with two African American members, included "America Must Die" on their 1983 album *The Sound of No Hands Clapping*, which was produced by Klaus Flouride of Dead Kennedys. Two years later, "America's Dying in Her Sleep" was recorded by Pig Children for their *Blood for the State* EP. Whipping Boy's track, which included an emphatic "America must die!" between each verse, addressed the hypocrisy surrounding the "land of liberty" idea that was very much at the core of the Reagan White House narrative. This was followed on the album by "Hero," a crawling tune that, while not mentioning Reagan by name, appears to run through the thought process of a mentally disturbed person intent on "Gunning down the president." In Pig Children's more suggestive track, it is specifically Reagan and his war-oriented diplomacy that is "Bringing people to their knees" throughout the world. "Bombs dropping in the East / Reagan's lying through his teeth" is followed in the second verse with "People dying left and right / Reagan thinks it's fucking right," clear denunciations of what would become known as the Reagan Doctrine. (Songs related to this are discussed in chapter 5.) If that wasn't enough, the group ripped into Reagan one more time with the final track on the EP, "Grand Ole Flag." Again critically assessing his approach to foreign affairs, it begins with the lines, "People dying in a land too far from home / Reagan sending aides to help, real truth not shown," before a final claim concerning the sleepy ignorance of most Americans and the possible effect of this: "The real people in this land don't understand / Nuclear war's in Reagan's hands."[5]

With those using Ks in place of Cs, obvious attempts by bands to associate America with the violence, racism, and hate-oriented politics of the Ku Klux Klan, one of the earliest was found on the *Not So Quiet on the Western Front* compilation. (Songs specifically related to racism are discussed in chapter 7.) 7 Seconds, a straight edge group from Reno, Nevada, had recorded a song titled "Fuck Your America" for their demo cassette, which was also included on the compilation. On the back of the cover it was relisted as "Fuck Your Amerika," although in the lyric booklet included with the double LP it remained in its original form. While lead singer Kevin Seconds asked throughout it plenty of concerning questions as Reagan entered office ("Do you want power, do you want freedom . . . Do you have justice, are you a proud one?"), special attention was paid the president in his notes included with the lyric sheet, where he wrote, "it's hard enough getting by in this world with people and things like Ronald Reagan, the K.K.K., the Moral Majority, [and] police . . . fucking things up." In terms of legacy, "Fuck Your Amerika" made punk authority David Ensminger's top twenty protest songs in 2012, thirty years after its original release. "Such vintage 7 Seconds proves," Ensminger wrote, "that portions of the country, even in backyard Nevada, were sick and tired of monotone so-called truths," and that "unbridled power" as well as "the fake security of patriotism," which according to punks informed Reagan's rhetoric about America, were causes enough to rail about in song.[6]

In addition to 7 Seconds' contribution, others with an alternative-lettered national moniker in the title were many, including one by Butylated Hydroxy Toluene (BHT). From just outside San Francisco, their 1986 *Prime Directive* cassette with "Amerika" as the first track also included the cultural commentaries "Mowing Down the People," "Fuck Law Enforcement," "Mr. Politician," and "We're Being Tricked." After a distorted guitar lick of the final notes of the "Star Spangled Banner," listeners of "Amerika" could make out a few familiar words like "government," "schools," "fascists," "KKK," and "FBI," leading up to an emphatic "Fuck Amerika!," all before a final question is offered that many Americans during Reagan's tenure, and not just punks, were seriously concerned about: "Will there be a next generation?" Also contributing to this narrative was The Lookouts!, a group from Northern California that would include Larry Livermore, cofounder of Lookout Records and *Lookout* magazine, and a young Tré Cool, future drummer for Green Day. Their debut 1987 album, *One Planet One People*, included plenty of punk punches like "Catatonic Society," "Fuck Religion," and the contentiously titled "Fourth Reich (Nazi Amerika)," a nearly one-minute, rapid assault that harrowingly asked, "Now we live in a nuclear ghetto / We don't even need gas chambers anymore / Fourth Reich Nazi Amerika / Is this what you want for the U.S.A.?"[7]

Down in Houston, a group that had moved between there and New York City released their second album the same year Reagan began his second term, with plenty of bombastic battering about the country. Stark Raving Mad titled their sophomore effort *Amerika* and had plenty to say about it as well as the president. Much is made in the brevity of the first song, "Are You Sleeping," concerning the general sense of apathy among Americans that many bands wrote about. Like Pig Children, Stark Raving Mad expressed frustration in their lyrics that not only might the end of times be near, a common theme in punk music (discussed further in chapter 5), but that the cause of this was a comatose citizenry, 54 million of whom had returned Reagan to the White House for another go around in '84. Something could be done if people would actually "Take a Stand," the title of the next track, which suggests to listeners in its final lines, "Take a stand / Question Uncle Sam / It's time for you to think." Although an *MRR* reviewer thought the album was "in many ways a disappointment" compared to the group's previous release, its "ranting and raving about social rebellion" could still be heard throughout it in songs like "Social Sickness," "Racist Pig," "Politishit," and "Fuck the

Army." While each offers insight, it is the first track on the second side of the LP where the band lays down its most telling lyrics about the country and Reagan's leadership. In the opening of "S.O.S.," singer Jeff Tunches, in a Biafra-esque vocal style, inquires of listeners, "Four more years of Ronald Reagan / Are you happy with friendly fascism?" Returning to the theme of indifference and lethargy among the American populace, Tunches states in the spastically sung closing verse, "We're Stark Raving Mad at apathetic slobs . . . Don't let us down." Over 37 million Americans, all of whom voted for Walter Mondale over Reagan in the previous year's election, tried not to and likely felt the same.[8]

The Land of the Free

Historian Eric Foner once wrote, "No idea is more fundamental to Americans' sense of ourselves as individuals and as a nation than freedom." It is the "central term of our political vocabulary" and "is deeply embedded in the record of our history and language of everyday life." Kevin Coe, in his 2006 historical analysis of the language of freedom used by presidents throughout most of the twentieth century, concurred with this assessment. "Given the cultural resonance of the concepts of freedom," he stated, "it is unsurprising that the language of freedom (and liberty, freedom's rhetorical counterpart) is a staple of political discourse. . . . In particular, American presidents have made use of [it]." Occupants of the Oval Office, "America's primary political storytellers," according to Coe, have used such language as a way to help Americans construct meaning and formulate understanding of their world. It has allowed them to situate their programs and policies within a larger narrative about America's cause, helped them define who our friends or foes in the advancement of this cause are, and been used as the justifying foundation upon which their decisions are made. While every president between FDR and George W. Bush used a freedom-laced discourse, few did so as much as Ronald Reagan. In comparison with others during the years of Coe's study, only Truman and Eisenhower referenced it more in their addresses.[9]

When Reagan spoke, it was clear he was passionate about freedom and America's role in securing it at home and abroad. Donald Regan, his chief of staff, would even go so far as to proudly boast in 1986 that "President Reagan has opened our eyes to the importance of America's place and mission . . . as the bastion of human freedom in our time." His first official political address as governor of California was riddled with references to it, including the well-known iteration that "Freedom is a fragile thing and it's never more than one generation from extinction." He would continue this narrative in nearly every public address given during his presidency, bolstering the notion of its critical importance with statements like "The United States and the freedom for which it stands . . . must endure and prosper," spoken in 1982 during a ceremony at Arlington National Cemetery. From the time he entered politics until his exit, Reagan spoke about and referenced freedom as often if not more than anything else. To him, and to many of his supporters, it was what defined the country, what made it different, what made it exceptional above all other nations of the world. Speaking to students and faculty at Moscow State University, he would explain the idea as he came to understand it near the end of his presidency and Cold War. "Freedom is the right to question and change the established way of doing things," he told them. "It is the understanding that allows us to recognize shortcomings and seek solutions." Ironically, by the time he spoke these words, punks had been spending nearly a decade doing this in exact opposition to everything he stood for and did while president.[10]

Throughout the 1980s, Reagan's frequent usage of "land of the free" language presented a unique opportunity for bands to be parodic. In particular, punks used the repeated line or a variation of it in song titles with lyrics serving as candid expressions of an interpreted hypocrisy. One of the earliest came from Hüsker Dü, the three-piece group from St. Paul, Minnesota, that would successfully cross over into major label alternative rock by the end of the decade. Fronted by the celebrated guitarist and songwriter Bob Mould, along with Greg Norton and Grant Hart, their second release, in 1982, included the track "In a Free Land," a nearly three-minute probe into the mind-numbing nature of living in America, where the government will "teach you what they want you to think" and "saturation, stars and stripes" will be the main experience of the populace. According to Mould, who wrote the lyrics, "the only freedom worth fighting for is for what you think," something few Americans seemed to care about in Reaganland, where "everybody's an authority" and no one bothered to actually read up on things. While Hüsker Dü would become frustrated with the punk politics of the period and become less assertive in their lyrical pronouncements, a point Kevin Mattson made in his book, *In a Free Land*, with the Statue of Liberty's torch burning an American flag on its cover, made clear the band's early opinions about what life looked like in the America of the first years of the '80s.[11]

A number of bands wrote songs simply titled "Land of the Free." The aptly named Patriots, a short-lived hardcore foursome from West L.A., would release *The Land of the Free* EP in 1983 with an opening track titled the same. It warned listeners, "In the land of the free it's a call to heed / To do whatever we must / Because it's a difficult thing to remain free / Of the chaos which surrounds us." That same year, Warboy, from Portland, Oregon, put out the *Futile Living* cassette with their own "Land of the Free," the typed lyrics on the insert covering part of a photograph of a grimacing Reagan. On the cover was an upside down drawing of Lady Liberty, a Bible in one hand and her torch replaced with a cross in the other. As the final verse explained, "Complete control isn't what we want / Complete control is what they've got / Complete control of church and state / Complete control that thrives on hate," a description of a land apparently not as free as some liked to think. Other "Land of the Free" appraisals would be offered by San Antonio's Fearless Iranians from Hell as well as Cape Cod's Crash Course, whose version would be included on their 1986 *Pilgrimage to Hell* cassette with a chorus repeating "It's the land of the free and the home of the brave" between verses citing all that's wrong with the country.[12]

In the Midwest, Unified Field, a lesser-known group from the Chicago suburb of Arlington Heights, recorded a demo cassette in 1988 with "Land of the Free" and other critiques like "Death of Miss Liberty," "Religious Right and the P.M.R.C.," "Barely Breathing," and "Government Waste." While the lyrics are relatively indecipherable (and do not appear to be available in sheet form), listeners can make out a few phrases expressing the group's concerns about "toxic waste dumping, freedom, religion, and more," as an *MRR* review informed readers. And not far away in Detroit, Angry Red Planet, who took their name from one of the anti-communist B movies of the 1950s, included a "Land of the Free" on their compilation cassette *Get Me a Shovel*. Released the same year as Unified Field's, it appears to be lost to time, not recorded for any other album by the group nor available on any streaming service. What can be found and listened to is their "Mummy from Hollywood," one of four tracks on the cassette from their 1983 EP *Too Much Knowledge Can Be Dangerous*. While it doesn't directly take on the idea of freedom, as one can assume their "Land of the Free" did, it does afford fans an "uncommonly intelligent" assessment with "anti-Reagan sentiments" on a release labeled in *MRR* as "Highly recommended." One of the catchier presidential parody tunes from the period, its opening verse, with references to MX missiles and eliminating food programs for the poor, explained how many saw Reagan during his rise to power. "Comes riding through in a blaze of glory / He's the latest cover story / Fueled by jellybeans in a jar / He's the mummy from Hollywood, Hey! Hey!" According to Angry Red Planet, and most other punk bands, this is what things looked like with Reagan at the helm in the land of the free.[13]

Home of the Brave

On January 28, 1986, Americans witnessed on live television a national tragedy as the space shuttle *Challenger*, seventy-three seconds after its takeoff from Cape Canaveral, Florida, violently exploded over the Atlantic Ocean. The following day the *New York Times* reported, "Wherever they were when they heard the news, at work, at school or at home, Americans shared in each other's grief over the death of seven astronauts." The evening of the explosion, President Reagan, who had been scheduled to deliver his yearly State of the Union address, decided instead to speak to Americans about the "truly . . . national loss." "The future doesn't belong to the fainthearted," he told viewers, "it belongs to the brave." In moments where the strength and resolve of Americans were challenged, Reagan often turned to a courage-oriented narrative. While punks appeared to pay the *Challenger* disaster no attention, they did frequently criticize the notion that American exceptionalism was somehow rooted in a courageous nature few other nations professed so publicly to have. To them, America was not the "land of the free and the home of the brave" that the national anthem and Reagan expressed it to be. In fact, it wasn't even close.[14]

While not many songs included "Brave" in the title, those that did were rather revealing in terms of how punks interpreted the Reagan-Era notion of courage as a unique and distinct American characteristic. One of the earliest was released in 1981 by a band from Tustin, California, called Saigon on their *Annihilation* release. "America (Home of the Free and the Brave)" brought the president into the picture almost immediately, the first two lines stating, "America the home of the free and the brave / Nuclear war is what Reagan craves." Between the possibility of dying in El Salvador or in another world war (songs concerning both of these are addressed in chapter 5), there was no place, according to Saigon, where one could be truly free, particularly because of the "U.S. fucking A." A similar theme was expressed the next year by Madison, Wisconsin's Mecht Mensch. Loosely translated as "Mechanical Man," the group's 1982 EP *Acceptance*, which included "Land of the Brave," was actually recorded by Butch Vig, drummer for the mid-'90s alternative band Garbage and legendary producer of Nirvana's *Nevermind*. Beginning with "They want you to die for your country . . . for what / Feeble fucker gonna die for your flag . . . fuck!," it offers a strong critique of the idea that bravery in America was only exemplified by the willingness of young people to sacrifice their lives and was the ultimate essence of national symbols such as the flag.[15]

Three years after Mecht Mensch's release and just a few months before the *Challenger* disaster, Reagan delivered a brief radio address on Flag Day in which he discussed the Stars and Stripes' storied past and historical significance. It was a constant reminder of the hardships the nation endured as we advanced the twin causes of freedom and democracy throughout our history. Asking all listeners to stand with him that evening at 7 P.M. to proudly recite the Pledge of Allegiance, he punctuated his request with an all-too-familiar enunciation of American awesomeness. "We are, after all," he firmly reminded them, "the land of the free and the home of the brave." That same year, Chicago's Naked Raygun released its second full-length album, *All Rise*, with the opening track titled "Home of the Brave," a roughly two-minute testament to the ridiculousness and hypocrisy of the idea that courage somehow informed the doings of all Americans. Described as "one of the most important punk bands to emerge in Chicago during the Reagan era," Naked Raygun, whose name was determined before he became president and apparently has no connection to his, became well known throughout the country and across the globe during the 1980s for its melodic tendencies and choruses of "ohs" and "ahs" powerfully belted out by frontman Jeff Pezzati. Briefly recounting the experiences of two people—Jeanie and Stu—disgruntled in a country they can't seem to understand and pondering the possibility of leaving it behind, "Home of the Brave" concludes with Pezzati singing about America, "Broken dreams and promises / These are things they have and hold," and sardonically asking, "A country that even persecuted the Weavers / Did you ever see the Weavers?"[16]

Led by the famous folklorist and activist Pete Seeger, the Weavers, a quartet whose work included classics like "If I Had a Hammer," "On Top of Old Smoky," and "Goodnight Irene," were blacklisted in the 1950s after being investigated by the House Un-American Activities Committee for suspicion of communist affiliation. A few years earlier, Reagan, then president of the Screen Actors Guild, testified before the same committee as a "friendly witness" and responded to questions about possible communist infiltration into the union. While the Weavers would be barred from recording, he would go on to act in dozens of films and television shows. The same year he testified, 1947, ten Hollywood insiders would refuse to, all of whom were imprisoned for contempt and, like the Weavers, blacklisted by studios. One of these was screenwriter Dalton Trumbo, who after spending eleven months in jail went on to write under a pseudonym. Robert Rich, the name Trumbo chose, would win an Oscar in 1957 for best story, the last ever given in this category, with a film about a young Mexican boy trying to save his beloved bull from being used and killed by a famous matador. Its name, ironically, was *The Brave One*. Trumbo's fellow blacklisted artist Seeger would go on to a successful solo folk singing and songwriting career, which included a performance at the Lincoln Memorial during the inaugural festivities for Barack Obama. One of his most well-known songs was the English nursery rhyme and counting song "This Old Man," which he supposedly would change the lyrics to in live performances to reflect his distaste for Reagan. As one listener recalled the parodied lyrics, "This old man, he played one / He cut back in Washington," "This old man, he played six / He was better in the flicks," and "This old man, he played nine / B-1 bombers all in line," were plenty of evidence of Seeger's opinions about the HUAC conspirator who would go on to play the role of a lifetime as the most powerful person in the world. Although they said it with a bit more punch, punks like those in Naked Raygun clearly concurred with the old folklorist's sentiments.[17]

Fuck Your American Dreams

Beyond bravery and freedom, Reagan often spoke to Americans about their country being the land of dreams. In his first inaugural address he proclaimed, "It is time for us to realize that we're too great a nation to limit ourselves to small dreams," and "We have every right to dream heroic dreams." "Your dreams, your hopes, your goals," he promised them, "are going to be the dreams, the hopes, and the goals of this administration, so help me God." Just a few months earlier, candidate Reagan delivered a Labor Day address at Liberty State Park in which he encouraged voters to look to him to renew their capacity to dream. As he emphatically iterated, "This country needs a new Administration, with a renewed dedication to the dream of an America, an Administration that will give that dream new life and make America great again!" A Reagan presidency would work hard to restore and revitalize this dream, would "take bold action" to ensure it was not swept away in the crisis of confidence Carter had spoken of the year before. With the Statue of Liberty standing tall across the harbor, the symbol of hope for so many who came to the United States with big dreams, Reagan promised his audience, "We can make the dream that brought so many of us or our parents and grandparents to this land, we can make that dream live once more."[18]

No one believed in this more so than Reagan, his life—from humble Illinois small-town origins to Hollywood film star to president of the United States—reflected this dream come true, and his public remarks constantly reiterated the idea that this could happen to anyone. Speaking about this at a White House ceremony to celebrate Hispanic Heritage Week a year after entering office, he reminded attendees, "We are a nation of freedom, living under God, believing all citizens must have the opportunity to grow, create wealth, and build a better life for those who follow. If we live up to these moral values, we can keep the American dream alive for our children and our grandchildren, and America will remain mankind's best hope." While Reagan may have enthusiastically believed in the American Dream, for others who looked at the country and the world through less rose-colored glasses than his, it seemed to be more like a nightmare. Punks in particular took on the idea that America was *the* place where everyone could fulfill their dreams. They rather chose to illuminate how it was a shallow promise, denied many, and took to decrying it in song.[19]

The same year Reagan reiterated to Hispanic Americans the importance of keeping the dream alive, a band from Los Angeles, home to the largest Hispanic population in the country at that time, many of whom lived in circumstances that could be described as less than dreamy, expressed a different take on things. Bad Religion, formed in 1980, would release their first album two years later titled *How Could Hell Be Any Worse?* on Epitaph Records, founded and owned by guitarist Brett Gurewitz. Included on it were songs about life in America in the early 1980s like "We're Only Gonna Die," "Voice of God Is Government," and the poignantly titled "Fuck Armageddon . . . This Hell." (More concerning the album and the last of these is discussed in the next chapter, whose title it shares.) The band also recorded for the album "American Dream," a penetrating appraisal of the failed promises of the Reagan Era. In true punk fashion, it begins with a typical assault upon all things American—"I hate my family, I hate my school, speed limits and the golden rule" is followed with "Hate people who aren't what they seem, more than anything else, American Dream." For Bad Religion, the dream had become about material consumption, as frontman Greg Graffin announced: "Promise me today I'll have a Chevrolet." A few years earlier Reagan would refer to the car as "the last great freedom" Americans had, the mobility it offered empowering them more than anything else. While the power to purchase cars, among other things, was what many wanted, Bad Religion also warned that it came and went rapidly and without pity ("It'll sweep you away, so enjoy it today, tomorrow you'll be old thus useless"). A similar theme ran through "American Dream" by Human Therapy, a group from La Verne, California, just east of L.A. Released on their 1983 7" by the aptly named Doctor Dreams Records, it reiterated the notion that the only measure of success in Reagan's America was financial prosperity and the ability to accumulate wealth. To Human Therapy, the American Dream was explained in a simple way that many Reagan supporters would likely have concurred with: "You've got to have a big house, Mercedes Benz, country club, a few friends." Their suggestion to listeners frustrated by the vapidity of this was as simple: "Don't waste your time on the American Dream."[20]

Beyond Human Therapy and Bad Religion, a few others tackled the Reagan-Era interpretation of the great American Dream. One of the bands to emerge from the Windy City made their listeners aware that the idea of a happy and plentiful future was far from the reality most Americans experienced. Chicago's Articles of Faith, led by frontman Vic Bondi, whose comments concerning Reagan in the opening minutes of the *American Hardcore* documentary were discussed earlier, wrote in their "American Dreams," "Look what's happened to my dreams / My nightmares speak in voices seen / We came to burn in the city on the hill / Prescribe me faith, but give me pills." Reagan spoke often about America being a "city on a hill," believing there was something special about Americans, that they were blessed by God to be a beacon of light for humanity to admire and look to. Bondi and Articles of Faith appeared to be done with the idea that the United States had some kind of divine origin that elevated it above all others, a model for the rest of the world to marvel at and emulate. As the chorus clearly announced, "I've had enough of American Dreams / I've had enough of American Dreams." Similar sentiments could be heard in "Fuck Your American Dreams" by Econochrist. Transplanted from Little Rock, Arkansas, to Oakland, their 1988 EP *It Runs Deep* was a later release that candidly assessed America in the final years of Reagan's tenure. Accompanied by "Think for Yourself," "Blind Faith," and "Ignorance," their condemnation of the dream of America rings similar to those expressed by Bad Religion and Human Therapy, "blind selfishness" being really at its core. As the second verse iterated, "I don't want to be rich like you / I don't want a suburban home / Materialism is not happiness / And I am no goddamn clone." Speaking to those who bought this narrative, which was aligned with the Reaganaut philosophy, the chorus emphatically stated, "Fuck your American Dream / I say it's a lie."[21]

Like Econochrist, another transplanted Bay Area group illuminated the fallacies of the grand American idea with its own "American Dream." The suitably named Corrupted Morals, originally from Palmdale just north of Los Angeles, was one of the bands that made the Berkeley 924 Gilman Street club a late-era punk mecca. In 1987, a year after forming, they put out a four-song demo tape that included their sneering study of the national fantasy. On a fold-up sheet peppered with images of Reagan on one side and Reagan, his wife, Rambo, and Colonel Oliver North of Iran-Contra fame on the other, are the handwritten lyrics for an unreserved review of what's wrong with the country. "Whatever happened to the American dream / The alarm went off and now it's gone / I'm awake and don't like what I've seen / This isn't the way it's supposed to be" was a sentiment shared by most punks. "American Dream" would be included on the group's 1989 LP *Cheese-It* along with others like "Freedom to Express," "Weapons of War," "I'm Not Smiling," and "Thoughts of Smog and Slums." In between they would release their *Chet* EP, named after the shotgun-toting, asshole older brother from the film *Weird Science* and described in *MRR* as a "darn swell tape" with "war and conformity" as the lyrical focus. On the opening track, titled "Be All You Can Be," a critique of the increasing impact on American youth of Reagan-Era militarism, the president is given a quick mention in the third verse with. "Sign on the dotted line and sign away your life / You belong to Ronnie now, your gun's your fuckin' wife." For many young Americans, this wasn't a dream but their nightmarish reality.[22]

Humorously, the EP concluded with a hysterical homage to a member of Reagan's cabinet that deserves brief mention. Edwin Meese had been part of Reagan's inner circle for years, serving as chief of staff during his governorship as well as in the 1980 campaign. During his time with Reagan in California, he would be well known for his strong stance against the Free Speech Movement at UC-Berkeley, having sent in 800 riot-dressed officers to violently clash with protesters in what would become known as the Battle of People's Park. As one author later wrote, "Practicing Reaganauts invariably favor government authority over individual rights and liberties wherever conflict occurs," and there were few persons surrounding Reagan who were more Reaganaut than Meese. He would eventually become attorney general and led the Commission on Pornography created by Reagan during his second term. Corrupted Morals, whose name could well have been one of the many societal ills mentioned in the Commission's report, took aim at Reagan's right-hand man and his censorial efforts in "The Adventures of Edwin Meese," opening with frontman Rick Morgan sarcastically singing as Meese over a slow buildup and Suess-like cadence. "'This country,' he shouted, 'I've now rated X / By smut, we're polluting youngsters learning of sex / A serious crisis of great proportions we've got / Perverting our morals with mind-warping rot.'" What became known as the Meese Report was a nearly 2,000-page document discussing the history and harmful effects of pornography, and with Meese at the helm of the Justice Department, it would eventually lead to a reduction in the sale and distribution of some pornographic materials. Corrupted Morals would not be alone in criticizing Meese's work, with a *New York Times* editorial response stating that the Commission relied on "questionable evidence" and that "its cure of censorship is worse than the disease." Ironically, Meese would eventually resign while being investigated for improper conduct—corrupted morals, one might say—although Reagan, in support of his longtime friend, would say, "If Ed Meese is not a good man, there are no good men." In assessing Meese along with other members of the Reagan regime, most punks would agree with the last part of that statement.[23]

Conclusion

While campaigning in 1984, Reagan's team ran an ad to remind Americans how good things were compared to four years earlier, and that to change White House occupants now would be ruinous. "It's morning again in America," it said in a calm and comforting tone, "and under the leadership of President Reagan, our country is prouder and stronger and better." Not everyone felt this to be the case. Likely part of the nearly 40 million persons who did not put an X next to Reagan's name on their ballots that November were the members of Agent 86, if—like many punks—they voted at all. The Arcata, California, group released a few months later their *Scary Action 7"* with a violently angry man holding a gun to his head and the above-the-fold portion of a newspaper stating in bold letters REAGAN LANDSLIDE on the cover. On it were clear responses from the group concerning the prospect of four more years of Reaganism, particularly "Raygunomics" and "Amerikan Way." That same year Social Unrest, an East Bay five-piece band, would release its first full-length album including the appropriately titled "Good Morning America." By that time they had firmly established themselves as "not just another three chord band" and lyrically articulated their intense frustration regarding the country and the man leading it. The "general enemy," as they had labeled him a few years earlier, was back. "Ronald Reagan's on the march to fuck the world up with heart," they told listeners. And with another electoral victory, punks would have more time to take him on in song.[24]

A few years earlier, experts had come together to assess his work and inform Americans about "the effects of Reagan's policies on the economy, foreign policy, women, minorities, neighborhoods, crime, health, education, and welfare." The result was the *What Reagan Is Doing to Us* essay collection mentioned earlier. In one of the chapters, Ira Glasser, director of the American Civil Liberties Union, told readers, "What Reagan is trying to do is clear enough. What we must do is also clear." Punks appeared to embrace a similar mindset, and in the months surrounding his reelection released a plethora of albums, all of which included critical commentary on the rule of the Reaganauts. Coupled with outpourings from members of the intellectual community like Glasser, one would have thought the election results would have turned out differently. With over 58 percent of the popular vote and 525 votes in the electoral college, Reagan won the '84 election in a landslide. The only state he lost was Minnesota, where his opponent was from. Only George Washington had won them all. For many punks, Chicago's Naked Raygun summed things up well with a song on their 1985 album *Throb Throb* — "Only in America."[25]

CHAPTER THREE

Fuck Armageddon . . . This Is Hell

> We made the city stronger—we made the city freer—
> and we left her in good hands.
> —RONALD REAGAN

> How can hell be any worse? Life alone is such a curse!
> —BAD RELIGION

All in All, Not Bad

Four years after helping him secure his second term, Americans turned on their radios and televisions to hear Ronald Reagan deliver his farewell address. It was his revolution that he would speak to them about during his final broadcast from the Oval Office, although, as he stated midway through the address, he saw it more as "a rediscovery of our values and our common sense" than something truly revolutionary. He was proud of what he achieved during his eight years in the White House, most importantly of the "new national pride . . . the new patriotism" that he and his supporters helped restore. The America he grew up in was different from the one he was asked to lead; the positive changes made under his watch would only be sustained through continued vigilance on the part of parents and schools, and "a greater emphasis on civic ritual." Speaking again through his favorite metaphor for the country, "the shining city upon a hill" was better off than it was eight years ago, standing strong and true, happier and more prosperous, and still a beacon of freedom for the world to marvel at. "All in all, not bad, not bad at all," he reminded them.[1]

While Reagan left office with a public approval rating upwards of 60 percent, not everyone looked back on his time with such affection. Tip O'Neill, former speaker of the House of Representatives who spent half the decade as leader of the Democratic opposition, said in the last years of his presidency, "I hate to say it about such an agreeable man, but it was sinful that Ronald Reagan ever became President. . . . I've known every president since Harry Truman and there's no question in my mind that [Reagan] was the worst." To many people, Reagan was the paradoxical president O'Neill's statement well described, likable as a person but despised for his policies and the impact they had on the country, a sentiment captured accurately in the earliest days of his presidency by journalist Arthur Rowse in the title of his book *One Sweet Guy and What He Is Doing to You*. As he wrote in the first pages (before spending the next 200 tearing year-one of his presidency apart), "It is easy to like Ronald Reagan." The seventeen experts who would come together a year later to produce *What Reagan Is Doing to Us* discarded any sense of likability for an all-out assault on Reaganism. "The Reagan approach," the editors iterated, "is the more mean-spirited for its hypocrisy." Looking back on the Reagan presidency, political scientist Hugh Heclo may have articulated things best: "However friends and foes of Ronald Reagan may parse his life, all must surely agree that he was a remarkable American. They may disagree on the honor due him, but they could hardly deny the significance of his life for good or ill."[2]

Whatever journalists and historians have said about Ronald Reagan, one thing is certain, and that is that punks might have been the least inclined people to even hint at the prospect of Reagan's presidency being anything less than awful. Not fooled by his charisma and charming, grandfather-like personality, they railed on him and his America without reservation. But while songs about both are meaningful, there is more evidence to consider if one wants to get a clear picture of punk as a grassroots, intentional reaction to Reaganism. Besides hating on Reagan and America, they also expressed a sense of disaffection for life in the 1980s, influenced by the policies of his administration. Like their songs about Reagan and America, they also used lyrics as a means to express the estrangement and increased anxiety many felt. First, punks wrote about life in the suburbs, the sprawling communities where many influential figures in the scene grew up and lived. Second, they wrote about the one place they spent more time in daily than anywhere else, which also became a place of concern for the Reagan administration—schools. Evidence of a deeper sense of awareness beyond their immediate lives, punk bands across the country also took on an issue not many artists at that time did—environmental abuse. Interestingly, and with an underpinning philosophy that seemed in line with the right-wing moralism of many Reagan supporters, they also wrote about straight living and avoiding the self-indulgent pitfalls that many punks themselves had fallen victim to. Songs concerning these themes, although they may seem disconnected from one another, are insightful introspections of youth disaffection in Reaganland and evidence of an intentional narrative within punk about life in the 1980s.

Suburban Wasteland

On April 13, 1984, New World Pictures released a film by Penelope Spheeris, director of the landmark 1981 punk documentary *The Decline of Western Civilization*. Described in a *New York Times* review as "a clear-eyed, compassionate melodrama about a bunch of young dropouts," it offered viewers a look into a Los Angeles area punk scene "more picturesque than dangerous" and made up of "refugees from broken, lower-middle-class families." Called *Suburbia*, it starred Chris Pedersen, guitarist for the Southern California band The Patriots, as the jocosely named Jack Diddley, and a young Flea of Red Hot Chili Peppers fame as a rat-loving punk named Razzle. Both belong to a group of social outcasts living communally in an abandoned neighborhood outside the city whose lives revolve around stealing food from open garages, going to punk shows, and general displays of teenage angst and aggression. With live show footage from Orange County bands D.I., T.S.O.L., and the Vandals interspersed throughout, *Suburbia* provides a unique perspective on the punk experience at a time when scenes were popping up all over the country. If it is an accurate depiction, frustration about living, particularly in the suburbs, was an essential aspect of being a punk in the 1980s.[3]

Suburbia, the sprawling and densely populated communities around cities like L.A., had by the time of Reagan's election become a far cry from the bourgeois utopias original planners had hoped they would be. They had grown in the wake of World War II as urban dwellers and veterans yearned for a quiet and more peaceful existence outside of the city but close enough to commute in for work. Rows of cookie-cutter homes dotted the landscapes surrounding cities as more and more Americans, mostly white, looked for their middle-class dream life in the manicured cul-de-sacs of these Edenic enterprises. A piece of paradise was what many were looking for and thought they had found, away from the hustle and bustle (and increased diversity) of the urban areas that had been home to most Americans since the late nineteenth century. By the end of the 1960s, what started as Eden became *sprawl*, a term used to describe the overextensive and haphazard development of these areas. With this came serious issues for individuals and the communities they had hoped to find. In books attempting to explain what happened, phrases like "alienated, isolated, and alone," "an oppressively isolated existence," "a polarized and fragmented society," and "the root cause of many of our personal and societal woes," describe a suburban world gone wrong where loneliness and depression became common. Both would resonate in punk songs about life in the suburbs, but also in schools and the world as a whole.[4]

Lisa McGirr, in her book *Suburban Warriors: The Origins of the New American Right*, saw the suburbs as fertile ground for the rise of a new conservative revolt, one that would eventually have Ronald Reagan as its standard-bearer. Her work specifically concerned Orange County, California, a region just outside of L.A. described as having "few central public spaces except those dominated by consumption activities" as well as "spatial isolation and an absence of community," both of which helped it become a conservative stronghold by the 1970s. Using it as a case study, McGirr posited that it was in areas like this, with "unending miles of suburban sprawl" and "an ethos of individualism," that the New Right found its base. In many ways, she was describing the fertile ground upon which Perlstein's Reaganland took root. Ironically, she was also describing the place where punk took off, Orange County being one of the earliest and most well-known scenes to emerge at that time. As the decades changed, in its villages sprang up bands like T.S.O.L., Social Distortion, Agent Orange, Adolescents, the Vandals, and Middle Class, all singing about individual estrangement and disconnectedness—middle-class life in suburbia—with the immediate world around them. They would not be alone as songs about depression, isolation, and an increasing sense of personal disaffection were common across scenes. Titles like "Depression," "I'm Not a Loser," "Bored to Death," "A Cry for Help in a World Gone Mad," "Mental Breakdown," "Troubled Times," and others like these found themselves on the track listings of every punk album produced during the '80s. With these also came a number that cut straight to the point, making the suburbs as big a target for their lyrical ire as Reagan himself. Void, a group formed around the time Reagan was elected and from the Baltimore-Washington metro area suburb of Columbia, Maryland, succinctly put into words what many of these bands expressed in song: "Suburbs Suck!"[5]

"The suburbs," according to Evan Rapport in his work on race in early punk, "are a cornerstone of punk in myth and reality," and "suburban geography and middle-class life is embedded in punk's genealogy and terminology." While Ronald Reagan is obviously not responsible for the emergence of suburbia, the sprawl that came to characterize it, or the many psychological and social issues suffered by those living there, particularly among the kids who would find welcoming spaces in the punk scenes that emerged near the end of the 1970s, the two are directly connected. So when punk bands sang about their frustrations with life in these places, they were again critically assessing the Reagan presidency, albeit indirectly. These songs concerned a number of issues that would have resonated with punks across the country. While many specifically mentioned "suburbia" in their titles and lyrics, others centered on emotional issues like depression, which environmental psychologists were connecting to the feeling of alienation stemming from life in these areas. Most famous among these was "Depression" by Black Flag. From Hermosa Beach, a South Bay suburb outside of L.A., it was likely first heard by many in Spheeris's *Decline* with the group's second singer Ron Reyes belting out the lyrics with a spastic and gyrating passion. "Right here, all by myself / I ain't got no one else / The situation is bleeding me / There's no relief for a person like me," the song's first verse, expressed a feeling of isolated helplessness that can definitely be sensed among the many scenesters interviewed by Spheeris for her film. The band would eventually rerecord the song with Henry Rollins out front for their seminal 1981 album *Damaged*, and while "Depression" would be one of its more powerful tracks, others like "Rise Above," "I Want to See," "No More," and "Police Story" offered insightful intonations on youth existence in the suburbs as well.[6]

Long before Black Flag came to be, the English author George Orwell described the mundanity of life in suburbia in his 1939 novel *Coming Up for Air*. Orwell's suburbs were, according to one reviewer, "a series of enclosed personal spaces in which the characters internalise their anxieties, frustrations, and feelings." For many young Americans growing up in the '70s and living in these spaces, boredom lay at the root of this phenomenon. Punk, in many ways, allowed them to "come up for air" and express frustration about their mundane existence in places like Fullerton, the Orange County suburban home of the bands mentioned above, or on the other side of the country in any one of the neighborhoods, towns, and villages of the DC metro area that spawned its own early unique and influential scene. From one of these, Rockville, Maryland, came John Stabb, lead singer of Government Issue. Their *Legless Bull* EP included a song that took this head on, with "Bored to Death" and Stabb's usual punchy vocal treatment repeating in the chorus what many kids felt and likely used as motivation to get involved in their local punk scenes. "Nothing to do, I'm bored to death / I'm so bored, I'm bored to death." Up the coast in Northampton, Massachusetts, a suburb of Springfield, the Teenage PhDs included a similar-themed tune on their 1980 self-titled EP. Between "Eat the Poor," "Punk Rock Is Dead," and "Eat, Sleep and Fuck" was "Too Bored to Die," a slow-moving song with a seemingly bored lyricist singing about being "Too bored to stay / Too bored to leave / Too bored to do nothing / Too bored to breathe." Apparently for some punks, even coming up for air seemed challenging, the excessive boredom of suburbia having an asphyxiating effect on their lives.[7]

Coupled with songs about depression, boredom, and the many other psychological issues stemming from life in what historian Kenneth Jackson called the *crabgrass frontier*, with its centerless cities, loss of community, and drive-in culture, are the many—and there are many—that expressly cite the suburbs or suburbia as a root problem in America. Some did this with the band names they chose. In Green Bay, Wisconsin, a city witnessing significant sprawl as punk was coming into its own, Suburban Mutilation was formed. Their 1984 *The Opera Ain't Over until the Fat Lady Sings!* listed such Reagan-Era tropes as "Twisted Cross," "Police State," "El Salvador Stomp," and "Don't Psychoanalyze Me." Down south, in the suburbs surrounding Columbia, South Carolina, some classmates at Irmo High School started the perfectly named BSY, or Bored Suburban Youths. Included on their 1988 record, titled *Red Menace—Farewell Suburbia* and released after the group parted ways, were their own "Police State" as well as other critical reflections like "Contaminated" and "Living in America." Things must have been really dull in the part of the country where they lived, as a 1986 *Columbia Record* article describing an upcoming show with the band stated bluntly, "Where'd it get that name, Bored Suburban Youths? Hey, these guys are from Irmo." Similar to BSY, out of the St. Louis metro area came a band with the burnishing moniker White Suburban Youth. On their demo tapes from the mid-'80s were the songs "White Suburban Youth" and "Suburban Streets," both barely comprehensible attestations of disaffection. In the latter, listeners can make out an utterance that would have resonated well with many of the suburban youth who turned to punk during the Reagan years: "No one knows, and no one cares."[8]

Expressing ire for the mundanity of life in the soulless sprawl of suburban society reached every corner of the country. Seattle's The Lewd sang about being a "Suburban Prodigy" ("I don't give a fuck, I don't like a thing") while 3,000 miles away in the fun and sun of Bradenton, Florida, just south of Tampa, Belching Penguin's (B.P.) "Suburban Life" announced, "Suburban life, nothing to do / Suburban life, does it bore you / I beat my head against the door / Suburban life, just another war." In the borough of Elmwood Park, a self-described bedroom suburb of New York City, Adrenalin O.D. released an EP in 1983 titled *Let's Barbecue*, the front cover including a photo of the band sitting on a back porch engaged in the favorite weekend recreational activity of many suburbanites. The first song, aptly titled "Suburbia," analyzed issues surrounding life there as well as any environmental psychologist could. Lines like "Too many cars," "Everyone works and everyone hides," and "Too many stores" were generalizations most suburban punks would have well been familiar with, regardless of where they were living. Around the nation's capital, along with Void's plainspoken pronunciation, was "Suburban Wasteland" by Artificial Peace, a band that, according to their Dischord Records page, always made it a point to let people know they were from Bethesda, Maryland, a suburb of DC. For them, the "isolated apathy" associated with life there was defined by "two cars and four T.V.s," "sterile walls," "a job and . . . a wife," and a "pre-fab junkyard" that must be escaped if one wanted to be truly free.⁹

Really Red, from Houston, wrote about being immune to "Suburban Disease," while New York's False Prophets sang about what happened when the "Suburbanites Invade." Up in Albany, The Morons, in a song called "Suburbanite," wrote about the "plastic houses," "artificial lights," "bridge, the lodge, the social club, [and] bowling Wednesday nights" that dominated the abhorrent existence of those who proudly wore the name. And just north of Chicago, the Evanston quartet of Darrel Lichtt, Pat Thedic, Lead Zeapplin, and Jug Head, also known as Heavy Mental, wrote in their "Suburb IA" about the "houses that look alike" and "condominiums in oblivion" lived in by "suburban refugees." These and others describe well the anxiety associated with youth life in suburbia and the sense of frustration experienced. But, ironically, not all punks felt that way. Back on the Pacific Coast, in the South Bay suburb of Manhattan Beach, the Descendents included on their pioneering album *Milo Goes to College* the song "Suburban Home," with its opening lines of "I want to be stereotyped / I want to be classified / I want a suburban home." A seemingly sardonic take on the suburbanite fascination for peace and tranquility, it allegedly had a deeper meaning. Written by Tony Lombardo, the group's bassist who was actually thirty-seven at that time, nearly two decades older than the other members, it wasn't so much a critique of suburbia but rather a reflection of his desire for a life of quietude and simplicity. As he mentioned in a later interview, Lombardo, like many punks, had come from a broken family and witnessed the childhood pain associated with divorce and an alcoholic parent. For him, suburbia was a place where he might "get lost." This attitude of removal would be mirrored in "I'm Not a Punk," also on *Milo*, where Lombardo presciently took note of the conformity that was already creeping into the hardcore punk scene, particularly the violence that would soon come to define it. As he said later in an interview, "that whole thing just turned me off. I just wanted to play the music." For Lombardo, suburbia didn't appear to be the wasteland his younger counterparts believed it to be. Not surprisingly, he seemed to be very much alone in the punk community when it came to thinking this way. What likely influenced this was his age, because, unlike his bandmates and so many punks, he wasn't spending up to eight hours a day in the other spaces they seemed to despise . . . schools.[10]

I Hate My School

Not long before Spheeris's film debuted, a taped radio address from Reagan was heard by the American people about an apparent issue of grave national importance. Referencing a commission report that had been published a few days earlier, he pleaded with listeners to join with his administration in facing the crisis head on. A unified effort was needed if the country was going to successfully overcome the calamity it faced. A course change was essential to get things moving forward once again. Two decades of decline had to be reconciled; the efforts of all were necessary if control was to be reestablished and disaster evaded. "For the sake of all our children, our country, and our future," he beseeched those tuned in, "we must join together in a national campaign to restore excellence in American education." The country, it seemed, was under attack from within, and a faltering school system was apparently the culprit. The solution, according to Reagan, was to put the education of America's youth back at the top of the list of national priorities where it used to and always should be.[11]

Reagan stepped into the Roosevelt Room of the White House to prerecord his remarks, having been made aware of "A Nation at Risk: The Imperative for Educational Reform," a report produced by the National Commission on Excellence in Education. Created two years earlier by Reagan's Secretary of Education Terrel Bell, a lifelong educator who had previously served in the Nixon and Ford administrations, its charge was simple—"to examine the quality of education in the United States and to make a report to the Nation and to [Reagan] within 18 months of its first meeting." Bell had replaced Shirley Hufstedler, the first secretary of the newly created department under Jimmy Carter in 1979, expecting to dismantle it. This was in tune with Reagan's federal education policy at the outset of his tenure, specifically the drive to disestablish any cabinet-level department that did not oversee programs of "overriding national interest" or were "Presidential in scope and responsibility." As two scholars wrote in the *Phi Delta Kappan* during his first year in office, "Education simply does not fit these criteria in Reagan's

Administration." Things seemed to change quickly in Bell's tenure with his newfound concern about "the widespread public perception that something is seriously remiss in our educational system." The Commission, created on August 26, 1981, would report on its findings roughly two years later with an emphatic opening line that no reader could misinterpret. "Our Nation is at risk." Ironically, although maybe not with the same causes in mind, most punks agreed.[12]

The Reagan years were not alone in seeing songs written about school, as every decade since the emergence of rock and roll witnessed artists paying homage to their hometown educational haunts. In the late '50s and early '60s, groups such as the Watts-banned Beach Boys released songs like "Be True to Your School," infused with a strong sense of spirit in celebration of the all-American high school experience. While Gary U. S. Bonds in "School's Out" sang about the joys of another year coming to an end, it was a far cry from the nihilistic tone provided in Alice Cooper's song of the same name released in 1972. Only a few years before the birth of punk and with lyrics like "We got no intelligence," "We might not come back at all," and "School's out completely," it reflected the growing frustration of many with an educational system that had gone through some radical changes during the previous decades, the most notable being forced integration. In terms of punk, it was the Ramones that first took on their schooling experiences with 1979's "Rock 'n' Roll High School," a catchy '60s-style pop tune and title track from the film released that same year. Opening with "Well, I don't care about history . . .'Cause that's not where I wanna be," it said what many students seemed to be feeling at that time—that they would rather be doing anything other than studying. In less than twenty years—the same time frame in which Terrel Bell recognized something amiss—schools had gone from places of pride to penitentiaries in the minds of some hyperbolic teens. And very quickly, Joey Ramone singing about "I hate the teachers and the principal / Don't wanna be taught to be no fool" would become punk par for the course when expressing disaffection with learning environments during the Age of Reagan.[13]

While no songs about how badly punk kids disliked their educational experiences mention Reagan specifically, two things are important when considering their inclusion as part of the lyrical assault on his presidency. First, nearly every band that wrote about schools also wrote about Reagan. He was clearly on their minds, and their frustration concerning his administration and leadership of the country can be recognized as one of the most consistent strains of thought across records from that era. Second, this is a chapter about the general sense of disaffection punks felt at that time, and in songs about no other topic could they—nearly all school-aged kids—express this most clearly. For them, life in America was directly connected to the hours spent every day sitting in classrooms under the watchful eye of teachers and administrators, immediate figures of authority (like their parents) easily juxtaposed with Reagan. Schools were the places where Reaganism was experienced firsthand by young people, its impact trickling down into their classrooms and hallways as educators felt increased pressure to perform under the weight of reports like "A Nation at Risk." Many were massive in size, where youths could easily get lost in the crowd, and as much a part of suburbia as the shopping malls close by. After a decade of schooling, described by one author as "not healthy for learning, excellence in education, or intellectual daring," schools in the 1980s appeared primed and ready to return under Reagan to their halcyon days where students were respectful, healthy competition was infused into nearly every aspect of life, and rigor was once again the cornerstone of every classroom. Yet, as the songs about education testify, school apparently sucked more during the Age of Reagan than at any other time in the nation's history.[14]

Songs about schools were nearly identical in tone with those about suburbia, and of all written about the awfulness of academic experiences, the most common title was as straight to the point as bands could get: "I Hate School," or some variation of it, was a forthright declamation used by kids since the first schoolhouse doors opened. But whereas most students reservedly retorted about their lack of affinity for academic affairs, punks—as they did about all things—screamed loudly and with a passionate rage that went unmatched. Simple and straightforward iterations, they were forceful assessments concerning education in the '80s. "I Hate My School" by Maumee, Ohio's Necros, another by Hawthorne, California's Redd Kross, "I Hated School" by the guilefully named No Rock Stars from Charlotte, North Carolina, and "I Hate School" by Charlottesville, Virginia's Landlords, are all insightful and ire-infused songs of discontent concerning American classrooms. For members of the Necros, hatred went beyond their teachers, all of whom were "insane," and included the other students, "fools" who were as much the cause of their daily strain as anything. "Why don't you just leave me alone? / All I wanna do is go home," while definitely not a feeling punks had a monopoly on, became a common thread among the school songs. They would double down on this with "Public High School" on the same release, describing it as "home of the fools" with an uncool and lame student body all centered on the Friday night football game more than anything else. Humorously, the

Maumee PTA (Parent-Teacher Association) was less than pleased with the group. A statement from them describing their music was included in an issue of *Touch & Go*, describing them as influencing the "unadulterated violence in our youth today" and proclaiming, "They must be stopped before our school is destroyed."[15]

Out West, Redd Kross would express sentiments similar to their Ohio comrades', with a disgust for "rah-rahs," "surfers," "jocks," and "bookworms" fueling their ire-laced lyrics. Having grown up in California, their school experiences would have been directly affected by Reagan's governorship and the educational policies he initiated. Similar to his presidency, as chief executive of the state he advocated for a limited central government, more local control, spending cuts, and no increases in funding for schools. The result of all this, according to one scholar, was "the deterioration of California's public schools," with "overcrowded classrooms, ancient, worn-out textbooks, crumbling buildings, and badly demoralized teachers." Reagan, according to the same scholar, left the California public education system in a worse state than it was in when he entered office. For many punks living there, they would have witnessed firsthand during their formative years the strained school circumstances listed above. For Redd Kross and others growing up in the suburban landscape surrounding L.A., things were apparently so bad that they felt compelled to express this frustration through their music. For their debut EP they would include "I Hate My School" as one of their first six songs recorded. With future Black Flag frontman Ron Reyes on drums and Greg Heston of the Circle Jerks and Bad Religion on guitar, the group, founded by brothers Jeff and Steve McDonald, gave listeners with their catchy and nearly sixty-second song an early anthem of academic angst. "I hate my school / Can't hardly wait to graduate / I hate my school / Better get out before it's too late" was a chorus that school-aged punks beyond California would have found to be an apt description of feelings.[16]

Not to be outdone by their California counterparts, a few Southern bands on the other side of the country joined in the critical appraising of school life during the Reagan ascendancy. The Charlotte quartet No Rock Stars would find their work released on the 1982 compilation tape *No Core* along with fellow North Carolinians Colcor, No Labels, and Corrosion of Conformity. Including a front cover image of a Confederate flag being burned, the cassette, according to an *MRR* review, was enough evidence that punk was thriving in the American South, a region of the country that had voted en masse for Jimmy Carter in 1976 only to switch over to Reagan (save Carter's home state of Georgia) four years later. If the lyrics of No Rock Stars' "I Hated

School" are accurate, classrooms in Dixie weren't much different from those in California, Ohio, or any other state where punks were railing against education. Again, a dislike for athletes and the school spirit surrounding them is expressed in lines like "Didn't play sports, ain't no jock" and "I hated school colors, I hated their banners," both sandwiching a homophobic iteration that was also common in songs from the era. (Songs concerning this are discussed in chapter 4.) Not far away in Charlottesville, the Landlords released *Hey, It's a Teenage House Party*, described in *MRR* as "one of the better US releases" in 1984, with "wild, crazy stuff that is abrasive and raw." Included on the twenty-one-song LP was "I Hate School," possibly the shortest song in the history of a genre well known for musical brevity. In a rapid four seconds that any inattentive album listener could easily miss, singer John Beers barked, "Teacher's a jerk / I hate homework / Let's burn the school / 'Cause I hate school." Thankfully, Beers had been drawn to punk when first seeing Dead Kennedys' "Kill the Poor" single at a local record store. His intrigue led him to buy it, which led him to start writing his own lyrics, including the group's educational invective. For many kids like Beers, who had graduated from high school and was headed to the University of Virginia, punk offered what nothing else could. "I'd found what I had been looking for," he said in a 2018 interview. And between the lyrics of "I Hate School" and caricatured images of Reagan included on their show fliers, it's clear that what Beers and the other members of the Landlords found was an outlet of expression for the disaffection they felt coming of age in the land lorded over by Reaganism.[17]

There are so many songs about school that it is impossible to adequately consider what few should serve as the best examples of polemics against Reagan-Era educational practices. Beyond those already discussed, JFA's "Out of School" could just as easily been included, with its chorus announcing "No more chicks to love / No more classes to ditch / No more jocks to hate / No more teachers that bitch." So too could have been one from Minneapolis's The Replacements, who went on to achieve renown as alternative rock pioneers. Their acerbic assault was rather simple, with "Fuck school, fuck my school" the most common lyric belted throughout by singer Paul Westerberg. Hüsker Dü, also from the Twin Cities, got in on the action with a strong "Fuck you!" concluding the first verse of "Guns at My School" from 1982's *Land Speed Record*. Back in L.A., Overkill, one of the earliest groups to fuse punk with metal, released on their 1982 SST album a torching tirade suggesting "No more dances, football games / Break the rules, burn the school." And up in the Chicagoland area, the slapstick quartet of teenagers known as Rights of the Accused provided another example with their simply titled "In School." While the lyrics for the song on the album insert tell listeners in true punk fashion to "Make up your own lyrics. God knows we do," it's clear from the chorus that punks, many growing up in the massive suburbs surrounding the Windy City, had similar feelings about their education experiences. "Having fun in school / Follow their rules / Having fun in school / Jocks are so cool," was a sarcastic description that most likely would have resonated with every punk kid in America walking the hallowed halls of their local educational institution.[18]

While all of these, and others like Pedestrian Abuse's "Fuck School," Chemical Waste's "School Sucks!," Sin 34's "Forced Education," and No's "American School System," to name but a few more, are grassroots takes on how young people involved in punk scenes perceived their educational experiences during the Age of Reagan, none took on the president himself. Again, that doesn't matter as each offers listeners intentional assessments of a school system that, like many other social services, was subject to both harsh rhetoric from the Reagan administration in the form of reports like "A Nation at Risk" as well as even harsher cuts in funding. As one scholar wrote looking back on his legacy, "As governor and president [Reagan] demagogically fanned discontent with public education. . . . As governor and president he bashed educators and slashed education spending while professing to value it. And as governor and president he left the nation's educators dispirited and demoralized." The results of this contributed to a public school environment where many kids felt increasingly disconnected and disinterested, a lot of whom became punks. The Reagan years did not constitute a "revolutionary federal disengagement" from public education as many thought it would, but did leave a lasting impact on how the public perceived teachers and the teaching profession in general, a perception that in some ways continues today. For punks throughout the 1980s, singing about school was just one more way to express their frustration and growing sense of disaffection with the times they were living in, which were influenced more by Reagan than anyone else.[19]

Toxic Shock

While the 1970s may have been a decade of educational decadence, it was in many ways *the* environmental decade, kicked off by the first Earth Day on April 22, 1970. But while Reagan would attempt to fix American schools, he would take a much different approach to issues concerning nature. Twenty million Americans occupied the streets that first Earth Day to protest the continuing devastation of the natural world. Just a few months earlier, many had seen images of the largest oil spill in American history up to that time off the coast of Santa Barbara, California, including Wisconsin Senator Gaylord Nelson, whose visit to the site became the inspiration for the April moment and the modern environmental movement. That year alone would see Congress pass the National Environmental Policy Act and Clean Air Act, as well as the formation of the Environmental Protection Agency. Other acts concerning water, endangered species, forest management, and marine mammals would follow. Jimmy Carter would keep things going, tripling the size of the Wild and Scenic Rivers system, doubling the size of the national parks, and getting legislation passed to protect endangered wilderness areas. After signing a law that set aside over 56 million acres of Alaskan wilderness, Walter Cronkite announced, "Environmental groups said Carter has now replaced Teddy Roosevelt as the greatest conservation president of all time." Added to all this would be the 1977 creation of the Department of Energy, whose job would be to implement a comprehensive strategy regarding resources in this area, the nation's first. For those concerned about the natural world, things seemed to be headed in a positive direction with the election of 1980 looming on the horizon.[20]

It was clear even before he took the oath of office that Reagan's thoughts on the environment were much different from his predecessor's and that his tenure was going to be a problematic one for nature enthusiasts. "The environmental movement has had a nightmare and awakened to find it is true: Ronald Reagan is President-elect and the Senate is in Republican hands" was how science journalist Constance Holden described things just days after the election. For Holden and environmentalists, Reagan's utterances even before being voted into the White House were cause for serious concern, many of which showed a rather callow appreciation of the values people held about the natural world. He had once remarked when asked about expanding Redwood National Park, "A tree is a tree. How many more do you need to look at?" and during the 1980 campaign insinuated to an audience in Youngstown, Ohio, that trees were more responsible for air pollution than anything else. While comments like these displayed a "lack of intellectual sophistication" as well as a "willingness to embrace 'facts' of indeterminate origin" concerning environmental issues, it was the clear notion expressed in his campaign that protecting the environment was not compatible with growing the economy—the top priority of his administration—that was the most alarming. Reagan ran on a promise to get America out of its rut, to end the stagflation that had been sapping it of energy, will, and pride. Deregulation was at the core of this promise, and agencies associated with environmentalism were in his crosshairs.[21]

While it would not turn out to be the ruinous eight years activists anticipated, a new course concerning environmental policy was laid out, one problematically shortsighted. And like their responses to so much of what Reaganism encapsulated, punks did not sit this battle out. Songs focusing specifically on environmental issues are not nearly as numerous as those directly attacking Reagan and the country under his rule, but like those about life in suburbia and schools, they were meaningful expressions of youth disaffection and concern. One early example came from San Francisco's Flipper, once described by Henry Rollins as "harder than anything" and immortalized by Nirvana's Kurt Cobain, who wore a shirt with the band's name hand-drawn on it during their 1992 Saturday Night Live performance. As one fan later commented about the group's legacy, "Flipper were a frightening band. . . . They came out of an '80s culture, Reagan's America, that was about death, the different ways death can be processed and fed to our country." One of these ways, industrial pollution, was expressly handled by the group on a 1981 single titled "Love Canal," a name, albeit not in reference to the song, that many Americans would have been well familiar with. A few years earlier, public awareness had grown concerning a Niagara Falls neighborhood and elementary school built on land previously used by the Hooker Chemical Company as a waste dump. Filled with over twenty tons of waste including various cancer-causing toxic chemicals, the unexplained illnesses, high birth defect rates, and numerous miscarriages among residents caused the Carter administration to get involved. He would eventually sign the 1980 Comprehensive Environmental Response, Compensation, and Liability Act, more commonly referred to as the Superfund, to hold groups responsible for cleaning up sites like Love Canal that had been contaminated with hazardous waste. This was a definite step in the right direction. Then Reagan was elected.[22]

Flipper's revulsion-infused response began with an innocuous description of a group "floating," "sailing," and "drifting" peacefully down a watery wonderland ride. This sense of serenity is quickly disrupted as singer Bruce Lose announces, "We seem strange," a feeling many from the Niagara Falls neighborhood likely had when news concerning the toxicity of the land started to spread. Similar to the residents of Love Canal, Flipper's canal commuters witnessed the environmental harm caused by hazardous waste dumping in the form of personal violence. With "bodies breaking down" and "poison killing our very cells," their lyrical struggle mimicked that of those who saw firsthand what living in a toxic environment could do. One passage in particular expressed the great sense of suffering that must have been felt by mothers such as Lois Gibbs, who went on to start the Love Canal Parents Movement and Love Canal Homeowners Association. Her oldest children, Michael and Melissa, were born there and suffered a series of serious physical ailments. Near the end of the decade, a 300 percent increase in miscarriages in the area was recorded along with 56 percent of children having some sort of birth defect, including an extra row of teeth. The lyrics to "Love Canal," sung in Lose's harrowing voice, retell the local agony without assuagement: "Our children look like monsters / We are breeding / Not to children but to monsters / We feel pain." A year after the single's release, Gibbs would disrupt a meeting of President Reagan's Cancer Panel, abruptly requesting the resignation of his appointed chairman. This was Armand Hammer, CEO of Occidental Petroleum Corporation, parent company of Hooker Chemical. While Reagan wasn't president when the news first broke about Love Canal, his actions—such as the Hammer appointment—were enough to spur punks on, and more songs about issues regarding toxicity would be recorded after Flipper's '81 effort.[23]

Compared to other scenes, New York seemed to have more bands lyrically expressing concerns about the effects of the hazardous material dumping done at places like Love Canal. Although Niagara Falls was on the opposite side of the state, what seems clear is that bands in the Big Apple were tuned in to what was happening there and across the country regarding chemical waste issues. These songs conveyed a sense of concern about living in a country where serious physical harm could be the effect of where one innocently resided. Groups like Armed Citizens and Heart Attack, both from Queens, as well as Staten Island's Ultra Violence, all wrote about the horrors of toxicity. Lyrics like "Have a taste for toxic waste / Causing a slaughter of the human race" and "Toxic waste, toxic waste / We're all gonna die from toxic waste . . . What to do, what to do / There's nothing to save our race" made listeners succinctly aware of the tragic end of existence these groups saw as the ultimate result of continued corporate chemical dumping. Heart Attack's take on things, included on their 1984 *Subliminal Seduction* EP, was a bit more adroit, as the title, "Toxic Lullabye," suggests. Reiterating the impact of waste dumping on pregnant women, the second verse alarmingly states, "The birds no longer come here, for the stork the trip's a waste / With still born births from mothers' wombs it's just nine months extra weight." To Heart Attack, the dumping being done was "the scum of rapists' lustful hate" whose Darwinian tendencies were clear—"the fittest will survive." While not personally implicating Reagan, such lines become interesting when coupled with statements like "Mr. Reagan is a spontaneous Social Darwinist," written in a *New York Times* piece just a few years earlier and suggesting that Reaganism was very much in line with the turn-of-the-century philosophy that elevated the wealth and well-being of the few, who were considered genetically more fit, over the greater good of the commonwealth.[24]

Agnostic Front, often referred to as the godfathers of New York City hardcore and from the famed Lower East Side scene, took up the environmental cause in 1986 on their *Cause for Alarm* album, an early crossover thrash release. Like Flipper and Heart Attack, their lyrics also enumerated the horrifying effects of decades of dumping industrial waste by companies like Hooker Chemical on pregnant women. In "Toxic Shock," frontman Roger Miret, beginning with a chilling scream of pain, informed listeners about the ultimate end of such a practice in lines like "Toxins buried underground seep into the water / Dioxin she drank for nine months deformed her unborn daughter." A few years before "Toxic Shock" was recorded, the *New York Times* reported that Dow Chemical, one of the largest producers of toxic chemical waste, had been trying to avoid responsibility for two decades worth of dioxin contamination in Michigan. The company found in President Reagan's Environmental Protection Agency a colluder in their cover-up, with damaging passages concerning hazardous waste removal deleted from a 1983 report. Although members of the EPA would claim they were ordered to do this by their Washington superiors, Reagan would attempt to deflect any responsibility away from his administration, blaming instead an overactive and exaggerating press. That didn't stop Congress from investigating, which led to the firing of numerous top EPA officials and the eventual resignation of Anne Gorsuch, chief administrator of the agency who had refused under subpoena to deliver documents related to the Superfund program. Miret might have expressed best the feelings of many upon hearing about the collusion: "Politicians allow the dumping must be forced to stop / I hope they live on an abandoned waste site and die of toxic shock."[25]

In the wake of the EPA controversy, Reagan famously announced concerning environmental advocacy groups, "I do not think they will be happy until the White House looks like a bird's nest." Statements like this help explain why scholars from the era came together in 1984 to release *Environmental Policy in the 1980s: Reagan's New Agenda*, a strong critique of policy during his first term that also confirmed much of what punk bands were saying. Armed with ideology and twenty years of fighting for conservative causes,

Reagan went to work almost immediately in breaking down what had been built up the previous decade. Punks recognized what was happening, and the lyrics of the above songs and many others are evidence of an intellectual understanding that seemed to be alarmingly lacking among the Reaganauts. Not long after the publication of *Environmental Policy*, a band from Idaho, of all places, summed up the feelings of many on "Public Lands," a rapid-fire attack included on their 1986 album *6.3 Million Acres*. After reminding listeners that "Pubic lands are owned by you and me," a claim that Reagan, the professed Sagebrush Rebel, would likely push back against, and that all efforts should be made to "Save the wilds for my children to see," singer Pat Schmaljohn of Boise's State of Confusion enumerated the concerns shared by most environmentalists opposed to Reagan's policies. "What are we gonna do when it's all gone / Destroyed by corporate greed it's like a bomb / You rape the land for profits / But I say NO WAY / You say it is gonna create some jobs / But I say NO WAY" could just as easily have been written by one of the many groups starting to engage in environmental justice advocacy more actively during Reagan's tenure. While other bands would write similar songs, State of Confusion would be one of few specifically playing "environmental hardcore," as bassist Wayne Flower labeled the group in a later reflective blog piece.[26]

From Dead Kennedys' "Cesspool in Eden" ("We built our ticky-tacky houses on landfill soil / To cover up a gift we left you years before / Of toxic chemicals and leaking gas / Just dig a little while you'll find your acid baths") to Reagan Youth's "Acid Rain" ("Danger, danger, danger . . . your public be aware / The factories are dumping toxic poisons in your air") to Corrosion of Conformity's "Poison Planet" ("Because you're old and rich / You don't care about this earth / Only about your filthy profits") to Capitalist Casualties' "Nuclear National Park" ("Rape the environment for your greed / Plant your highly toxic seed / Bury your troubles underground / Don't worry they'll never be found"), bands across the country powerfully asserted their understanding and awareness of what was happening while Reagan was in office. They, as much as anyone, were part of what one author in *Environmental Policy* called the "environmentalist counterattack" against the Reagan Revolution. They were clearly disturbed by the administration's agenda, and they expressed this lyrically to a significant extent. As the group Bedlam wrote in "New Jersey; Chemical Dump State," a rather candid critique of their home that was supposed to be, according to its nickname, a garden, "My body is breaking down they don't care / Industrial progress, chemical nightmare." A year earlier Steve Cohen, who would serve as consultant to the Environmental Protection Agency during Reagan's entire time in the White House, had said, "much greater strides must soon be taken if we are to defuse the toxic time bomb and preserve our lands and water." Toxic time bomb—that would have made a great name for punk band or song.[27]

Drug Free Youth

As the above songs about life in suburbia, educational experiences, and environmental concerns show, in terms of expressing their discontent with Reaganland, everything that punk bands sang about seemed to be oppositional. Nearly. By the time punk emerged in the mid-'70s, sex, drugs, and rock and roll were like the holy trinity of popular music culture. And while punk was clear in its original intentions to avoid being corporatized like the arena rock bands that dominated the airwaves, it had a harder time removing the hedonistic accoutrements that were as much a part of the music scene as the music itself. Drug usage was connected to punk culture in its founding moments as much as anything with early icons like Darby Crash and Sid Vicious, immortalized for their substance abuse and related insolence. Alcohol and sex were also prominent, although the latter would eventually appear to be less important as the rise of hardcore drove away many of the girls in the scene with its hypermasculinity and aggressive/violent tendencies. While punk proclaimed itself an oppositional force to the cultural decadence of the 1970s, as the decades changed hands, punks, like many young Americans, were doing drugs, drinking alcohol, and having sex, engaging in the same destructive and decadent behavior as those they professed to be opposing. For Ronald Reagan, who was a moralist for sure, this was a terrible troika and more evidence of a nation that had lost its way. Interestingly, a subgenre within hardcore would mirror his moralism, one of the few instances where punk in the 1980s and Reagan seemed to be speaking the same language. This was straight edge.

The rise of straight edge coincided with Reagan's decision to make the fight against drugs a central aspect of his administration. In October of 1982, Reagan co-delivered a radio address from Camp David along with the First Lady about the "drug problem" the nation was facing and what he planned to do about it. According to Nancy, alcohol and drugs were having a profound effect on young Americans. Reagan, whose masterful communication skills included a penchant for the simplistic, stated near the end of the address, "Drugs are bad, and we're going after them." Many punks who were frustrated by the prevalence of substance usage in the scene would agree, although their mechanism for "going after them" would be much different than the president's. "The mood toward drugs is changing in this country," Reagan told listeners, as the growing number of straight edge adherents at that time would suggest. As with premarital sex, Reagan would advocate for abstinence, and by the beginning of his second four years in the White House, his wife Nancy (herself the target of a number of punk songs not discussed in this book) would be the most public face of the anti-drug campaign and armed with a slogan few who lived through that time will likely ever forget. "[Nothing] captures the mood of the Reagan era quite like 'Just Say No,'" wrote one author in the wake of her 2016 death. It was "the motherly battle cry of the anti-drug movement" embraced by professional musicians, artists, athletes, and many others who took to TV in support of the First Lady's crusade. On a September 1982 CNN piece, she would look viewers in the eye and heartfeltly plea, "Say yes to life, and when it comes to drugs and alcohol, just say no." sXe (straight edge) kids couldn't have said it any better.[28]

In *Straight Edge: Clean-Living Youth, Hardcore Punk, and Social Change*, sociologist Ross Haenfler explains, "Straight edge's unyielding, black-and-white strictures on behavior were similar to fundamentalist religion's rigid, clearcut beliefs." In simplest terms, straight edge was a conservative moral movement within punk and with rules for living that were similar to those espoused by many of Reagan's supporters. While they would have hated the music, they would most have likely approved of the lyrics. These rules, although he would challenge that description, were first written into song by Ian MacKaye, lead singer from the seminal band Minor Threat. In 1981 the group would release two EPs, a self-titled debut and *In My Eyes*, both on their Dischord label. On the former would be the track "Straight Edge," from which the movement got its name. One of the most forceful anti-drug use songs ever recorded, with references to the various recreational drugs available to youths at that time, it opens with a proclamation that would resonate with punk adherents looking for a cleaner way to live. "I'm a person just like you / But I've got better things to do / Than sit around and fuck my head / Hang out with the living dead," a declaration of defiance, would be added to on *In My Eyes*' "Out of Step," a one-minute-and-fifteen-second statement of the strictures Haenfler refers to above. Over the distinct distortion of Lyle Pressler's guitar, MacKaye passionately professed, "I don't smoke / I don't drink / I don't fuck / At least I can fucking think." Repeated in the second verse, along with the chorus stating, "I can't keep up! / Out of step with the world!," it rang out as a call to arms, something its writer never intended it to be. What began as MacKaye's expression of personal frustration would become the foundational principles of a lifestyle that in many ways out-Reaganed the Reaganites in terms of moral constraints.[29]

The bands that were part of what Haenfler refers to as the straight edge *Old School*, including Minor Threat, were connected with the "more conservative national climate" that informed the Reagan Revolution, as their lyrics attest. While they might not have agreed with tax cuts for the wealthy, massive increases in defense spending, cutbacks in social services, and the possibility of being drafted to fight in Reagan's proxy wars throughout Latin America, they did seem to agree with the moralism of the Reagan camp, albeit of a nonreligious type. Their lyrics were characterized by Nancy Reagan's plea to "Say yes to life" and to reject the consumptive and destructive lifestyle deemed an albatross around the necks of American youths. Bands like Orange County's Uniform Choice, who, according to Youth of Today frontman Ray Cappo, "single handedly whipped Southern California into a straight edge frenzy," would record *Screaming for Change*, a full-length album filled with anthems advocating clean living. Their "Straight and Alert" would mirror the message of Minor Threat's similarly titled paean of personal empowerment in lines like "The best thing to know is to know one's fate / It's easiest done when the person is straight." New York's The Abused would appeal to listeners with words the Reagans would most definitely have applauded, concluding "Drug Free Youth," with "Shape up man, before it's too late / Got one life to live, do it straight." Describing the group as "outcasts within outcasts," singer Kevin Crowley noted in a later interview that it was "the idea of not having anything control me" that turned him on to straight edge as well as the prevalence of drugs in New York's Lower East Side. Not far away in Boston, SS Decontrol, whose 1982 album *The Kids Will Have Their Say* was described in *MRR* as having "fired the shots heard 'round the world and generated a thriving hardcore scene," included such straight edge tunes as "Wasted Youth" and "Headed Straight." Though the First Lady might not have used the same language, she would definitely have agreed with the sentiment expressed in the final lines of the former—"When you gonna wake up and get off your ass / We better change this and fuckin' fast."[30]

Out west in Reno, 7 Seconds, who had been raging against Reagan since the earliest days of his presidency, would chime in with "Straight On" from 1984's groundbreaking *The Crew*, an album that was far less aggressive in terms of style and tone but with a message just as powerful as any other from the era. With lyrics like "Thumbs down to all those drugs you need" and "Just more false starts, it tears apart / Your heart, your head, your soul, your brain," it sounds eerily like the public service announcements '80s kids got a daily television dose of. The group would double down with 1986's "Drug Control," a forty-five-second blast reiterating the point. ("Drugs make you turn on me! / Drugs will not set you free!") Not long after, a nonprofit organization called Partnership for a Drug-Free America would be formed and launch its famous *This Is Your Brain on Drugs* campaign, its message identical to 7 Seconds'. A year later the Reagans would return to television to confront the issue again, Nancy advocating for "an outspoken intolerance" and imploring viewers "to be unyielding and inflexible in your opposition to drugs." The band would most likely have pushed back regarding the First Lady's entreaty, as singer Kevin Seconds once told an interviewer, "I'm just not trying to lay down laws to people or telling people how I think they should live their life. For me personally, not doing drugs or drinking is just a personal choice." Reagan would advocate for a different approach. In the 1986 television remarks he outlined his plan to help usher in a "drug-free America," which would include not only an expansion of educational and awareness programs, which most straight edge bands would have supported, but also aggressive action on the part of the government connected to prevention and criminal punishment. While few of the early straight edge bands were so militant as to agree with Reagan's claim that "Drug abuse is a repudiation of everything America is," all shared in the concern that drugs were a significant problem and were harming young people. The Cleveland band Confront would resolutely pronounce on their 1989 demo cassette, "One Life, Drug Free." The Reagans could not have said it any better.[31]

Conclusion

Punk, at its core, was about disaffection. In the OED, this is defined as "Alienation from or dissatisfaction with an authority, government, system of organization, etc.; disenchantment with the status quo; hostility or disloyalty to a controlling power; dissent." There may be no better word to characterize the music punks produced, particularly during the Age of Reagan. He was the authority, the government, and a large part of the system they railed against in song. The country he came to represent and rule informed their disenchanted discourse, his control over it fueling their enraged ruminations. This chapter barely touches the surface, as every song produced by every punk band was in many ways an expression of dissent. They all were, to paraphrase the title of one by Fullerton's Agent Orange, cries for help in a world gone mad. Depression, anxiety, anger, but more importantly concern, resonated across scenes, and so many bands that emerged took to expressing this through lyrics. They felt alienated in an America many considered in decline. Their songs expressed disquietude about what was happening around them, which, ironically, their main mark held as well. In 1981 diary entries regarding affairs in the Middle East, Reagan twice mentioned concern that the end of days might be near. "Sometimes I wonder if we are destined to witness Armageddon," he wrote, contemplating the possibility of the reign of hell on earth happening during his lifetime. Not long after Bad Religion would release its first album with a fiery red sleeve including an image from Dante's Inferno on the back. As if responding directly to Reagan's private ruminations, frontman Greg Graffin cantillated, "How could hell be any worse? Life alone is such a curse / Fuck Armageddon, this is hell." Very few lines expressed as clearly the general punk sentiment about life in Reaganland.[32]

CHAPTER FOUR

Religious Vomit

> Religious America is awakening, perhaps just in time for our country's sake.
> —RONALD REAGAN

> All religions make me wanna throw up. All religions suck.
> —DEAD KENNEDYS

God's Instrument in Rebuilding America

On August 22, 1980, a little more than a month after receiving the Republican nomination for president, Ronald Reagan delivered what might have been the most important speech of his pre–White House career. He was in Dallas to address the Religious Roundtable's National Affairs Briefing Conference and 2,500 evangelical pastors in attendance. Sharing the stage with what one historian called "the superstars" of conservative Christianity, he used the opportunity to assure the audience he was their man in the upcoming election. Although pitched as a nonpartisan gathering, Reagan roped them in in the first few minutes. "I know that you can't endorse me," he told the eager listeners, "but I only brought that up because I want you to know that I endorse you and what you're doing." According to Jeffrey Hadden and Anson Shupe, experts on the rise of evangelicalism in America, "Those words worked their magic."[1]

With that statement, Ronald Reagan became the candidate of the Christian Right, an amalgamation of fundamentalists and evangelicals that would include such notable religious figures as Pat Robertson, James Robison, and Jerry Falwell. According to Reagan, and the 16,000 attendees, the Christian tradition in America was under attack. "If we have come to a time in the United States when the attempt to see traditional moral values reflected in public policy leaves one open to irresponsible charges," he warned his listeners, "then the structure of our free society is under attack and the foundation of our freedom is threatened." He reminded them, in case any had forgotten, that America's heritage was Judeo-Christian and that the First Amendment was being used not to protect this, but rather move the country further from it. "We can still become that shining city upon a hill," he assured them, if only they would join with him in fighting to protect this sacred goal from the tyranny of government. "Religious America," those in attendance especially, "is awakening, perhaps just in time for our country's sake," and Reagan assured the audience he was ready to lead when it finally came to.[2]

The merger of Ronald Reagan and the Christian Right was one of mutual benefit. From them, he got the support of what was becoming a powerful and influential force, what one author described as "conservative evangelicals who abandoned the long-held belief that political activism is incompatible with their religion and assert that the church has a role, indeed a duty, to change America." From him, they got a powerful instrument to support the changes they were hoping for. While Reagan had been a bit less socially conservative during his time as governor regarding the two primary areas of concern of his new supporters, abortion and gay rights, he was primed and ready by 1980 to become the agent of change Christian conservatives hoped he would be. He made sure to remind them of this in his Dallas address: "The perils our country faces today and will face in the 1980s seem unprecedented in their scope and consequences; but our response to them can be the response of men and women in any era who seek divine guidance in the policies of their government and promulgation of their laws." Reagan, with the Christian Right behind him, was just such a man.[3]

What historian Daniel Williams described as "an unlikely alliance" in reality became a productive relationship for both Reagan and the conservative Christian leadership, the former gaining the continued support of social conservatives and the latter a presidential pulpit from which to preach their message about America. Abortion, gay rights, prayer in schools, pornography, traditional family values, American military strength in opposition to international communism—all of these found their way into the political discourse of the decade, with both Reagan and his fundamentalist following often speaking the same language. While the ties that bound them together were actually less tight than they seemed, the unbridled approval afforded Reagan by the Christian Right at the 1984 Republican Convention spoke volumes about the perceived connection between the two during his first four years in office. Reagan was, according to Jerry Falwell in his closing benediction, one of "God's instruments in rebuilding America."[4]

Historian Andrew Hartman in his work on the culture wars stated regarding the rise of the Christian Right in America and its connection to Reagan, "Given the mobilization of religious conservatives during the 1970s, and given the biblical inspiration upon which their triumphant nationalism rested, the Christian Right's enthusiastic embrace of Ronald Reagan's 1980 presidential candidacy should not have been surprising." Whether punks were among the ranks of the unsurprised, they were definitely spurred into action and motivated to write. And while all that went into the rebuilding of the country during the Reagan Revolution was something they had sung frequently about, the rise of the Christian Right and its attempt to remake the nation in its image was afforded special attention by more than a few. Punks recognized what the Christian Right was attempting to do: turn the country hard right in terms of morals, values, and social norms. They, more than most artists at that time, displayed a willingness to speak truth to power concerning conservative Christianity's real agenda, to remold the nation in its image. Fear was not a factor as they lambasted many of its central figures and the institutions they represented, their lyrics often explicit, vulgar, graphic, and at times disturbing. Like their songs about Reagan and the America his supporters were helping him build, in those about religion they held nothing back. Dave Dictor from M.D.C., repackaged as Millions of Damn Christians by Reagan's second term, would remind listeners about this group's newfound power and influence: "Now they're wealthy and in control / Got you by your balls, by your soul."[5]

We've Got a Bigger Problem Now

Three main groups that emerged the year before Reagan was nominated provided the foundation for what became known as the Christian Right: the Christian Voice, founded by two California ministers as a merger of West Coast religious groups concerned about gay rights, pornography, and the decline of the American family; the Religious Roundtable, sponsor of the 1980 Dallas conference and a forum for conservative clergy to discuss political affairs; and the Moral Majority, a loose alliance of primarily Southern Baptist churches with a mission to advocate for conservative social values on a pro-family/pro-America platform. Although all three played an important role in helping shape the conservative Christian narrative during Reagan's administration, it was the last that became the most influential and garnered the most popular attention. As sociologist Robert C. Liebman wrote not long after its founding, "the Moral Majority became the byword for the entire New Christian Right. . . . When the ACLU, Planned Parenthood, and other liberal organizations lashed out at [the movement], they attacked Moral Majority by name." The same could be said for the punk bands that took them on, but in a much more aggressive and assertive tone.[6]

"Jerry Falwell," according to Liebman, "came to personify the [Christian Right] in the eyes of millions of Americans." Dead Kennedys, one of the leading bands in the lyrical assault on the rise of religious influence in politics, appeared to feel the same. They, and a few other of the movement's leaders, found themselves rightly situated at the center of one of the strongest punk song assessments of religion at the onset of the Reagan Era. The album on which the track was included was the band's 1981 EP *In God We Trust, Inc.*, an eight-song critique of America released in the immediate wake of Reagan's election. Falwell, the founder of the Moral Majority and one of the Christian Right's earliest public supporters of Reagan, found his name mentioned prominently, among others, on the second track of the EP, the aptly titled "Moral Majority." Clocking in at one minute and fifty-five seconds, "Moral Majority" is a rapid and stinging assault on major personages of the conservative Christian movement and their newfound affinity for political activism. Its lyrics are some of the most pointed in terms of drawing direct attention to individuals, all of whom in some way were involved in the Christian Right's attempts to rebuild America. "Masturbating with a flag and a Bible" was how singer Jello Biafra described the movement's mindset, with "Circus-tent-con men and Southern belle bunnies," using God and country to prey upon the nationalistic faithful for financial support. Finishing most of the verses with a pronounced "God must be dead if you're alive," the song uses the Nietzschean notion that morality, which leaders of the Christian Right were advocating for a return to, is actually being destroyed by those proclaiming to advance it. A number of other bands from the era would follow suit, with the phrase "God is dead" being used quite often in punk lyrics.[7]

In terms of others beyond Falwell, the song mentions North Carolina Senator Jesse Helms, one of the leaders in the push to restore prayer in public schools; Terry Dolan, a leader in the Christian Voice and chairman of the National Conservative Political Action Committee; Phyllis Schlafly, an outspoken opponent of the Equal Rights Amendment; Anita Bryant, a leading anti-gay activist; and, of course, Reagan. For each, with the exception of Bryant, they are afforded the forceful directive to "blow it out your ass" prior to their names. An even more assertive "ram it up your cunt" is reserved for Bryant, a former music star who in the '70s went on to lead the Protect America's Children campaign, one of the first oppositional organizations to the movement for gay rights. These individuals, with their pay-to-play Christianity, were the real problem in America according to Dead Kennedys. "It's the new dark ages with the fascists toting Bibles," Biafra warned listeners. And the Moral Majority is "Trying to rub us out."[8]

Before "Moral Majority," *In God We Trust, Inc.* begins with another scathing critique, the sardonically titled "Religious Vomit." A total of sixty-three seconds, it is one of the group's fastest songs, with its focus on religion in general rather than any one specific group or individual. Similar to its album mate, "Religious Vomit" draws attention to an aspect of faith-based institutions that a plethora of bands would cite as well: money. "Free for a fee" is how Biafra described the spiritual exchange between believers and their faiths. "They all claim that they have the truth that'll set you free / Just give 'em all your money and they'll set you free" is the first of two verses that highlight the idea that salvation will only come through monetary contribution. Like other songs from the era discussed below, Dead Kennedys illuminated lyrically the hypocrisy behind this. Biafra iterated a feeling of disgust with the rather candid lines "All religions make me wanna throw up / All religions make me sick / All religions make me wanna throw up / All religions suck." He would bring the president in on the jazzy reboot of the band's 1979 single "California über Alles," the title changed to "We've Got a Bigger Problem Now," with Reagan taking the place of the previous version's target, Governor Jerry Brown. After introducing him as "Emperor Ronald Reagan / Born again with fascist cravings," a stab at the president's often mentioned spiritual conversion, Biafra quickly turned to the religious implications of his elevation to the highest office in the land. "Now I command all of you / Now your gonna pray in school / And I'll make sure they're Christian too," the closing lines of the first full verse, drew a clear connection between Reagan and the conservative Christian movement. Reagan had, with full support from the Christian Right, made prayer in schools a central aspect of his social agenda. "We've Got a Bigger Problem Now" served as a reminder of what both "Moral Majority" and "Religious Vomit" emphasized for the listener, that religion in America at that time, particularly the Christian Right and its connection to President Reagan, was the real problem.[9]

Beyond its lyrics, *In God We Trust, Inc.* deserves a special place among punk records released at that time for the artwork included on the front sleeve. Like Wasted Youth's *Reagan's In*, it is iconic in terms of imagery and recognizability. Situated prominently in the middle of a shiny silver foil background covering the whole front is an image of a gilded Jesus nailed to a cross made out of folded one-dollar bills. Known as *Idol*, it is a piece by Winston Smith, a surrealist well known for his political montage art. Forever associated with the band, he also came up with its iconic black-and-red DK symbol. Regarding *Idol*'s connection to the group's 1981 EP, Biafra reflected in a later interview upon his first impression, "That is one of the best record covers I've ever seen in my life. Now I gotta go make the record." With "Moral Majority," "Religious Vomit," and "We've Got a Bigger Problem Now," the *Idol* album cover makes *In God We Trust, Inc.* one of the most insightful cultural artifacts of the era and Dead Kennedys leaders of the punk assault on the rise of the Christian Right. But they would definitely not be alone in this.[10]

Moral Majority, Not for Me

The year 1979 was a pivotal one in America, especially for Christian fundamentalists and evangelicals looking for ways to bring the country back from what they perceived to be a cultural and moral decline. It was particularly important for Jerry Falwell, who had been hosting "I Love America" rallies on the steps of state capitols across the country since 1976. As founding pastor of the Thomas Road Baptist Church in Lynchburg, Virginia, Falwell had been using radio and television since the 1950s to spread his message through the *Old Time Gospel Hour,* and by the late '70s he was becoming more engaged in politics than fundamentalists had traditionally been. In 1978 he wrote *How You Can Help Clean Up America,* a manual for how to combat the triple threat of homosexuality, abortion, and pornography, and was starting to talk publicly about the need for people of faith to do more to help restore the country's moral compass. As he presciently stated in an interview that year, "I see the church getting very involved in moral issues in the next few years." The following May, Falwell was invited to a meeting held in Lynchburg of conservative Christian leaders, out of which was born the Moral Majority, a political action committee (PAC) whose purpose was to endorse and help fund conservative candidates. Published a few months later was his *Listen America!,* a political manifesto that went well beyond the three issues religious rightists had traditionally focused on. According to Falwell, "strong moral leadership at every level" was needed to dig the country out of the moral hole it was in and return it to its rightful place of prominence among the nations of the world. "Americans have been silent much too long," he told his readers, and it was only through the ballot box that real change would actually occur. A few months later, Falwell would find his moral leader in Ronald Reagan and would work tirelessly to help see him into the presidency.[11]

While the size and scope of the Moral Majority was never as grand as it appeared to be, its impact on the American political landscape during the Age of Reagan was still significant. As Daniel Williams, author of *God's Own Party: The Making of the Christian Right,* noted, "the Moral Majority did more than any other organization to launch the Christian Right," and Falwell had provided it a national voice through his "masterful use of publicity" and the access this afforded him. Dead Kennedys clearly recognized this early on, prompting the release of *In God We Trust, Inc.* Other bands, like Houston's Really Red, did as well. Although their 1980 7" release had no songs that directly took to task the Falwellian faction, its title, *Despise Moral Majority*, voiced their opinion clearly enough. In Tempe, Arizona, there also formed a group a year later that unfortunately left no recordings but still offered insight into the distaste punks had for the rising influence of the Christian Right and its recognized leader's increasing authority. The band's name was Moral Majority, and the title of one of their songs, which he likely would agree with, was "Jerry Doesn't Like It." Beyond these, the Moral Majority found itself rightly situated front and center of the lyrical attention paid religion by punks. Along with Dead Kennedys, both Youth Brigade and Circle Jerks produced songs using the group's name as title. The latter, led by former Black Flag frontman Keith Morris, released "Moral Majority" on its 1982 album *Wild in the Streets*, a quick interjection on the cultural conformity being pitched by the followers of Falwell. According to Morris, in his iconic nasally whine, the Christian Right had moved beyond the scientific concerns that informed its past political participation, a possible reference to the 1925 Scopes trial on the teaching of evolution in schools, which reemerged during the Reagan Era, and into more personal areas. As he stated in the first verse concerning this intrusion, "First there was biology, then pornography / So says the moral majority / Telling you and me, what we can watch and read."[12]

It was just two years before Circle Jerks' release that Tim LaHaye, one of the cofounders of the Moral Majority, had published *The Battle for the Mind*, a call to action concerning what the Christian Right viewed as the continued encroachment of secular humanism into American society, something the faithful felt they had a divine duty to stamp out. For LaHaye and others, what was truly at stake was the right to freely exercise their religious beliefs as enumerated in the First Amendment. Reagan expressed his support for their cause when in 1982, the same year Circle Jerks recorded "Moral Majority," he stated at the Annual Convention of the National Religious Broadcasters, "The first amendment was not written to protect the people from religious values; it was written to protect those values from government tyranny." Keith Morris, in his concluding verse, saw things a bit differently. "What ever happened, to the first amendment / They way these people talk, they've never even heard it."[13]

On the other side of the country, Youth Brigade, the Washington, DC, rather than L.A. band by the same name, had its "Moral Majority" included on the Dischord *Flex Your Head* compilation. Released the same year as Circle Jerks', it too took aim at Falwell's flock, also mentioning both him and Reagan by name. Like Morris's lyrics, those sung by Nathan Strejcek highlighted the conformist tendencies of conservative Christians and their continued attempts at cultural control. "If you wanna go to school, you gotta play," the last verse begins. "They'll tell you what to be and what to say / If it's right for them, then it's right for you / Whatever made you think you had the right to choose?" Concerning Falwell and Reagan, they found themselves mentioned in the first and second verses with a similar critique. "A godless society, full of moral decay / But Jerry Falwell knows the way" and "Ronald Reagan is quite a man / A part of new morality, tryna rule this land" are clear expressions of distrust concerning the connection between the two and their expressed intentions for a religious revolution in America. Youth Brigade also mentioned a third individual, Bailey Smith. Pastor, evangelist, and the youngest person to ever serve as president of the Southern Baptist Convention, Smith presided over the largest Protestant Christian denomination in the country and was instrumental in spreading the faith throughout the 1980s with his Real Evangelism Bible Conferences. His name was dropped in the song's second verse along with Reagan, where Strejcek sings "Bailey Smith, the big conservator / Help destroy liberals, go to Heaven, for sure." Smith was briefly embroiled in a controversy concerning comments he made at the 1980 Dallas conference where Reagan had issued his endorsement of the fundamentalist movement. Regarding Jews, Smith had mused that it was pointless for them to pray at political rallies since God didn't want to hear what they had to say anyway. "How in the world," Smith queried, "can God hear the prayer of a man who says that Jesus Christ is not the Messiah? It's blasphemous." Such comments might explain the lyrics used by Youth Brigade for persons like Smith and the other members of the Moral Majority, described in the chorus as "right-wing knights" with clear intentions to "take away your rights." With that, the song ends with the same personal pronouncement it begins with: "Moral Majority, not for me."[14]

While Dead Kennedys, Circle Jerks, and Youth Brigade were well-known groups whose releases found themselves in record stores across the country, other lesser-known bands also took aim at the Moral Majority in their music. From Boulder, Colorado, White Trash's "Piss on the Moral Majority" was on a self-released 1982 cassette that also included the group's homage to the president, "Ballad of Ronnie Raygun." And 1983 would see a live compilation released called the *SF Sound of Music Club Live, Vol. 1* that included the track "Moral Majority" by ELF, as well as one titled "Dancing with Ronnie" by the Defectors, both San Francisco bands. That same year in Seattle, Washington, Mr. Epp and the Calculations recorded "Moral Majority" on its *Live As All Get Out!* album. On Long Island a band emerged with the humorous name the Moral Majority Dance Band, described in *MRR* as "raunchy" and "demented," with lyrics that were "very provocative," far from what the real Moral Majority would have considered wholesome entertainment. Modern Warfare, from Long Beach, had a "Moral Majority" listed on their 1983 album *Life Is Boring So Why Not Steal This Record*. In Clifton, New Jersey, Sacred Denial included its own "Moral Majority" on their *Extra Strength Tylenol Anyone?* LP. Clearly, Jerry Falwell's following caught the attention of bands across the country, a testament to his perceived influence and potential impact on the affairs of the nation during Reagan's tenure of office.[15]

In the month after Reagan was elected, *US News & World Report* put out a special edition titled *Outlook '81*. In it was an editorial that referenced efforts by the American Civil Liberties Union to draw attention to the increasing political influence of religious fundamentalists. In newspapers across the country, accompanying a cartoon of a cross-wielding Falwell astride Uncle Sam, was a warning: "If the Moral Majority Has Its Way, You'd Better Start Praying," readers were alerted. "Their agenda is clear and frightening. They mean to capture the power of government and use it to establish a nightmare of religious and political orthodoxy." Punk bands across America agreed, but let their listeners know with just a bit more descriptiveness than the popular magazine would likely have allowed in its pages.[16]

Homo-Sexual

Interestingly, on one subject of interest to the Moral Majority, punk outpourings from the period seemed at times in line with their social views as well as the narrative coming from the White House. With lyrics eerily similar to what many Reagan officials and conservative religious leaders were saying, some bands wrote not only about homosexuality using defamatory language, but also the AIDS crisis that was tightly connected to it during the 1980s. While most would stop short of describing it as "a symptom of a nation coming under the judgement of God," Jerry Falwell's words from the year of Reagan's first inauguration, some expressed sentiments that seemed at odds with punk's inclusive origins and acceptance of alternative lifestyles. Although Reagan professed to have no issue with persons being gay, including those friends from Hollywood he knew were, his administration was apathetic toward the struggle for queer rights. In Lou Cannon's biography he wrote, "Reagan thought homosexuality 'a sad thing' but he had no antipathy toward gays and lesbians." While that might have been true, what he apparently also did not have was a desire to use his power as president to advance their cause or help bring an end to the discrimination they continued to face. In light of Reagan's support from Christian fundamentalists and their public professions regarding homosexuality, his lack of effort in this area should come as a shock to no one. What is shocking are the punk songs that, rather than drawing attention to Reagan's insensitive apathy, appear to embrace the position that many Reaganites took on the issue.[17]

Songs from the decade that mention homosexuality range from the downright offensive to the blatantly absurd, many even being both. One of these came from Los Angeles' Angry Samoans, a group that got its start a few years prior to Reagan's election and would go on to become one of the earliest hardcore punk bands in the country. After releasing their first album in 1980, the six-song record *Inside My Brain*, they would put out a four-song EP as The Queer Pills. While the name of the company the record was released under, Homophobic Records, along with the pseudonymous moniker were expressions enough of the group's apparent lewd and offensive posture, it was the 1982 release *Back from Samoa* that hit sharply, albeit confusingly, with the song "Homo-Sexual." In a little more than fifty seconds, the group produced what appears to be one of the most intolerant songs from the era. With lines like "Living in your fa**ot world" and "Sucking dick your pants on fire," the lyrics are easily interpreted as openly intolerant of gay men. But with a chorus that states "Homosexual—I'm one too / Homosexual—So are you," as well as "Homosexual—We love you," things get rather confusing. Coupled with something few listeners are likely aware of, that the person given credit for writing the song on the record sticker is none other than "J. Falwell," the absurdity of the lyrics become more evident. The group even announced in a 1988 issue of *Ink Disease*, "we thought no one's going to even think this is falling in line with all the other idiots, [so] we'll credit it to J. Falwell," going so far as to send a copy of the record to the Moral Majority as a joke. Regarding the source of their misjudged offensiveness, one later reviewer wrote, "The Samoans . . . were full of self-hatred and loathing that turned insecurity and rage upon everyone and everything in the world 'cause it was just there to be hated." Singer Mike Saunders would confirm this. "Our way wasn't that funny, but stupid and mean," he told *Juice* magazine in 2008. "We wrote about living in LA—hell on earth. . . . It was very ill tempered. We didn't want to make anyone laugh." Persons in the queer community definitely would not have, particularly as the lyrics seemed to brazenly ape the homophobia that many witnessed firsthand, seemingly more acceptable while the Reaganauts ruled. But, when listened to in light of the listed lyricist, the group might have had a bit more complex way of thinking than the lyrics appeared to show.[18]

Another example of punk's problematic approach to addressing issues of sexuality came from Durham, North Carolina's wonderfully named Ugly Americans. On their second full-length album, 1985's *Who's Been Sleeping . . . in My Bed*, with lyrics described in MRR as "creative and slightly twisted," the foursome included the song "Homophobia." After a thrash-influenced buildup, the first verse insensitively intoned, "Let's beat up some fa**ots / Cause they really make me sick / We all know it's a man's world / And real men don't eat dick / No way!" In the second, frontman Simon Bob Sinister continued, "I know some funny AIDS jokes / They make me laugh like hell!," rounding out the song's discomforting locutions prior to a few melodic "Homophobia" chants and concluding with a firm "Up my ass!" To the untrained ear of a listener uninterested in digging, these, and the remainder of the second verse ("And if you don't like ni**ers too / I'll tell you about sickle cell"), can make the Ugly Americans easy targets for accusations about punk's homophobic, as well as racist, tendencies. But when one does delve deeper into the group and their larger body of work, a different story emerges. Concerning the usage of the N-word, while written by guitarist Danny Hooligan, who is White, accompanying him on the track is Jon McClain, one of handful of African American drummers in the punk scene. While this doesn't excuse the word, it does shed some light on the group's intentionality. (More on this is discussed in chapter 7.) As far as the song's blatant usage of homophobic language is concerned, their ironic nature becomes clear when one realizes they stood firmly in opposition to Reagan and those who supported him. In the months leading up to the '84 election, the Ugly Americans would headline a Jam for Justice/Rock against Reagan rally at Duke University sponsored by a coalition of left-wing groups that included the campus Democrats. "Homophobia," in light of this, as well as the fact that they clearly chose an ironic band name, should be taken as it is—an insensitive-sounding and absurdist critique of the ridiculousness of the New Right's moral musings, a common practice among punks that often gets misinterpreted.[19]

Angry Samoans and Ugly Americans were not alone in using homophobic language that without context easily appears insensitive at least, downright mean-spirited and inhumanly offensive at most. One explanation for this might stem from those same words being used by non-punks to insult and belittle them. In every documentary about the scene there are references to punks being called "f*g" or "homo" or "gay" or "queer" by one of the many "cowboys" or "jocks" or "rednecks" who got riled up by their very presence. Often these stories are accompanied by accounts of punks getting pummeled, other times about punks doing the pummeling. The documentary *Clockwork Orange County: The Rise of West Coast Punk Rock!* talks of the many disputes between patrons of Zubie's, a cowboy bar and grill, and the punks from the Cuckoo's Nest, a legendary Costa Mesa club located across the parking lot, where Angry Samoans had even played. Ian MacKaye and Henry Rollins, in *Salad Days: A Decade of Punk in Washington DC (1980-1990)*, talked about how members of the DC punk scene were constantly harassed by Georgetown jocks whose masculinity they apparently offended. In the first three minutes of *You Weren't There: A History of Chicago Punk, 1977-1984*, members of some of the earliest Windy City bands described being called "f*g" or "fa**ot" constantly. A tale of one episode is even recounted by Jello Biafra on Dead Kennedys' 1987 *Give Me Convenience or Give Me Death* compilation. On "Night of the Living Rednecks" he describes a narrow escape from the clutches of some Portland "jocks" whose fun for the evening consisted of yelling at the singer, "Hey, fa**ot!" before pulling up alongside in their "giant Hot Wheels car" to douse him with water. Such homophobic-inspired harassment was a common occurrence for punks in the late '70s and early '80s, which could explain why some would use similar language in their songs and band names. In a disturbing way, doing so afforded them the chance to take ownership of the words, transferring agency as well as lessening their impact when used against them. If the cap fit, and for queer punks it actually did, it seems they embraced a "might as well wear it" mentality.[20]

While using homophobic slurs in their songs did not necessarily mean those that did were guilty of homophobia, this is not to say some punks weren't and didn't express this sentiment lyrically. This is also not to say that those who used such epithets deserve a pass for doing so. Like those who used insensitive and derogatory racial terms, the challenge of considering this in light of contemporary interpretations of such language is evident. There is no acceptable reason today to use it. Regarding the 1980s, rather than claiming outright that those who did were homophobic, which is interesting in light of the fact that many had friends or knew of other scenesters that were, or they listened to bands like the Dicks who had openly gay singers, knowing that punks were often subjected to such labeling might help us understand better why a group might call themselves Gay Cowboys in Bondage and record a song like "Cowboys Are Gay" or why another, Sockeye, front Kent, Ohio, would label a cassette tape *Music That Gay People Would Like* (they would accurately be described in a *Trouser Press* review as "tasteless, horribly amateurish, and delightfully ridiculous"). It might also explain the thought process behind songs like "Homo Truck Driving Man" by the Pajama Slave Dancers or why the Descendents would wrap up "I'm Not a Loser" with the apparent and tasteless anti-gay diatribe, "Your pants are too tight / You fucking homos / You suck / Mr. Buttfuck, you don't belong here / Go away, you fucking gay / I'm not a loser." (The band, still touring and considered one of the most important punk groups ever, no longer sings the lines, drummer Bill Stevenson describing them as "the distasteful humor or points of view handed down to us by our suburban, white fathers" and a joke they thought no one would ever hear when they wrote it.) On a more personal note, it helps me understand how Naked Hippy, the local hardcore band from my hometown of Normal, Illinois, could flip the script and write "Conservative f*g, what a drag / Man I hope I'm never like you." It might also explain why three guys from Philadelphia, two of whom were African American, would choose a band name like Homo Picnic. As Tony Tigre, drummer for the group, clarified in a 1988 interview with the zine *Threatening Society*, "Hell, HOMO PICNIC started as somewhat of joke. . . . And it's funny."[21]

"Animosity toward homosexuality was typical in many sectors of American society," explained Raymond Patton in his work on punk's global revolutionary reach throughout the 1980s. "[It] was certainly not an invention of punk." The many instances of punk bands using homophobic language should be taken for what they are: immature and ridiculous, but often innocent of vile intent, and potential evidence of a defensive strategy on the part of punks who themselves were ridiculed with similar language. Although frustratingly hard to listen to today because of their blatant offensiveness, it becomes easier (just a bit) when the listener is aware of the historical circumstances and context in which they were used. There were homophobic punks, for sure, but there were also plenty who were eager to listen to and share the stage with bands like the Dicks, who proudly accepted the label "a commie fa**ot band," as was written above their photo on the cover of an '83 *MRR* edition. There were also bands like The Dickies, around since the late '70s and known for their slapstick silliness, who would write humorous and catchy tunes such as "Going Homo," with lyrics like "I can't find a dame / They're always the same, I'm going to shame my family name / 'Cause I'm going homo." But there were also bands like 7 Seconds who used their music as a medium to attack homophobia, as they did with 1986's "Regress No Way." On the unity-inspiring album *Walk Together, Rock Together*, the group expressed to listeners what should have been the standard punk pronouncement on sexual orientation discrimination: "Get hip, there's nothing you can do / Why should that bother you . . . Wake up to human rights and see / The truth and your hypocrisy." Unfortunately, most bands seemed less inclined to approach the topic of gay rights in America with the same intellectual acumen as the Reno, Nevada, quartet.[22]

While the songs described above appear void of any real sense of maliciousness, some, particularly those that directly confronted the AIDS crisis, were so insensitive and maligning, as well as in line with the thoughts of many Reagan conservative supporters, that it's hard to take them at anything but face value. AIDS hit America and the world by storm in the early '80s and was quickly associated with gay lifestyle, particularly that of men. To certain Reaganites like Pat Buchanan, it truly was the "gay plague," as it was being referred to. In a 1983 column, Buchanan, who would become the director of communications for the Reagan administration, would write regarding the preponderance of AIDS cases in the gay community, "The poor homosexuals. They have declared war on nature, and so nature is exacting an awful retribution." His boss in the Oval Office did little to support efforts to address the epidemic, the effects of which were severe. "Reagan's response to [AIDS] was halting and ineffective," wrote Lou Cannon, and even after the death of his movie star friend Rock Hudson, "[he] was slow to join the battle against AIDS." Sean Wilentz offered a bit more critical interpretation of Reagan's lackluster response. "The president's failure, until late 1985, to address seriously the spreading contagion," he candidly stated, "reflected both a deep-seated public antagonism toward homosexuality and a political determination by the White House not to rile its supporters in the religious right."[23]

Nonsensically, the bands that wrote about the crisis expressed a similar antagonistic sentiment, aping the attitude of Reaganites like Buchanan regarding AIDS and attacking gay men in particular. Jack Tragic, formally of Jack Tragic and The Unfortunates, would exemplify this well in his 1989 song "Homo Parade," with the chorus ringing out, "You are gay / You got AIDS / You will march in the homo parade." Amazingly, this is the least insensitive lyric of the first track on an equally offensively titled album, *White Ni**er Rising*, which was only found on Discogs and no streaming services. As brutal was the hardcore thrash band M.O.D. (Methods of Destruction) in their 1987 song "A.I.D.S." Explaining the acronym as the "Anally Inflicted Death Sentence" at one point, sounding exactly like Jerry Falwell, singer Billy Milano stated emphatically, "AIDS like a plague is from God / For he sees something wrong in his eyes." A few years earlier, The Left, whose compilation album in 2006 would ironically be called *Jesus Loves the Left*, included the song "AIDS Alley" on their second LP. From Hagerstown, Maryland, described by one writer as "their strange redneck hometown," the group's music was characterized as "Sarcasm, black humor and pessimism . . . rolled into one brutal attack, powerful, offensive, fierce and fun as hell!" If taken seriously, the lyrics of "AIDS Alley" ("Fifty bucks will make their butthole quiver / Ready and waiting for you to deliver" as well as "People call them sleezy, fa**ot trash" and "People are afraid of f*gs, can't you see") were as offensive as anything that came from the mouth of a Religious Right Reaganite at that time. Along with these, East Coast hardcore band Bedlam shared in the offensiveness. On their "A.I.D.S.," interestingly (purposefully?) left off of a 2021 Beer City Records reissue of the band's work as well as the Spotify track listing, the group energetically chanted in unison: "A is for your anus, that feisty little hole / I is for infection, that's on your cock / D is for the dick, that spits the disease / S is cause you suck, the tool of life." While painful to listen to and with levels of insensitivity to human suffering that are incomprehensible, these songs offer unique insight into the era, specifically regarding what had become an acceptable message among some Reagan sympathizers about AIDS. And although M.O.D.'s Billy Milano would later say that Reagan "sucked" and that "Jimmy Carter was the best President we've had," his lyrics, as well as Bedlam's, The Left's, and Jack Tragic's, seemed at odds with this. As Milano fan and journalist Sean L. Maloney would later ask, "could these songs actually be satire of . . . the anti-gay sentiment that passed for political discourse in the late '80s?" In the same review Maloney characterizes these and the many other songs that might appear to be homophobic in a rather poignant and summarizing statement; "They're songs that, however ineloquently, capture a portion of the Reagan Era zeitgeist that most would rather ignore." One can only wish they had used the chance to express this with lyrics less malicious, even if absurdist and ironical, than they come across today.[24]

God Is Broke

One of the most common themes across songs about religion concerned money, which was directly connected to the emergence and growth of televangelism. The two decades prior to Reagan's election had witnessed an unprecedented rise in religious broadcasting. By the end of the 1970s, Pat Robertson had started his Christian Broadcasting Network Satellite

Service, the first of its kind, laying the foundation for others to follow and cash in on. By the middle of the 1980s, according to Jeffrey Hadden (who supposedly coined the term *televangelism*), close to 25 million Americans watched religious programs, a massive increase from the roughly 5 million who did so two decades earlier. According to Reagan historian Haynes Johnson, between 1978 and 1989 the number of Christian TV ministries jumped from twenty-five to 336. "The electronic church formed a multibillion-dollar televangelist empire serving what the Christian evangelical movement claimed to be sixty million Americans." Punks were clearly concerned about this, especially its embrace of the Reagan-Era moneymaking mentality that in many ways contradicted the purported principles of Christianity, a hypocrisy they were more than willing to point out. A common message would be delivered from punk bands like New York City's The Silent Age, who sarcastically sang, "Bless my soul, bless the holy vision / Bless the sound of the video Christian."[25]

One of the earliest groups to critically consider the emerging presence of televangelism in America was a punk outfit that disbanded before Reagan was even elected. The Controllers, a three-piece band from Los Angeles, had their song "Electric Church" included on a 1979 compilation titled *Tooth and Nail*. With others by the Germs, Negative Trend, and Middle Class, it remains a classic album forecasting punk's eventual metamorphosis into the faster and more aggressive style of the 1980s. The Controllers' contribution, a rather lengthy three-plus-minute, blues-riff tune, sheds light on the ridiculousness of how a person of questionable morality and limited capacity to comply with the law can wake up Sunday morning, turn on their television, and be absolved of sin. As the opening lines by singer Kid Spike expressed, "I can cheat and I can steal / I can rape and I can kill," followed by the chorus, "But come Sunday morning I'll be looking right at you / And my savior comes right into my front room." These were added to midway through the song with "God bless me, my TV / My TV will save me," a reiteration that salvation lies within . . . the television, that is. Although the group disbanded the year "Electric Church" was released, they did much to help lay the foundation for what came after, with songs like "Neutron Bomb," "Suburban Suicide," and "White Trash Christ" in their body of work. With their 1979 stinging critique of televangelism, they were followed by a number of bands seriously concerned about the Christian Right's newfound affinity for small screen sermonizing, and the money associated with it.[26]

One of these was another California band, San Jose's Los Olvidados, whose song "Pay Salvation" was included on the 1982 compilation *Not So Quiet on* the Western Front. Described as "one of those legendary punk bands that everyone agreed would put their town on the map," they were one of the most important in the skate punk scene, although their songs had more of a political edge than others in it. "Pay Salvation" definitely falls into this category, with some of the clearest and most assertive vocals on a punk record. After an opening crunchy guitar riff, singer Mike Voss began with some apparent sermonizing, confirming what Haynes Johnson would say about the omnipresence of televangelist broadcasts during the era. "It's Sunday morning you just got up you go to turn on your TV / I'm always here on every channel there's no escaping me" is followed in the second verse with "I'll take your dime or dollar bill whatever you can afford / Assuring me a new Rolls-Royce in the name of Christ our Lord." While not all televangelists were using viewer donations to feed their less-than-Christlike conspicuous consumptive habits, a few were and even flaunted it publicly. One in particular, Jim Bakker, would actually purchase two vintage Rolls-Royces in 1984, one not even to be driven, but rather to be placed in a glass display case. By the end of the decade, charges would be brought against Bakker, who would go to jail after being found guilty of fleecing his flock for upwards of $150 million. It took punk bands like Los Olvidados a lot less time to see him and others for what they really were: faith-peddling frauds.[27]

A year earlier and on the opposite side of the country, Government Issue would also point out the absurdity behind the televangelist phenomenon on "Religious Ripoff," the first song on *Legless Bull*. In the second verse, John Stabb reiterated the ridiculousness of the pay and pray practice of Christian broadcasting with the lines, "T.V. evangelist put on a show / Trying to tell me what they know / Just send us money and you'll be saved / Pretty soon you'll be our slave." While Jerry Falwell had been the target of most songs on the subject, G.I. drew attention to two others, Ernest Angley and Billy Graham. Angley, host of the weekly *Ernest Angley Hour*, owned the Winston Broadcasting Network, which served as a moneymaker for his larger ministry. It would bring in so much over the years that in 2005 he was able to purchase a Boeing 747 for $26 million to use for mission trips. Graham, whose evangelical career began four decades earlier, by the 1980s was considered by many to be one of the most important Christian figures of the twentieth century. A dear friend of the Reagans, he would be on the platform at the 1981 inauguration and was presented the Presidential Medal of Freedom two years later. While G.I. would lump him together with the "Gospel scam" televangelists of the era whose "slime if I watch in prime time" was only good as "gospel crime," Graham would come out of the turbulence of the decade relatively unscathed compared to his fellow pastors. Angley would not fare as well, the last years of his life being marred by sexual abuse allegations, including a taped admission to having a sexual relationship with a male employee, a significant finding considering Angley's years of preaching against homosexuality. Again, while many Americans were giving millions of dollars to televangelists like Angley, punks were recognizing that something just didn't seem right.[28]

It was Houston's Dirty Rotten Imbeciles that provided the most straight-to-the-point assessment of the money/religion relationship with their track "God Is Broke," included on 1985's *Dealing with It!* Like most songs by the band, it clocked in at around one minute, packing a punch with rapid guitar riffs, pounding drums, and lyrics that left listeners well aware of the corrupt connection. "Salvations around the corner / Just dig into your soul / Donations for the holy word / A paycheck for god's goal," the song's opening lines, could just as easily have been uttered by one of the many televangelists asking for money on the countless programs that cropped up in the '80s. Its chorus, "God is broke / The well ran dry / Pay up while you can / Or you'll end up in hell," reflected a message presented on Christian TV programs across the country that one's soul could be saved, not through repentance, but through monetary contribution. Projected into the living rooms of millions of Americans, these programs were huge moneymakers for their hosts. Jim Bakker, with his wife Tammy Faye, raked in millions of dollars using similar language on his *PTL Club* show, carried by over 200 stations, often openly praying that home audiences and listeners would make immediate contributions to their holy war chest. This would inspire one band from Boston to even name itself the P.T.L. Klub, and on their 1985 *13 Commandments* record they included the song "Join P.T.L." Like D.R.I.'s quip about dollarless damnation, they would sing, "Join PTL / Or you will rot in hell." On the same album the group would take a direct stab at Reagan, albeit on the nonreligious "M.X.," the short name for his LGM-118 Peacekeeper missile with intercontinental nuclear capabilities, first deployed the year *13 Commandments* was released. Claiming that "MX stands for peace," singer Dr. Death implored to listeners, "We gotta go along with Ronnie . . . Good for the economy." Ironically, what wasn't good for the personal economic position of the Bakkers was some less than moral behavior. Prior to his eventual imprisonment for defrauding his followers, the Bakkers, not God, would go broke in the wake of a sex scandal involving Jim and his former secretary, Jessica Hahn, though both he and Tammy Faye would eventually repent, on television, of course.[29]

There to pick up the pieces of the Bakkers' evangelical empire was none other than Jerry Falwell, who not only was the founder of the Moral Majority that punks so often raged against, but also of the *Old Time Gospel Hour*, a syndicated television show recorded at his Thomas Road Baptist Church. (The fall of the Bakkers and their association with Falwell was humorously addressed in the song "Jim and Tammy" by the Surrogate Brains from Stockton, California, with lines like "Goddammit, I earned that money the American way" and "People say . . . You're going to straight to hell / Just like Jerry Falwell.") Situated on the campus of Liberty University in Lynchburg, Virginia, which Falwell had also founded, it was a megachurch with over 20,000 members and upwards of $72 million in contributions brought in each year. With close to 400 stations carrying his show, Falwell was able to reach millions of Americans every Sunday. While most punk bands took on the Moral Majority, one not far from Falwell's backyard decided to make him their personal center of lyrical attention. Just a few hours east in Richmond, a band called the Prevaricators recorded "Jesus H Falwell" for their 1985 *Snubculture* LP, a satirical berating of the Baptist minister and evangelicalism in general. The opening lyrics, "I watch TV and all those preachers try to recruit me / I made my choice, I fell in love with Jerry Falwell's voice," were followed with "I paid his fee, he said that he would talk to God for me / So I'm saved from sin, those pearly gates are gonna let me in," both clear denunciations of the pay-to-play salvation narrative that had become associated with televangelism by the middle of the decade.[30]

Falwell's church would continue to gather more members as well as more money, although his *PTL* takeover would eventually fall through. With this came more influence, particularly political, which often blurred the line between his ministry and the Moral Majority, a conflict of interest that often put the tax-exempt status of the former in question. The Prevaricators, like so many punk bands, saw the line as it truly was, nonexistent, and in the second verse of "Jesus H Falwell" they illuminated this well: "Jerry Falwell says all the f*gs are gonna burn in hell / So vote right wing, you just might get to hear his angels sing" brought the Christian Right's position on homosexuality and gay rights to the front of the discourse concerning political participation. A vote for Ronald Reagan, whom Falwell unabashedly supported, was a vote against what he openly referred to as the "homosexual revolution" taking place in America. "With God as my witness," Falwell wrote the year after his Moral Majority helped Reagan win the presidency, "I pledge that I'll continue to expose the sin of homosexuality to the people of this nation." Although the Prevaricators called him on the carpet for mixing his pulpit with politics, they, like bands mentioned above, found themselves at times mirroring the homophobic rhetoric of Falwell and others in the Christian Right in songs like their "Jesse's (a) Girl."[31]

In the final year of Reagan's presidency, Jeffrey Hadden and Anson Shupe wrote, "[There] is no more profound multiplier effect in American politics than 3,500 religious broadcasters disseminating the social and political agenda of the New Christian Right on their respective radio and television programs." But in 1987, the televangelist revolution almost came to a crashing halt. The Bakker scandal and conflict concerning who would take over his evangelical empire, as well as Oral Roberts's claim that if his followers did not raise $8 million God was "going to call him home in one year," seemed to get Americans to finally think critically about the pay-the-Lord practices of their pecuniary-principled preachers. As Hadden and Shupe noted, polls by the *Los Angeles Times*, *New York Times*, and *USA Today* all showed that televangelists were losing the support of the American public, with substantial percentages of respondents expressing disapproval of how they raised money as well as why, which was clearly to line their own pockets. Punk bands had been saying the same thing since before Reagan was even voted into the White House. They, more than anyone, attempted to illuminate the absurdity behind the pay salvation schemes of televangelist leaders like the Bakkers as well as the political pandering of Jerry Falwell and his Moral Majority. Unfortunately for many Americans, who were well-fleeced as members of these flocks, punks just weren't a group they would ever pay attention, let alone listen to.[32]

The Catholics Are Attacking

One of the more interesting things to happen during the Reagan Era was the newfound connection between Christian fundamentalists and Catholics. Historically, each distrusted the other, with the latter often described as "papists" whose allegiance to America was questionable. Once outcasts, by 1980 many Catholics had attained a degree of prosperity and found themselves, according to Robert Lekachman in *Visions and Nightmares: America after Reagan*, "by no particular coincidence securely located in the mainstream of American politics." In terms of their connectedness to the Christian Right, it was on issues like abortion, gay marriage, family values, and the spread of communism where Catholics found common ground in the 1980s with their fundamentalist counterparts. Although reared in the church of his mother, the Disciples of Christ, Reagan's father Jack was

Catholic. While he never joined the Church, he seemed to retain an affinity for the faith, surrounding himself as president with Catholics in various administrative positions including Secretary of State Alexander Haig and National Security Advisers William Clark and Richard Allen. He also appointed Antonin Scalia, the first Catholic in thirty years, to the Supreme Court. Reagan, always interested in speaking before a crowd, accepted a number of invitations to speak before Catholic groups, one of which was in 1984 at the St. Anne's Festival in Hoboken, New Jersey, where he affirmed his support for their faith and reiterated the importance of their continued involvement in politics. "I'm only the head of a civil government, a secular authority," he told attendees. "It's probably true that politics is the prose of culture, but religion is its poetry. Governments are passing things in the long history of the world, but faith and belief endure forever." With such support, Catholics were welcomed into the Reagan Revolution, emboldened in ways they had never been before.[33]

While the Moral Majority received the brunt of lyrical attention from punk bands, Catholics were given a fair flogging as well. Near Chicago, where Reagan had addressed the National Catholic Education Association in 1982 about the support his administration planned to provide private schools, the suburban group Negative Element spoke its mind a year later on the EP *Yes, We Have No Bananas!* Described in *MRR* as having "Youthful exuberance, chaotic instrumentation, and half-serious, half-silly themes" (one of the songs on it is titled "Anti-Pacman" and another "What Ever Happened to Elmer Fudd?"), it was an eight-song commentary with two specifically addressing the topic of religion, both highlighting Catholicism and its influence on Americans. In the first, "Temples of Corruption," singer Tom Faulkner drew attention to the suborning influence of all religions and religious leaders, Catholics and priests at the front of both lists. As the opening line informs, "They prey on the ill-fated / The poor, this misinformed / When they lead them blindly / With a hopeful hand." In the second song, "Pay the Lord," a title that would reflect the same concerns expressed by the above bands, Faulkner explained what the real institutional intentions of the Rome-influenced religionists were. Priests, the Church, and Catholic schools will "steal your money and your minds" if you let them.[34]

The same year Reagan let Chicago Catholics know he supported their educational endeavors, Cerritos, California's Channel 3, made listeners aware of what a Catholic education really entailed. Included on their *Fear of Life* album, which *MMR* labeled as "Southern California suburban angst," was an unbarred assessment of an American youth's experiences with parochial schooling titled "Catholic Boy." A little more poppy than their previous work, something noted in the review, its aggressive attitude concerning the religious educational experience of the titular figure can be well understood in the simplicity of its opening lines: "Father Finn, dressed in black / Slivers from his ruler lodged in my ass / Catholic boy, Catholic school / Live and die by the same ten rules" offered a concise yet clear explanation of the personal plight of many American youths enrolled in the country's plethora of parochial schools. While Reagan was praising the work of Catholic educators in his Chicago speech — "I'm grateful for your help in shaping American policy to reflect God's will" — Channel 3 was voicing concern about the corporal punishment policies enforced by many of these same educators, who likely thought it was doing some worldly good in shaping students' character.[35]

Also digging into Catholic schools was a band out of Winston-Salem, North Carolina, called Subculture, described by Tim Yohannan as "high quality straight-ahead hardcore. . . . Powerful has hell!" On their 1985 album *Fear of Life* was the track "Catholic Schools," a fifty-second chastising of the force-feeding moralism associated with Catholic education. "All I wanted was an education / But I got their morals shoved down my throat / Fascist nuns breed humiliation / In a catholic school there ain't no hope" is repeated twice for emphasis, with a "Catholic Schools / Home of fools" chorus capping off each as well as the song. Like Channel 3, Subculture's lyrics informed listeners about what many likely already knew, that attending a Catholic school would not be a pleasant experience for someone other than a young person ready and willing to conform to the rules of the Church. While Reagan is mentioned in neither tune, the empowerment Catholics and Catholic educators felt during his administration seems to have impacted the parochial school landscape to the point that bands felt compelled to lyrically respond. Ironically, while some were shedding light on the horrors of Catholic education, Catholics, who had gained a clear ally in Reagan, were sending their kids less often to Catholic schools than ever before. By decade's end, punks could be proud of having possibly contributed to fewer wooden fragments embedded in the backsides of kids.[36]

In his work on Catholics and their relationships with presidents since 1960, Lawrence McAndrews stated, "In some ways the American Catholic bishops never had it better than during the presidency of Ronald Reagan." This notion of Catholic empowerment as well as concern for it could definitely be seen in punk songs from the era. One of these, only thirteen seconds long, was "Smart, Tough, and Catholic" by Carmel, Indiana's Chemotherapy, a quick but clear commentary on American Catholics' newfound sense of significance and superiority. "I'm smart, I'm tough, I'm Catholic / That makes me better than you / I'm smart, I'm tough, I'm Catholic / I love beating on rich smart Jews," the song's only lyrics, said more than enough about this. Coupled to it should be "The Catholics Are Attacking," a slightly longer assessment of Catholic affairs by the San Francisco punk outfit Pop-O-Pies. Once described in the *L.A. Times* as "absolutely the worst band in California," their over-five-minute, 1950s pop-inspired denunciation was included on 1981's *The White* EP. With musings such as "They've got a big contention / Over a million strong / Someday they're taking over / You know it won't be long," as well as juxtaposing Catholics with both Nazis and the followers of fanatical cult leader Jim Jones, it added plenty to the already cautionary concern among punks about Catholicism during the Reagan Revolution. With Catholics, as McAndrews implied, having it better under Reagan than any previous president, they gave punks another religion-related target to hit in their lyrical lashings. And while they may have been on the attack, plenty of punk bands were ready and willing to hit back.[37]

Bad Religion

Of everything punk bands sang about, religion remained as constant a theme across scenes as anything else. The songs are so plentiful that a single chapter cannot do them justice. Beyond those assessed above, a band in every scene across the country most likely had a song that lashed out lyrically against what might best be described in punk terminology as *bad religion*. One group of teenagers from Los Angeles even went so far as to choose their name based on ill feelings about the dogmatic and nationalist tendencies of faith-based groups. That band was Bad Religion. Their logo, the Crossbuster, was a black Christian cross encircled in red with a thick red diagonal line striking through it. Formed in 1980, they would release their first full-length album *How Could Hell Be Any Worse?* two years later. Included on it was "Faith in God" and "Voice of God Is Government," both early punk tunes about the continued encroachment of religion into the political arena with Reagan coming into the presidency. With the group's early work, songs that could have been included in this chapter are too numerous to provide anything close to a complete listing. A few others worth mentioning are "Religion Is Recruiting" by Orange County's Uniform Choice; "Faith" by the youthful Chicago counterparts of Negative Element, Rights of the Accused; "God Is Dead" by Queens' Heart Attack; Seattle's The Fartz' "Bible Stories"; "Second Coming" by San Diego's Battalion of Saints; "7 Deadly Sins" by the False Prophets from NYC; or Poison

Idea from Portland, Oregon's "God Not God," whose 1983 EP *Pick Your King* had a picture of Jesus on the front and chubby-cheeked Elvis on the back, blasphemously prompting listeners to select between the two regal idols. Even Minor Threat got a jab in on "Filler," with Ian MacKaye's emotionally frustrated lyrics wondering, "What happened to you / You're not the same / There's something in your head / Made a violent change," followed by "It's in your head / Filler / You call it religion / You're full of shit."[38]

Also up for inclusion might have been "Religion Kills" by the aptly named Crucifix from Berkeley; "Religion Is the Opium of the Masses" by Boston's Marx-inspired foursome The Proletariat, which was included on 1982's *This Is Boston, Not L.A.* anthology; one of the best song titles of the era, "Praise the Lord and Pass the Ammunition" by San Francisco's (Impatient) Youth from the *Not So Quiet* compilation (which actually was a cover of a 1942 post–Pearl Harbor patriotic song by Frank Loesser); "White Lies" by Houston's Really Red; "Jesus Slaves" by Richmond, Virginia's Unseen Force; "Lord's Prayer" by Hayward, California's Social Unrest; and Cape Cod's the Freeze's "Warped Confessional," a strong lyrical attack about sexual assault on young parishioners by Catholic clergy, a tragedy that went on for decades before finally being acknowledged as a national scandal in the early 2000s. It, like so many more, was just another example of punk bands drawing attention to religious hypocrisy and injustice at a time when most Americans were willing to live quietly, turning a blind eye to the happenings around them, praying for salvation and paying plenty for it.[39]

Beyond the borders of the United States, religion was as vilified by international bands as it was by their American counterparts. To recognize just a few, in Sweden, Anti-Climex released "Game of the Arseholes," which prompted the faithful to put their crucifixes in a less than holy personal place. Sweden also saw Asocial record the straightforwardly titled "Religion Sucks" for its 1986 EP of the same name. In Canada, the Dayglo Abortions released the already mentioned "Religious Bumfucks," which included a special lyrical mention of "Reaganism" as one of the many forms of religion hated by the band. D.O.A. subtitled their 1981 release *Positively D.O.A.*, which included "Fucked Up Ronnie," *No God No Country No Lies*. Jerry Falwell's followers even received attention on the international front with bands like Australia's Fear and Loathing and Death Sentence, both recording songs titled "Moral Majority." In Spain, Porkeria T. released "Religion, Esperanza, Desperados" (Religion, Hope, Desperation) on its 1985 cassette *Represion, Maldita, Represion* (Repression, Damn, Repression), while the 1984 compilation tape *La Lucha Continua!!* (The Struggle Continues) included "Campos de Cruces" (Fields of Crosses) by the appropriately named Anti-Dogmatikss and "No Religion—No Poder" (No Religion—No Power) by Autodefensa. In Brazil, where the iconic statue of Christ the Redeemer has been a place of pilgrimage for Christians since its opening in 1931, Karne Krua included a live instrumental performance they titled "Jesus Is Dead" on their *Cenas de Ódio e Revolta* (Scenes of Hatred and Revolt) cassette.[40]

Across the pond in the UK, where punk bands were having as much fun ripping on the Thatcher regime as American bands were the Reagan Revolution, religion was also a main source of lyrical inspiration. Chaotic Dischord had the uncomplicatedly titled "Fuck Religion, Fuck Politics, Fuck the Lot of You" on an album of the same name, which also included the song "Anti-Christ." Stoke-on-Trent's Discharge had "Religion Instigates" on its 1980 *Fight Back* EP. A 1983 demo by Criminal Justice included "Victim of Religion." Another cassette from '83 by the group Suburban Filth included both "Smash Religion" and "Religion Is Shit." The anarcho-punk group A.P.F. Brigade (Anarchy, Peace, and Freedom Brigade) included on its 1982 *Sick Society* cassette the songs "Man Created God" and "Jesus Who." They would also release a year later another cassette titled *God the Tape: Last Will and Testicle*, with what appears to be an insert image of Reagan dancing with Margaret Thatcher over a stack of skulls labeled "Harvest 1982." One of the most well-known UK bands among US punks, Scotland's Exploited, released its EP *Jesus Is Dead* in 1986, with a title-track diatribe against the notion that belief and faith were meaningful in terms of real-life circumstances. As singer Wattie Buchan explained to those listening, "Jesus, Jesus sleeping on your cross / Fuck mankind you couldn't give a toss."[41]

It is evident from the abundance of songs on the subject that religion was a matter of serious concern within the global punk community. One song by an American band that summarizes this succinctly was "Downward Christian Soldiers," by DC's Black Market Baby. A lyrical parody of the evangelical fan favorite "Onward Christian Soldiers," it was released in 1983, the first year of Night of Joy, a contemporary Christian music festival held at Walt Disney World for more than three decades. Its second verse described the frustration and concern of punks throughout the world about the continued growth and influence of conservative Christians, and it deserves full inclusion here. "The Moral Majority and Club PTL / If that's the way to heaven, I'll spend my time in hell / Donations flow in, the ratings they soar / They can build a brand new church, why bother with the poor / They got so much money, they invade politics / Using smear campaigns and mudslinging tricks / A born-again army led by fascist direction / How long do we have before they control elections?" Unfortunately for many Americans, most of whom were poor and already suffering under the fiscal policies of the Reagan Revolution, it was too late before they realized what was really being done with their money in the name of God.[42]

Conclusion

In the month that Reagan was inaugurated, the president of Catholics for Christian Political Action, Gary Potter, boasted about what was coming. "When the Christian majority takes over this country," he began, "there will be no satanic churches, no more free distribution of pornography, no more abortion on demand and no more talk of the rights of homosexuals." If that wasn't enough of a warning, Potter continued, "After the Christian majority takes control, pluralism will be seen as immoral and evil, and the state will not permit anybody the right to practice evil." Such was the narrative at the begin of the Reagan Era, its tone and message offering more than enough reason for the lyrical lashing delivered by punk bands in the years that followed.[43]

Sociologist James Davison Hunter, one of the first scholars to use the term "culture wars" to describe the polarizing of America during the last half of the twentieth century, stated the following in his essay on the liberal response to the Christian Right: "What has long been a source of amusement or of superficial contempt has recently become the cause of serious concern on the part of the liberal community in North America. Those on the far right of American political theory and praxis have rarely been taken very seriously by those who fashion themselves the vanguard of social and political thought. But with the emergence of such groups as the Moral Majority . . . *and* the election of a conservative Republican president, such nonchalance has been rapidly laid aside." While most punk bands would never label themselves as leaders in the liberal community, their lyrics prove they were as concerned about the connection between Reagan and the conservative Christians that backed him. While these same lyrics were often amusing, and at times absurd and disturbing, the contempt they expressed for groups like the Moral Majority as well as their adherents was far from being superficial. With a rapidity unmatched in terms of music, there was no nonchalance to speak of. Punk songs about the Christian Right and religion in general are some of the most authentic expressions of concern we have about the fusion of politics and faith that truly took hold in the 1980s, which has since then never really dissipated. Again, not to sound like a broken record, maybe we should have been a bit more willing to listen to what they had to say.[44]

Reagan's In (Jackpot Records, 2021). Wasted Youth. A record store day reissue of the group's 1981 LP. Author's collection.

Bonzo Goes to Bitburg (Beggars Banquet, 1985). Ramones. Original 12″ UK release. Author's collection.

A Sensitive Fascist Is Very Rare (Vinyl Communications, 1987). A.P.P.L.E. Original 7″ release. Author's collection.

Let Them Eat Jellybeans! (Alternative Tentacles, 1981). Various. Original 12″ compilation. Author's collection.

Scary Action
(Arcatones, 1985).
Agent 86. Original 7″.
Author's collection.

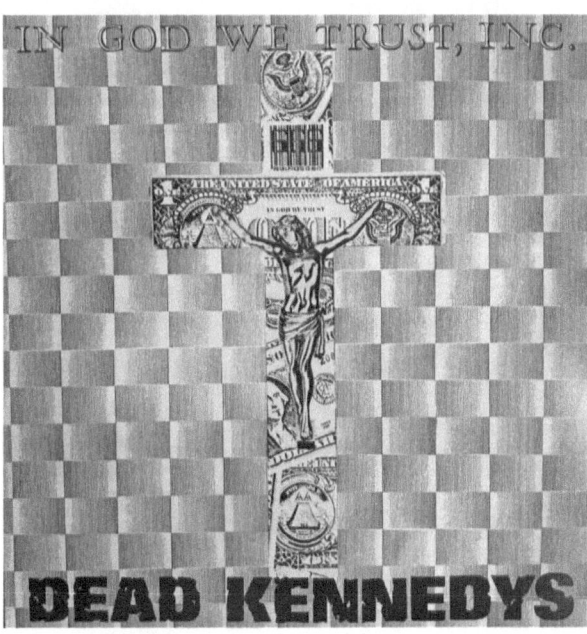

In God We Trust, Inc.
(Manifesto, 2003).
Dead Kennedys.
Reissue of the
group's 1981 12″.
Author's collection.

Kill by Remote Control (Alternative Tentacles, 1984). Toxic Reasons. Original LP UK release. Author's collection.

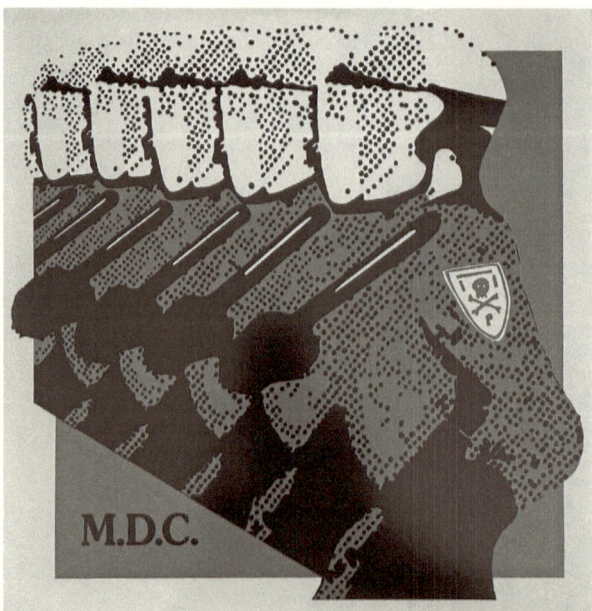

Millions of Dead Cops (Beer City Records, 2014). M.D.C. Reissue of the group's 1982 LP. Author's collection.

Mein Comp (Youth Attack, 2003). Compilation. Original 7″. Author's collection.

Fucked Up Donald (Sudden Death Records, 2016). D.O.A. Original 7″. Author's collection.

CHAPTER FIVE

War Is Bad

> My fellow Americans. . . . We begin bombing in five minutes.
> —RONALD REAGAN

> War is bad! / It's not very pretty / People get hurt / Some even die.
> —MUSICAL SUICIDE

A Matter of the Utmost Gravity

On August 11, 1984, at his Rancho del Cielo vacation home, Ronald Reagan sat down behind his desk to deliver a weekly radio address. Like presidents before and since, Reagan used the opportunity to speak directly to the American people about current and upcoming policy initiatives. No one there could have anticipated what happened when the president's mic went hot. Moments before delivering his speech and as radio stations across the country began recording during sound check, Reagan decided to crack a joke. "My fellow Americans," he began, "I'm pleased to tell you that today I have signed legislation that will outlaw Russia forever." An inappropriate jest for any president to make concerning any nation, let alone one with which the United States had an uneasy relationship since the end of World War II, he capped it off with an unimaginable line. "We begin bombing in five minutes." Those six simple words would cause fear and consternation across the nation and the world as many wondered how someone in his position, with fingers literally on the bombing buttons, could say such a thing, even humorously.[1]

"A matter of the utmost gravity," as one author described the situation between the two countries in 1984, seemed a cause to quip rather than take seriously. Unable to comprehend why others couldn't see this, Reagan witnessed a backlash as both concerned American citizens and global leaders spoke out. At home, his opponent in the upcoming election, Democrat Walter Mondale, criticized the president for being less than presidential. "People must understand that words like those live," he told the press. "And whatever was intended . . . many may not accept it as such. . . . He's the president of the United States." An official response from the Kremlin was a little more scathing, describing Reagan's offhand remark as "unprecedently hostile toward the Soviet Union and dangerous to the cause of peace." After waiting for a reaction from the administration, which came with a statement of support for the president's "frankness" in responding to the situation, the Soviets issued a frank statement of their own. "This conduct is incompatible with the high responsibility borne by leaders of state, particularly nuclear powers." Interestingly, punk bands had been saying the same thing about Reagan for quite some time. One in particular from Detroit, Dad and the Boys, asked a question not long after the gaffe that was becoming more pertinent. On their 1985 single "Reagan (in the White House)," vocalist Don Isler posed to listeners, "What would you do if there were nuclear war?" For many Americans post–Reagan bombing quip, this was seemingly becoming more possible every day.[2]

The Reagan Doctrine

Reagan's eight years in office were defined by the final stages of the Cold War. With distrust between the Soviet Union and the United States going back decades, by the early 1980s things seemed to be more tense than ever as the world's two superpowers sized each other up for what many thought could be the final moments of humanity. While there was less concern about the spread of communism at home than there had been in the past, significant attention was paid in the post–Vietnam War era to its spread across the globe. Humiliated by our loss in Southeast Asia, as well as the Iranian hostage crisis that plagued his predecessor's last years in office, the United States needed to restore its sense of pride and place of primacy on the international scene. Ronald Reagan truly took this to heart. Speaking before the Veterans of Foreign Wars Convention in August of 1980, then-candidate Reagan told the crowd, "America has been sleepwalking far too long." While we sat back, Soviet influence spread throughout the world and was continuing its creep into Africa, the Middle East, and Latin America. While we talked of peace, the Soviets were building up arms at a rate double or even triple our own. "When one side relaxes while the other carries out the greatest military buildup in the history of mankind," he reminded his audience, "the cause of peace has not been advanced." With their endorsement, the first given to a candidate in eighty years, Reagan promised to end the era of American complacency and usher in a new age of peace, prosperity, and pride in the nation.[3]

Charles Krauthammer, a political columnist for the *Washington Post*, would label the international interventionist policies born out of this rhetoric as the Reagan Doctrine, under which the government's involvement would be supplying support for anti-communist insurgencies rather than direct troop deployment. Coupled with a massive defense build-up, much of it nuclear, the Reagan Era constituted a time of great concern for many Americans. Writing five years after his death, political scientist Hugh Heclo wrote in an assessment of the mixed legacies of Reagan, "the Reagan doctrine . . . led to American support for brutal regimes and proxy wars that had nothing to do with moral clarity and everything to do with whatever seemed expedient as an anti-Soviet maneuver. The negative consequences were profound." Although he was most concerned about the greater impact of this doctrine over time, Heclo's evaluation concerning consequences was absolutely in tune with what bands across the country during the 1980s were saying about Reagan's military philosophy. In simplest terms, punks viewed Reagan's global outlook and the connected policies with serious concern and took to writing about this eagerly and often throughout the decade.[4]

While it's important to note that punk music began expressing disaffection for the state of world affairs before Reagan's presidency—one need only listen to the Clash's 1979 track "London Calling" or "We Got the Neutron Bomb" from 1978 by the Weirdos as examples—his time in office saw bands across the United States take to task his administration for everything it did in the realm of foreign policy. Songs from the decade fall neatly into groupings, as the draft, nuclear war, World War III, and the names of countries like El Salvador and Nicaragua, where the Reagan Doctrine was applied, found themselves as titles used by groups across scenes. And while a number of pop artists similarly expressed their concerns in song—Nena's "99 Red Balloons," "Ronnie Talk to Russia" by Prince, and Genesis's "Land of Confusion" come immediately to mind—none did so with the assertiveness and aggressiveness of punks. Their anger-laden lyrics, very much informed by fear, came through clearly, though often indecipherably. In the land of confusion where they were coming into adulthood, punks used music as a way to make their anxieties about the future live as opposed to keeping them locked inside, as many Americans did. Their songs on the subject never made it onto MTV, like those mentioned above, softened by corporate-influenced imagery to make them more palatable to the masses. They screamed, loudly as ever, about how it all might end in their lifetimes, with singers like Dave Dictor of M.D.C. proclaiming what many punks were feeling in that moment: "I'm born to die."[5]

I Hope You Get Drafted

Concern for their lives among many young people during Reagan's administration, and not just punks, was directly connected to the possibility of being forced to join the military and fight, maybe even die, for their country. While the Selective Service System had been around since the Civil War, for American youth growing up in the immediate wake of Vietnam it was a serious matter. Although Jimmy Carter had pardoned all draft evaders in 1977, two years later he revitalized the system after the Soviet Union invaded Afghanistan. That same year, Reagan, in pursuit of the Republican Party nomination for president, spoke out hotly in opposition to Carter's decision. "[Conscription] rests on the assumption that your kids belong to the state," he announced. "That assumption isn't a new one. . . . The Nazis thought it was a great idea." A year later he would affirm his position in a letter sent to congressional draft opponents. "Perhaps the most fundamental objection to draft registration is moral. Only in the most severe national emergency does the Government have a claim to the mandatory service of its young people." While punks might have agreed with Reagan on this issue, they would soon have cause to call him on the carpet as well.[6]

While many thought one of the first things Reagan would do upon entering office would be to end Selective Service registration, it wasn't until midway through his first year that the Military Manpower Task Force would take up the issue for review. In January of the following year, Reagan issued a statement the *New York Times* described as a "marked reversal of the position he took in the election campaign." Now President Reagan sang a different tune about the government's power to force young Americans to register for military service, even in times of peace. "We live in a dangerous world," Reagan announced. "In the event of a future threat to national security, registration could save the United States as much as six weeks in mobilizing emergency manpower." Although Reagan tried to assure Americans that a continuance of registration did not constitute the draft's return, for many of service age, punks particularly, the damage was done. This would only add fuel to an already raging fire, and the draft would find itself a topic of interest lashed out against lyrically. Expressing early on what many would feel was New Orleans' the Sluts, who the same year Reagan made his announcement would release *12" of Sluts* with "Draft Song" included. "So you want to draft me, why / Suck my cock / I ain't gonna go fight" would be followed by plenty of other irreverent lyrics concerning conscription during Reagan's eight years in the White House.[7]

Although it came out before Reagan's flip-flop, "When Ya Get Drafted" by Dead Kennedys, released in 1980 on *Fresh Fruit for Rotting Vegetables*, provides one of the earliest interpretations of post-Vietnam Selective Service and is a foundational song on the subject. Described as "one of the most important albums to emerge from punk," *Fresh Fruit*'s track listing included such notable anthems as "Kill the Poor," "Chemical Warfare," "California über Alles," and "Holiday in Cambodia." These and the respective others marked a watershed in the history of punk, as much of what followed became more politically charged and threatening in terms of lyrics. "When Ya Get Drafted" is no exception and affords listeners a critique of the circumstances surrounding conscription in the moments leading up to Reagan's election. From the influence of the military-industrial complex to making poor kids the primary targets of the Selective Service System, it holds nothing back in drawing attention to the draft's realities with lines like "Yeah, what Big Business wants Big Business gets / It wants war (when ya get drafted)," and "Call the Army, call the Navy / Stocked with kids from the slums (when ya get drafted)." The last verse is the most insightful, particularly regarding what the group perceived to be a post-Vietnam apathy among young Americans. As singer Jello Biafra warned, "Forget your demonstrations / Kids today sit on their asses (when ya get drafted) / Just a six-pack and you're happy / We're prepared for when ya get drafted." With all of the anti-draft songs that popped up in its wake, at least punks appeared to have gotten the message about the need to be more engaged in oppositional activity.[8]

With a slight change in title from Dead Kennedys' tune, the Dicks, relocated from Austin to San Francisco, released "I Hope You Get Drafted" on their 1984 7" *Peace?* Also included on the *International P.E.A.C.E. Benefit Compilation* released the same year, it offered an interesting take on not only the draft, but also the circumstances surrounding the increased possibility of there being a nuclear war, as well as who would be doing the fighting if/when it comes. A little less than ninety seconds, its Johnny B. Good guitar intro is followed by the powerful and soulful voice of singer Gary Floyd. His verbal assault on apathetic Americans begins with the strong accusation, "You don't care about nuclear war or how many people die" and continues into the second verse with, "Your privileged life shows itself when you speak / Your education is lies." Like a number of songs connected to Vietnam, Creedence Clearwater Revival's "Fortunate Son" being the most recognizable, the Dicks insinuated that wars are most often fought by marginalized Americans while the comfortable classes sit back and watch it all play out. To this latter group, who were enjoying personal prosperity during the Reagan Revolution, Floyd had a clear message: "I hope you get drafted / I hope you burn and fry / You apolitical asshole / I hope you're the first to die."[9]

On the same 7" was "No Fuckin' War," a nearly five-minute tune with a rather simple yet emphatic titular expression of the band's thoughts, an art the Dicks mastered throughout their career. It also included the track "Nobody Asked Me," sixty-three hard-driven seconds of rage about how the government under Reagan was making the same mistakes it had during Vietnam, most notably the spread of misinformation and lack of transparency concerning military affairs. The year before the record was released, Reagan had appeared in October on national television to speak to the American people about Grenada, a small island nation in the Caribbean Sea with a population of little more than 100,000, less than 1 percent of that of the United States at that time. The crisis there, according to Reagan, was a Marxist military coup with alleged ties to Cuba and Moscow that now threatened the lives of 800 American students at St. George's University Medical School. Operation Urgent Fury commenced on October 25 with 7,500 soldiers taking only four days to liberate the island. A few weeks later, the United Nations would adopt a resolution stating that it "deeply deplores the armed intervention in Grenada," and described Reagan's actions as "a flagrant violation of international law." The Dicks, whose frontman Gary Floyd was a Marxist, appeared to agree, as "No Fuckin' War" announced, "Well here we go again / Another war to win / It's the American dream," and "Nobody Asked Me" included lines like "The army came today / We saw the bastards land / Another U.S. plane / God is at work again / Just like in Viet Nam!" Taken together, the three songs that make up the Dicks' *Peace?* release reflect a growing sense of concern among punks that America under Reagan was becoming more adventurist in its foreign policy and willing to sacrifice lives to achieve its publicly professed goal of stopping the spread of international communism.[10]

Of the 7,500 American troops that fought in Grenada, nineteen were killed and over a hundred wounded. For punks that was enough to keep them raging against the possibility of being forced to fight in the future wars they saw as likely to happen under the Reagan regime. Houston's Dirty Rotten Imbeciles, who would soon move to San Francisco like the Dicks, included "Draft Me" on their 1983 *Dirty Rotten* EP. Only nineteen seconds, it is the quickest of the draft songs, with final lines sarcastically spewed by singer Kurt Brecht: "I want to help America keep the peace / I want to be a trooper in the world police — Draft me!" In addition, the record would include other expressions of anti-militarist angst such as "War Crimes" and "F.R.D.C." The second of these starts out "I'm a first round draft choice . . . 19 / A man without a choice . . . unseen," a mocking sports-related remark by Brecht that likely resonated with a number of disempowered young men of fighting age. Two years later, the band would put out *Dealing with It!*, which included "I Don't Need Society," "Stupid, Stupid War," and "Argument Then War," all songs with strong lyrical pronouncements about expanding military interventionist activity under Reagan. In the first verse of "I Don't Need Society," Brecht's lyrics provided powerful imagery regarding the draft. "Your numbers up you have to go / System says, 'I told you so' / Stocked on a train like a truckload of cattle / Sent off to slaughter in a useless battle / Thousands of us sent off to die / Never really knowing why" expressed a concern that some young Americans feared could become reality in the years following Reagan's decision to invade Grenada.[11]

In the body of punk work on war, songs about the draft were plentiful. In 1983, the same year American troops landed in Grenada, Bum Kon, a group from Denver, recorded "The Draft" for its *Drunken Sex Sucks* release, which would be included on a later compilation of the band's catalogue along with "Nancy Reagan Fashion Show" and "Reagan Sucks." The following year would see Atlanta's Neon Christ release a 7″ titled *Parental Suppression*, which included "Draft Song." Accompanied by a brilliant apocalyptic album cover with mushroom clouds, the grim reaper, a stack of skulls, and a Klansman joined by a heavily armed solider front and center of it all, it includes other Reagan-Era reflections like the title track and "Doom," a rather pessimistic take on the state of the world as Reagan's first term was about to give way to his second. A year later San Francisco's Christ on Parade recorded "Don't Draft Me" on a live radio show. It would eventually be added to a compilation of the group's work that included other notable expressions of disaffection and concern like "Drop Out," "Thoughts of War," "America the Myth," and "The Plague," one of the handful of punk songs from the period addressing environmental issues. That same year Santa Monica's Entropy on a non-label cassette chock full of cultural criticism included the song "Draft or Die," with a lyric that summed up the concerns of many of-age American men at that time—"It's your eighteenth birthday, now it's time to go war / It's time to die and you don't know what the fuck it's for." And on the other side of the country, Tampa's Belching Penguin (B.P.), with songs like "There's Gonna Be a War," "Better Off Dead," and "Forget the World," humorously titled their 1986 release *Draft Beer . . . Not Me*. Four years earlier in a statement defending his decision to retain Selective Service registration, Reagan proudly claimed, "I know this generation of young Americans shares the sense of patriotism and responsibility that past generations have always shown." For punks, their lyrics regarding the draft strongly suggested otherwise.[12]

While it's important to note that no one was forced to serve during Reagan's eight years in office, what matters is the punk perception at the time that his flip-flop, coupled with the sending of troops to places like Grenada, could have resulted in young men being forced to serve against their will. Worsening things was the thought that they might die for a country few felt any sense of attachment to. For punks who clearly hated Reagan and what his administration stood for, this was the worst of all possibilities. One band from New York City, Silent Age, would even get personal on this asking, "Hey Mister Reagan / What is the answer / Who is the dancer / Will this man die?," a reference to Reagan's son Ron, himself a dancer who, the band made sure to make listeners aware in the liner notes, "did *not* get sent to Grenada." "Reagan's election in 1980 was viewed with horror," the band claimed, and "Hey Mister Reagan" was their way of calling out the president for sending others' sons to die and not his own. While Silent Age and so many more bands assailed this in song, their lyrical attention also turned to those places where soldiers were sent in support of the Reagan Doctrine. One thing is for sure, and that was the sending of American soldiers to places like Lebanon, El Salvador, and Nicaragua provided punks an additional platform beyond Selective Service upon which to grill the Gipper.[13]

I Wish I Was in El Salvador

While the Vietnam War had ended five years before Reagan became president, it was still very much on the minds of the American people. Fifteen years earlier, not-yet-Governor Reagan, when asked about Vietnam, had said, "We should declare war on North Vietnam. We could pave the whole country and put parking stripes on it and still be home by Christmas." In his 1980 VFW address in Chicago, candidate Reagan spoke about "Vietnam Syndrome" and how it was high time we stopped wallowing in shame and regret. As he told those in attendance, "It is time we recognized that ours was, in truth, a noble cause." Punk bands would use much different rhetoric than Reagan's to reflect on the American military experience in Southeast Asia. One in particular, Boston's Jerry's Kids, would use "Vietnam Syndrome" for a song title, its message not about the loss of national self-esteem but rather the emotional and mental impact the war had on a number of veterans. "Lodged deep inside his head / Visions of war, visions of the dead" the chorus sandwiched between the opening lines, "Ten years back from Vietnam / He gave his mind to Uncle Sam," and the first lines of the closing verse, "So thanks very much for his kick in the face / He's not all right, he's in outer space" reflected a growing concern among many Americans, not just punks, that soldiers coming home from the war were having serious trouble returning to normal living.[14]

Interestingly, the first wave of Hollywood films about the war, such as *The Deer Hunter* and *First Blood*, would have themes similar to punk songs like "Vietnam Syndrome." As the Reagan rhetoric about service became increasingly more patriotic in tone, the movie industry appeared to follow along, with films like *Rambo: First Blood Part II*, *Uncommon Valor*, and the Chuck Norris vehicle *Missing in Action*, all calling for our return to Vietnam to restore our national sense of self-worth. Punks weren't buying the new narrative and stayed critical in their lyrical pronouncements, especially about the mental health impact of the war. One band that really drove the point home was Circle One, whose singer John Macias suffered from a mental illness that would contribute to his untimely death in 1991. (This is discussed in the next chapter.) They recorded "Vietnam Vets" for their *Patterns of Force* album, with an opening verse that not only described the tragedy behind the postwar trauma being experienced by soldiers now home, but also issued a warning. As Macias harrowingly sang, "V.V. syndrome doesn't stop their / Flashbacks, jitters, another nightmare / A war that people want to forget / Will happen again that's a sure bet." While he could not have foreseen what was to come, Macias's prognostication is interesting to think about, not only in light of the conflicts America would be involved in during the remaining years of Reagan's presidency, but also the perpetual state of war it appears to be in in the post-9/11 world. Concerning the Reagan Doctrine wars, punk bands like Circle One would speak their minds emphatically and aggressively.[15]

Only seven years after the last American soldiers left Vietnam, Reagan deployed troops to Lebanon in 1982. Responding to a request from the Lebanese government for help keeping the peace between the Israelis and the Palestinian Liberation Organization (P.L.O.) who had been fighting in the country's southern region, Reagan sent 1,800 Marines to be part of a UN-authorized multinational force. Supported by his State Department and National Security Council, the decision was opposed by the Joint Chiefs of Staff and made without congressional approval. After a year of being there, on October 23, 1983, a truck carrying explosives drove into the American barracks outside of Beirut, killing 241 service members, mostly Marines. The US mission in Lebanon, described by one officer as "80 percent political, 20 percent military," had been rather unclear beyond the peacekeeping presence Reagan had hoped for. Punk bands took notice of the confusion surrounding the conflict with one, Florence, South Carolina's Sex Mutants, going straight for Reagan on "Lebanon." Included on their 1985 non-labeled *Escape from Society* cassette, it puts the blame squarely on his shoulders in the first verse with the lines "People are starving, people are mad / Things have gone from worse to bad / Ronnie knows it but he won't show it / He just wants to rule the world." Fullerton's D.I., who had railed on Ronnie in "Reagan der Fuhrer," had their "Going to Lebanon" included on the 1987 compilation album *Rat Music for Rat People Vol. III*. In it frontman Casey Troyer intoned about "Keeping peace with M-16s," "Heads are flying, the enemies dying," and a repeated melodic chorus of "We're going to Lebanon / They'll be dead we'll be gone" wrapping things up. By March of 1984, the last Marines in Beirut left for home. By the end of their civil war six years later, nearly 100,000 Lebanese had died.[16]

A year before American Marines landed in Lebanon, the Reagan administration released a State Department white paper expressing concern about Soviet and Cuban influence in Central America, El Salvador specifically. For Reagan, Latin America was rapidly heating up as a front in the Cold War, with right- and left-wing revolutionaries fighting one another for control throughout the 1970s. While a number of American newspapers challenged the department's findings, including the Reagan-supporting *Washington Post*, the administration moved forward, sending both advisers and monetary aid to the right-wing military junta. Much of this support made its way into the hands of death squads whose murdering of civilians, including the 1980 assassination of Catholic Archbishop Oscar Romero and the violent rape and murder of several American Catholic nuns, was becoming more well known. While Reagan, whose office denied there was any Salvadoran military involvement in the death of the missionaries, tried to convince Americans that extremists on both sides were opposed by his administration, many thought differently as international reports condemned the displacement, torture, and murder of tens of thousands of Salvadorans by regime-supported groups. Included in those starting to express concern were bands whose songs about what was happening in Central America attempted to further illuminate the impact of America's Reagan-Era martial tendencies.[17]

El Salvador, which received more aid than any other Latin American nation at that time (Reagan actually increased aid while Carter had suspended it in the wake of the nuns' murder), became the spot upon which Reagan's Central American policy would be initially tested. As Reagan historian Haynes Johnson wrote about the administration and the region, "They were determined both to set a strong new example of U.S. willingness to meet force with force and not to permit a failure in their first foreign policy challenge." Punks couldn't ignore this and let loose their lyrical outpourings. Some songs directly criticized Reagan and the ideological foundations of his doctrine. "El Salvador" by the UK band the Insane, from their single *El Salvador*, released in 1982 while American intervention was ramping up, laid a solid foundation for the American bands that followed with lines like, "Dictator killing rebels with aid from the U.S.A.," "C.I.A. are in El Salvador," and "El Salvador! South Vietnam! / Maybe Cuba next for President Reagan." Their Fresno, Nevada, counterparts Capitol Punishment, whose "El Salvador" was included on the *Not So Quiet* compilation, went after the president as well in the opening lines, "Let's go to El Salvador / Be one of Reagan's conquistadors." Capitol Punishment would also target Reagan, though indirectly through his Secretary of State Alexander Haig, the primary author of the State Department white paper ("Got those commies on the run / C'mon Haig let's get it done") as well as the provisional president of the Reagan-backed military junta in power, José Napoleon Duarte ("Advisors who carry M-16's / Join the Duarte regime"). And on a 1983 non-labeled cassette described in *MRR* as "a blistering thrash attack, matched by very intelligent lyrics . . . [that] belies the current cliches about 'mindless anti-government' punk rock," Reading, Pennsylvania's Fatal Existence would write about El Salvador, "It's a beautiful country, where we don't belong / But Ronnie won't admit he's wrong." "A Living Hell" was just one of many songs on their *Life's Adventure Begins Here* that expressed the group's concern about foreign policy under the Reagan regime. As they warned on the track "American Interests," "If you let us into your country / We'll be big brother to you / If you let us into your country / We'll take control and tell you what to do." While supporters and members of the Reagan administration might not have publicly asserted such a claim, a good number would likely have confirmed the sentiment behind closed doors.[18]

Other bands paid less attention to Reagan and centered their lyrics around the conflict itself. Some, like Oxnard, California's Dr. Know, expressed confusion with the opening lyrics of their "El Salvador": "What are we doing here? / What are we fighting for?" were questions many Americans likely had while listening to Reagan speak in 1983 about the increase in support provided the Duarte regime to combat the supposed "Marxist-Leninist takeover" in the region. Others, such as San Diego's 5.0.5.1., whose numerical name was allegedly chosen because it was the police code used for situations concerning mentally unstable persons, including punks, drew a connection between what was happening in El Salvador and Vietnam. (The code was actually 5150, the group not realizing the mistake until after their first shows.) "El Salvador, it's just another war / Vietnam all over again, you're wasting good and innocent men" was the chorus repeated and rapidly sang by frontman David Klowden. It was followed in the song's final moments with the sardonically spoken line, "Meanwhile, back in the States," with a slowed down tempo and eerie guitar suggestive of the complacency of most Americans in terms of their concern for what was happening in Central America. Connecting the situation in El Salvador to the draft was the New Jersey band Detention on 1982's *Dead Rock 'n Rollers* release, which included their "El Salvador." After an opening military-march drumbeat, a list of everyone and everything that should not be sent to the country, including priests, nuns, Cuban-trained spies, Israeli jets, and American nukes, is capped off with "But most of all, don't send me / Amen!"[19]

Reagan finally got the democratic elections hoped for in 1988 after supporting Duarte for eight years, only to have his preferred leader replaced by the further-right-wing ARENA (National Republican Alliance). The civil war in El Salvador would continue for another four years, but by that time punk bands seemed to have said enough. One final assault, but concentrating its attention on issues a bit closer to home, was hurled by former Dead Kennedys' frontman Jello Biafra. Teamed up with D.O.A., the combo would record "Wish I Was in El Salvador" for their 1989 album *Last Scream of the Missing Neighbors*, a somewhat fitting title considering the prevalence of civilian disappearances during and after the Duarte regime. Told from the perspective of a former gang member given the choice of jail or the Marines, it is an insightful take on the impact of war on the mindset of a serviceman not even sent to El Salvador. A military police officer who becomes a civilian one, he continuously describes a desire to be there, "Where I could jerk off with my gun and kill the poor." Biafra expresses the character's excitement-laden hope for the freedom to do what the death squads have been doing for nearly a decade: "I wish I was down in El Salvador / We're just countin' days 'till we can do it up here." These lyrics and those from the other songs make it clear that to punks, what was happening in El Salvador was something people needed to pay much closer attention to. Not only was another prolonged American military adventurist affair entirely possible during the Reagan presidency, but its effect on the nation's psyche could be profound.[20]

By far the biggest controversy during Reagan's eight years in the White House concerned America's dealings in Nicaragua. Colonel Oliver North and the C.I.A. used proceeds from arms sold to Iran in exchange for US hostages in Lebanon to fund the Contras, a right-wing militia opposed to the Marxist Sandinista government. This scheme, which became known as the Iran-Contra Affair, would mar his second term as Congress investigated possible violations of legislation prohibiting further assistance to the Nicaraguan rebels. While the scandal came to light in the final years of Reagan's administration, which coincided with the waning of Reagan-inspired punk, some groups still recognized the significance of the moment and wrote about it in song. The Lookouts! from Laytonville, California, a three-piece outfit whose drummer Tré Cool would move on to pop punk fame with Green Day, rebuked Reagan specifically in their "Don't Cry for Nicaragua" track. The band suggested that Americans express remorse for themselves rather than the Sandinista-ruled nation, "Don't cry for Nicaragua / Cry for what we've become / The enemy of freedom and justice / Enforced at the point of a gun." The Lookouts! offered another reminder of the willfully ignorant attitude most Americans had toward what was taking place in Latin America, writing, "Ronald Reagan smiles as he kills / You look the other way." On the other side of the country, at Bennington College in Vermont, the quartet CBMT (Complicated Bone Marrow Transplant) raked Reagan's lackey in the scandal over the lyrical coals with their "Ollie North," included on 1988's *Speak 7″* as well as Mutha Records' *Music Only a Mutha Could Love* compilation. Labeling him a "blinded patriot with basset hound eyes / the weapons you supply cost peasants their lives," the group, while North was being investigated by Congress, made no mistake in letting listeners know how they felt, concluding the tune with "You tried real hard to subvert the nation / You can't be a creature of God's creation / You're a killer, Mr. North." To add insult to injury, *Speak* also include the band's "Monarch Reagan," which frustratingly pronounced, "Monarch Reagan has fucked things up / All us kids are out of luck." In terms of the legacy of the scandal, Reagan escaped relatively unscathed and North, considered by many Americans to be a true patriot for his efforts, would have his conviction reversed and all charges against him eventually dismissed.[21]

M.D.C., Concord, California's Sewer Trout, and Chicago's Naked Raygun also addressed the situation in Nicaragua. M.D.C.'s take on the situation, "Guns for Nicaragua," was on their 1987 release *This Blood's for You*. A blistering critique of America on a number of fronts, it also included "Massacred and Dismembered Culture," "Police Related Death," and a final farewell from the band to Reagan titled "Bye Bye Ronnie." "Guns for Nicaragua" begins with a mock phone call from a member of the Northern California chapter of the Young Republicans asking for donations to help fund anti-communist forces fighting in the Americas, among other right-wing causes. The final two minutes is a mix of Reagan sound bites, mostly from his 1987 news conference where he claimed that the media was responsible for the public's misunderstanding of the Iran-Contra situation. "I'm not going to tell falsehoods to the American people" is repeated along with other comments he made about freedom and democracy, all over a funk-inspired bass track accompanied by a surfeit of exploding bombs.[22]

On Sewer Trout's less seriously titled "Wally and the Beaver Go to Nicaragua," from the 1987 MRR compilation *Turn It Around!*, attention is put on the Coors Brewing Company. Owned by the Coors family, well-known supporters of conservative causes and groups like the Council for National Policy, a think tank created in the first year of Reagan's administration to promote and support conservative policy initiatives, who admitted during the Iran-Contra congressional investigations to having put money in a Swiss bank account to purchase a plane for the Contras. In his testimony, CEO Joseph Coors proudly proclaimed that he gave the donation to "the Nicaraguan freedom fighters." In their song, Sewer Trout exclaim, "Fight for freedom, fight for Coors / Drink their beer and fight their wars / Help the rich to kill the poor / Next stop is El Salvador." The band would take on the company again in the cleverly titled "Coors for Contras," directly labeling founder Adolph Coors a Nazi and suggesting to listeners they choose alternative beers to drink. As vocalist Jim MacLean sings, "Adolf [sic] ain't my kind of man / Profits go to contra-scam / Drink a Schaefer's to protest / Coors for contras—Schaef's for anarchists." While Coors continued to be a domestic beer of choice for many Americans, it was punks like those in Sewer Trout who were trying to cleverly reveal their involvement in the Reagan Revolution and its extension into Central America.[23]

In his book on Reagan's first years in office, journalist Ronnie Dugger wrote, "President Reagan has stealthily but steadily returned the United States to its postwar role as the world's policeman." Lebanon, El Salvador, Nicaragua, Grenada, Guatemala, Libya, Angola—all witnessed the Reagan Doctrine in action, whether assistance for troop development, provision of arms, financial and advisory aid, or CIA fomentation of rebellion. As Dugger continued, "[Reagan] has demonstrated that the use of military force abroad is the means that becomes the ends of his foreign policy. . . . There is an extremism at the base of his views that makes many people uneasy about having him in the White House." One group that definitely felt uneasy was the punk community. Rather than turning a blind eye to what Senator Barry Goldwater once described as Reagan's "surprisingly dangerous state of mind . . . that . . . will not seek alternatives to a military solution when dealing with complex foreign policy issues," punk bands lyrically lashed out against him and the doctrine he stood for, with some using his own words against him. Others were witty while illuminating connections many Americans deliberately ignored. Others, like Chicago's Naked Raygun, did so with a serene simplicity that went unmatched at that time. In the song "Managua," featured on their 1985 *Throb Throb* album and also the capital city of Nicaragua, Jeff Pezzati repeated the same lines for three minutes and forty-five seconds. "Gee wiz / Pretty pretty boy / Pretty pretty boy / Onward to Managua"; while uncomplicated, this was as formative a critique of the Reagan Doctrine as made by any punk band from the era. In simplest terms, Naked Raygun, among others, appeared to be saying, "Here we go again."[24]

Nuclear Holocaust

Beyond those about the draft, Vietnam, and Reagan Doctrine conflicts, the largest body of songs about Reagan's foreign policy centered around the prospect of nuclear war. Looking back on this as a catalyst for the urgent tendency of hardcore, punk chronicler George Hurchalla wrote, "No one knew just how crazy Reagan was, and how easily he might push the button and begin the end." For many Americans, the potential for a catastrophic global event to happen during their lifetime was as real during the 1980s as it had ever been. In the wake of the Cuban Missile Crisis in 1962, the *Bulletin of the Atomic Scientists* had set its Doomsday Clock to twelve minutes to midnight. By the end of Reagan's first term the clock had jumped forward to three due to the "accelerating nuclear arms race and the almost complete breakdown of communication" between the United States and the Soviet Union. This was the closest the two hands had come since 1953, when the latter had detonated its first fusion-based hydrogen bomb. The world, it seemed thirty years later, was teetering on the brink of destruction as both sides engaged in the most massive arms buildup in human history. The Reagan administration even appeared to accept that nuclear war was not only possible, but actually winnable. Because of this, punk bands made singing about potential nuclear war and the horrors of its aftermath central to their music.[25]

Of war-related songs, one of the most common themes addressed was the prospect of another major world conflict. At the center of this concern was the investment in defense that increased incredibly during Reagan's first term in office. Hundreds of new aircraft, tanks, and ships were procured along with an improved nuclear arsenal of intercontinental ballistic missiles known ironically as Peacekeepers. While the administration made drastic cuts to social services, billions of dollars were awarded the Pentagon. In 1981 Reagan proposed a five-year military budget twice as large as Carter had. With such an increase, the possibility of war seemed alarmingly real. One band, Orange County's Uniform Choice, described the feelings of many with the aptly titled "War Is Here." Recorded in 1982 for their *Orange Peel Sessions* demo tape, it was released later on a 7″ with imagery of an emerging mushroom cloud flanked by President Reagan and his U.S.S.R. counterpart, General Secretary Leonid Brezhnev. Like most from the era, the song highlights the potential for a nuclear exchange between the two superpowers. The band calls the former leader out in the second verse with, "The Commies launched some bombs today / Reagan launched some more they say." The result of such an exchange, a dying world, is iterated throughout both "War Is Here" and Agnostic Front's "Final War," released in 1983 on their *United Blood* EP. In twenty-two power-infused seconds, singer Roger Miret warned listeners, "Better look out / You've gotta move quick / They're coming to get you / Uncle Sam this is it / This is the final war . . . and there will be no one left."[26]

Throughout the decade, bands in every city expressed concern similar to Uniform Choice and Agnostic Front. In Boston, Negative FX screamed about "Government war plans!" in their song by that name, recorded for a 1982 demo that also included "Nuclear Fear." (The 2008 CD compilation of their work released under the same title used as cover art an image of Reagan delivering a speech with an X etched into his forehead.) Also in 1982, New York City's The Abused recorded a demo tape featuring "War Games," "We Need a War," and "Nuclear Threat." The first of these songs, which describes a youth playing a flight simulator war-related video game, would also become the name of a 1983 movie about a youth hacker who nearly causes a nuclear war because of his insatiable desire to play such games. Down in DC, Artificial Peace would record the song "Artificial Peace" as well as "War Path" during a 1981 demo session. Written initially by three members while still in the band Assault & Battery, the latter song resoundingly warned listeners in the chorus, "We're on the war path, drop the bomb / We're on the war path, to kingdom come / We're on the war path, no turning back / We're on the war path, till they attack."[27]

Quite a few bands used some fairly straightforward titular wording to express their concern about and opposition to war. Suburban Death Trip from Iowa City recorded one of many songs simply titled "War" on their 1985 *Mind Shattering Power Blasts* demo cassette. In the song the band pointedly declared, "I don't wanna die in war / I don't want to die in war." On their *Rest in Pain* LP released the same year, Houston's Really Red included a cover of "War Sucks," originally by local rock trio Red Krayola and including irony-infused patriotic lyrics like, "America, America, God shed his grace on thee . . . Sea to shining sea you know war sucks!" The award for most straightforward title and lyrics had to go to Cincinnati's Musical Suicide with "War Is Bad." Released a year earlier on their *Little Fish in the Big Sea* album, it is a two-minute, grovelingly sarcastic spoken-word rant about . . . how bad war is. In the opening verse the group tersely concluded, "War is bad! / It's not very pretty / People get hurt / Some even die." Another "War" was recorded by Richmond, Virginia's Honor Roll for the 1982 split cassette *Your Skull Is My Bowl!* alongside townmates Graven Image. It would call out Reagan by name in the opening lines: "Now it's time to go to war / I don't wanna live no more / Fighting for the land of the free / Would President Reagan die for me?" While the Reagan administration continued its military machine buildup, bands continued to convey their concern about the prospect of war through lyrical denunciations. As The Fartz made clear in their "War," "It's just a game the president plays / We're the ones who'll have to pay / He's killing people like you and me / Still believes it keeps us free."[28]

Although war in general was a topic for lyrical concern, a selection of songs used the possibility of another major twentieth-century global conflict happening under Reagan's watch as a platform for their denunciations. Out west, T.S.O.L. released "World War III" on their 1981 self-titled EP, which also included as an opening track "Superficial Love." A disparagement of America's emerging militant mindset, it concluded with the directive for the newly inaugurated chief executive: "President Reagan can shove it!" A year later their neighbors from Los Angeles, Bad Religion, had "Part III" on *How Could Hell Be Any Worse?*, which appeared to call out world leaders like Reagan in the opening lyrics: "The final page is written in the books of history / A man unleashed his deadly bombs and sent them overseas." Some bands figured that more than one world catastrophic event might happen in their lifetime and wrote about the war coming *after* the next war. San Antonio's Marching Plague recorded "World War IV" for their 1983 EP *Rock 'n' Roll Asshole*, with the distressing message for listeners in the chorus, "Can't you see that you're gonna die / I can't wait for World War IV." New Jersey's Adrenaline O.D., one of the earliest groups associated with the scene in New York City, had their "World War IV" released the next year on *The Wacky Hi-Jinks of . . .* LP. The song featured frontman Paul Richard singing about how in a post–World War III America, our hairless, glowing selves can't wait to "find some Commies / So we can start World War 4." And on the

Hardcore 84 Fresno compilation tape, Harsh Reality avoided numerically labeling the assured upcoming conflict and sang instead about the "Next World War." This was tellingly preceded by their "Ronald Reagan," which summed up the feelings of many: "I can't handle Ronald Reagan . . . It's too late the war is here now . . . Soon we're all going to die."[29]

With the shadow of another world war looming large over their heads, bands from the era went a step further and recorded songs that specifically centered around a global holocaust-level nuclear event. The environment in which this took place was created by the Reagan administration's casual consideration concerning the nation's ability to fight and win a protracted nuclear war. Journalist Robert Scheer wrote about this in his 1982 book *With Enough Shovels: Reagan, Bush, and Nuclear War*, intended to make Americans aware of what was really being discussed among high-ranking officials in the Reagan White House. Interestingly, it was recommended in a *Flipside* ad by the Women's Action for Nuclear Disarmament group as one punks should read to learn more about the nuclear arms race. "Reagan's first year was continuously marked by such comments about waging nuclear war in some form or other," Scheer wrote, and a 1982 Defense Department plan signed by Secretary Casper Weinberger detailed how one could be fought and won. "With enough shovels," a quote taken from Reagan's Deputy Under Secretary of Defense Thomas K. Jones, Americans could survive a nuclear attack. And according to Scheer, "Jones's views are all too typical of the thinking of those at the core of the Reagan Administration." It was in the wake of these and other statements made by persons close to the president that bands across the country felt inspired to let listeners know that under Reagan, the threat of nuclear war was real.[30]

As film, television, and literature took on the idea of a post–nuclear assault with examples like *Steel Dawn*, *The Day After*, and *The Fate of the Earth*, punk bands across the country waged their own war against the prospect of a human-induced apocalypse. In Seattle (by way of Washington, DC), Christ on a Crutch, described in an *MRR* review as "ferocious punk and thrash with angry lyrics slagging sexist goons, vigilantes, homophobes, and other lamos," added the perils of nuclear war to the list of targets on their 1988 album *Spread Your Filth* with the track "Nuclear Holocaust: A X-Mas Song." Following its bouncy jingle-bell opening, singer Glen Essary gave listeners a little lighthearted yuletide insight into what they could expect to find beneath their trees in the chorus: "Ho Ho Ho, missiles come streaming down / Merry Christmas, you've got another minute to live / Deck the halls and the government officials / What a wonderful present for them to give." Nonseasonal but similar denunciations about the impending global atomic end of days were made by Fullerton's D.I. in their "Nuclear Funeral," included on the same album as "Reagan der Fuhrer" ("You're destined for a nuclear funeral / Everybody that you know's dead") and Negative FX in "Nuclear Fear" ("If you think it's gonna stop / Just you wait for the bomb to drop"). "Nuclear Death" by Concord, California's Decline ("Nuclear death at your expense / Clouds parting, wind blowing / Temperature's rising / Your world's dead") as well as the Richmond, Washington, group Diddly Squat's "Nuclear Age" ("I see a change in things getting worse / I have my doubts about seeing tomorrow") illuminated this concern as well. While Reagan and the neo-hawks, a term coined by Robert Scheer, in his administration continued to convince themselves that it was possible for the country to win a nuclear war, punks were literally screaming about the stupidity of such a notion. Describing the warmongers around Reagan, Scheer was "struck by the curious gap between the bloodiness of their rhetoric and the apparent absence on their part of any ability to visualize the physical consequences of what they advocate." One thing for sure was that such a gap was nonexistent in the punk lyrics of the day.[31]

In October 1981, Reagan was asked by reporters about the prospect of an exchange of nuclear weapons happening in Europe only, a situation that would make citizens of those countries "proxy victims" for the two nations really at war, the United States and Soviet Union. Responding with "I honestly don't know. . . . I could see where you could have the exchange of tactical [nuclear] weapons against troops in the field," Reagan appeared to open the door for what became known as limited nuclear war. Toxic Reasons, a band from Dayton, Ohio, decried this as insanity in their song named after such a war, released in 1984 while Reagan was running for reelection. In the second verse, the band attempted to entice listeners to get to the polls in November and make a much-needed change in executive leadership: "The nuclear clock is ticking away / U.S. policy we're to pay / You can change it with your vote today." Included on their aptly titled *Kill by Remote Control* LP, which for the UK release on Jello Biafra's Alternative Tentacles label included an image of Reagan menacingly hovering over what can only be a bomb-release button, flanked by a smiling Margaret Thatcher, cartoon figures of Hitler and Mussolini, two British policemen, and nuclear missiles ready for launch, it was preceded by a song with a similar warning for the world. "Destroyer," the second track on the album, summed up the situation surrounding nuclear war and the Reagan administration: "30 seconds to Moscow and then it's bombs away / If you're waiting for tomorrow get on your knees and pray / Great birds of steel bring destruction from above / And a message from Ronald Reagan to Russia with love." Whether the missiles fired or Reagan himself were the "destroyer" didn't matter. What does is that punk bands like Toxic Reasons provided some of the most insightful critiques of the president's position on nuclear war.[32]

Conclusion

In his brief assessment of the Reagan presidency, historian Michael Schaller wrote concerning his foreign policy, "Ronald Reagan lived in a world of myths and symbols, rather than facts and programs." The myths and symbols that would dominate his time in office all centered around the alleged wickedness of communism, a fantastic idea that first germinated in his mind during his early days in Hollywood, and the potential for the Red Menace to spread across the globe with aid from the Soviet Union. Hoping to reduce Soviet influence throughout the world, Reagan used, according to Schaller, assertive rhetoric when discussing their quest for dominance and push into countries whose names few Americans could pronounce, let alone find on map. If rhetoric was all there was, the decade might not have witnessed the death toll it did. Nor would it have been characterized by constant fear of nuclear war and possible end of times. "At that time," Michael Azerrad remembered, "nuclear dread was making a sweeping comeback . . . it was hard to forget that [Reagan's] shaky finger could press The Button at any time." While the thought of a global thermonuclear holocaust lurked in the minds of many, covert paramilitary operations and a multibillion-dollar arms buildup, coupled with the aggressiveness of Reagan's rhetoric, were the foundations of foreign policy for his time in office that horrified punks. The American pathology concerning this can only be described in retrospect as both imperialist and militant, and the ripple effects of this agenda can still be felt today.[33]

Robert Lekachman wrote concerning a post-Reagan America that the buildup in defense during the decade, what he called "the prosperity of the Pentagon," entangled the country at almost every level. A "reversal of this momentum will be horrifyingly difficult for succeeding administrations." When listening to the outpourings of bands from the era, specifically the lyrics addressing the "persistence of imperialistic yearnings in the national political ethos" under Reagan, one clearly gets a sense that punks too understood the impact this would have. Unfortunately, like their songs about the many other issues connected to the Reagan Revolution, punk bands have been ignored and excluded from the larger historical narrative on this subject. This is unfortunate. From them we get a unique and original perspective about the United States and its late–Cold War ideologies and interactions with the rest of the world. While the Reaganites were not solely responsible for the deaths that occurred or the constant fear of a global holocaust, they had more than a strong hand in both. Punks made sure their listeners understood this. And the assertiveness of their rhetoric more than matched Reagan's.[34]

CHAPTER SIX

Police Story

> Every moment wasted is a moment lost in the war against crime.
> —RONALD REAGAN

> We're fighting a war we can't win. They hate us, we hate them. We can't win.
> —BLACK FLAG

Make America Safe Again

Ronald Reagan was elected governor of California in 1966, and one of the first speeches he delivered was at the University of Southern California during a Law Day luncheon. Its message was clear to those attending: liberty without law and order was impossible, and more support of law enforcement was needed to stem the rising tide of criminal activity, particularly among juvenile delinquents. Hoping to foster community cooperation and greater local citizen involvement, Reagan proposed his "master plan" to curb crime across the state. "I am convinced," he told those there, "that the enactment of this proposed legislation will help deter crime . . . will speed and strengthen the administration of justice and will assure California citizens the best and most efficient law enforcement agencies in the country." A few months earlier Reagan had stated at his inauguration that a crime bill would address the state's need to restore law and order, the essence of which was to enhance the capacity of local police to address criminal wrongdoing more effectively. "We lead the nation in many things; we are going to stop leading in crime," he firmly avowed. With technological innovation, the latest scientific techniques, a state police academy, and support from both the public and private sectors, policing would improve, and Californians would again be able to combat the lawlessness that was holding them up in their houses, afraid to walk the streets of their own neighborhoods. Reagan was clearly announcing he would be a law-and-order executive and supporter of police, an identity he would take with him into the White House a little more than a decade later.[1]

The Reagan presidency would have a profound and lasting impact on policing in America. His agenda was centered on getting control of crime, and this became evident in the first years of his administration. In a radio address delivered on September 11, 1982, he reassured the people of his seriousness. "We live in the midst of a crime epidemic," he told listeners, "[and] we must make American safe again." Swift action was needed from Congress in passing an anti-crime legislative package he would send to Capitol Hill. Lawlessness, apparently, was overrunning the nation, and according to Reagan, "Every moment wasted is a moment lost in the war against crime." The Reagan Era would be characterized by increased severity in punishments, worsening prison conditions, and an expanded policing apparatus. While his administration was cutting budgets for social services, funding for criminal justice efforts was increasing, with the largest amount spent on prisons and local needs. Concerning the latter, the move toward paramilitary policing was the most significant aspect of the president's war on crime. As one scholar noted retrospectively, "We have witnessed in only the last fifteen years a significant departure from the strong tradition in the United States of eschewing the military as a model for civilian police." While it might not have begun during Reagan's time in the White House, the militarization of the police further became a reality accepted without thought by many Americans during the 1980s. But not all.[2]

The central tenet of this chapter is that punk bands recognized throughout the decade that something was wrong about policing in America. They refused to turn a blind eye to injustice and abuse of power. And while they may not have witnessed the impact of this to the extent that members of minority communities did, they were very much aware of violence associated with law enforcement during the Reagan years, which they did experience firsthand. In typical punk fashion, they told their police stories the best way they could, through lyrics. They would write extensively about their interactions with police, from constant harassment on the streets for looking different to shows being stopped by cops who seemed to think that slam dancing was a form of ritualistic, punk gang violence. Describing one episode from a 1983 L.A. show, George Hurchalla hauntingly wrote, "Inside the police treated the punks like fur hunters going after baby seals, clubbing away with unbridled enthusiasm," a shared experience for too many kids across scenes. They got beat on and they made sure to write about it. Their songs would range from being informative, such as those titled "Police Brutality" by the bands Vicious Circle, Necros, and Urban Waste; to more accusative, like "Fascist Pig" by Suicidal Tendencies, "Cops Are Criminals" by America's Hardcore, and "Cops from Hell," by the Hated Principals; to action-oriented, like Final Conflict's "Abolish Police" and Disability's "Battling against the

Police"; and finally, to a few that actually promoted violence, such as "Cops for Fertilizer" by The Crucifucks and "Dead Porker" by Nazi Bitch and the Jews. While these songs are not directly about Ronald Reagan, they are about the police practices that punks witnessed throughout the years of his presidency.[3]

Meaningless Orgy of Bloodletting

Before getting into the police songs from the period, a brief mention of a pivotal event in the history of punk is warranted. In the year prior to Reagan's election, at a show held at the Elks Lodge Auditorium in Los Angeles, a critical moment occurred that would have a decisive impact on punk and the intensity with which bands would scrutinize law enforcement officials and their practices. Originally billed as the St. Patrick's Day Dance, it is now known as the Elks Lodge Riot from the violence that erupted, initiated entirely by police according to many in attendance. Described by Hurchalla as "one of the first unrestrained riots on the part of the police against punks," the events of that evening were horrifying for some in attendance and provided plenty of inspiration for songs that would emerge in the years that followed.[4]

The Elks Lodge Auditorium was located near MacArthur Park, in the massive concrete building belonging to the Benevolent and Protective Order of Elks, where on March 17, 1979, the punk bands X, Alley Cats, Go Gos, Plugz, and Zeroes were scheduled to perform. An all-ages show that attracted youths throughout the L.A. area, it began with the Go Gos but went not much further as midway into the Plugz' set all hell broke loose. "The cops just came in slamming. They just started beating everybody up," was how Go Gos guitarist Jane Wiedlin remembered that evening. Black Flag's Keith Morris saw it the same. "Suddenly cops flew through the front doors in full riot gear with shields and batons swingin'. They were cracking heads. Cracking skulls." The Elks Lodge Riot provides an illuminating glimpse into the interactions between punks and the militarized police force emerging in America at that time. The violence witnessed there and at other shows across the country helps explain why so many bands would take aim at the cops in their lyrics. Joe Nolte, a member of the band The Last, was at the show and provided a harrowing account of what he saw in his personal journal. Upon hearing the commotion and seeing 200 police in riot gear bust through the doors, a macabre scene unfolded in front of the club. "Everywhere we looked kids were being hassled [and] billy clubbed," Nolte remembered. "Kids were screaming 'Nazis!' and it actually sounded redundant—the inherent fascism of these fuckers was painfully obvious." What Nolte found most intriguing was how prepared the officers seemed to be. As he noted in his journal, "They had been obviously well trained for the night's activities. Strange. I thought it was spontaneous."[5]

Nolte's account of what happened was confirmed by Chris Morris, a music writer also there and whose piece in the *Los Angeles Reader* titled "A New Wave of Police Brutality" is just as revealing. Looking for any reason to shut things down, the police, as Morris remembered, "did what they do best and enjoy most—busting heads open." "I am appalled by the meaningless orgy of bloodletting," he wrote in reflecting on that night's events. His feeling of dismay would not be isolated as punks across the country were becoming more conscious of police brutality, and it was the tragedy at Elks Lodge that caused many to say *fuck it* and make boldly singing about these interactions a fundamental aspect of their music. As if a catalyst for their courage, for the ten years following the riot punks would let loose a torrent of lyrical scourges on those who were supposed to serve and protect. Through songs with titles like "Nightstick Justice," "Pigs Run Wild," "Fascist Cops," "Police Beat (On Me)," and "Police Related Death," punks throughout the 1980s were definitely clear on how they felt about law and order in Reagan's America.[6]

Here Come the Cops

Punk rock has always been anti-authority, but what made the post–Elks Lodge Riot music different was the direct attention given police and the vicious assertiveness of lyrics written about them. No other form of music at that time was as expressive and explicit as punk in critically assessing the practices of law enforcement officials. Moments like Elks Lodge made it clear that cops hated them and were free to express this through intimidation, harassment, and excessive force. Pick a scene and you will likely find a moment similar to what happened at Elks Lodge. Pick an album and you will just as likely find a song about police. Bands throughout the '80s stepped up when it came to singing about police brutality, a topic few major label artists considered touching. Sometimes macabre, often caustic, always mordant, their songs offer powerful depictions of police practices during the Reagan Era from the perspective of kids who were not only marginalized and harassed by the public for being different, but also by those whose express purpose was to keep them safe and secure.

Bands from scenes across the country wrote similar lyrics about their interactions with and perceptions regarding police, and there are some consistent strains of thought across scenes worth mentioning, the first of which is resentment. Almost every song about the cops contains lyrics that express this sentiment as punk kids across the country felt harassed and targeted, their shows constantly interrupted or shut down. "Here Comes the Cops" by San Francisco's Afflicted is a good example of one. Its sing-along melody and decipherable lyrics told a story that many fans knew all too well, the first verse relaying, "We were having lots of fun / A rad cool party had just begun / The mood was good and the night was young / Then they showed up with their guns." "Police Brutality" by the Necros of Maumee, Ohio, was similar in this regard. Calling out members of their local department, it began with "Most cops go to the academy / Where they learn to fight off crime / Maumee cops are all off the farm / And they just wanna waste my time." Both songs are far less hostile in spirit than others, yet still insightful as the most common depictions of what the many punks experienced and felt.[7]

Not without a sarcastic and comedic side, the era also saw some bands poke lighthearted fun at a stereotypically favorite pastime of police: eating donuts. San Francisco's Pop-O-Pies wrote "Fascists Eat Donuts," whose minimal lyrics are repeated four times during a lengthy four-and-a-half-minute runtime. "Make those donuts with extra grease / This batch is for the chief police," although far less assertive than most songs, does not lack punch as the potential post-consumption digestive effect of a well-greased batch of donuts is enough to make clear the group's feelings about cops. L.A.'s NOFX joined their northern neighbors in making the police passion for pastry worthy of song. "Cops and Donuts" recounts a drunk-driving episode foiled by a jelly-filled donut, the arresting officer bamboozled by the berliner-on-a-stick offered by the offender. "Cops and donuts / Cops love donuts," concludes the song, a reminder yet much gentler iteration regarding police than can be found in most of the others from the era.[8]

While songs about how much the cops were disliked and distrusted became commonplace during the decade, some bands took things much further. Those that did lyrically conveyed an unmatched revulsion and hostility, their detestation-ridden lyrics calling for violent action against the police, some even suggesting death as a form of retribution. Of those that embraced this approach, few did so with the assertiveness of Lansing, Michigan's the Crucifucks and Fresno's Nazi Bitch and the Jews. The former's "Cops for Fertilizer," as the title suggests, was forceful regarding how punks should respond to being constantly harassed. "So kill the policeman that gets in your way / It'll set a good example for the children today," begins a chorus that only gets topped by the lyrics of the latter's song, "Dead Porker." Included on the *Not So Quiet on the Western Front* compilation, it is one of the most lyrically suggestive in terms of retributive violence against police. Singer Annelle Zingarelli, one of only a few women to front bands at that time, coarsely growls throughout the song, "Dead porker, dead piggy / Die in a bloody scene." Not alone in doing so, the Crucifucks and NBJ were just two of many bands who felt emboldened enough to make violent retaliatory suggestions a common theme in police-centered punk songs.[9]

Again, while Ronald Reagan is not explicitly mentioned in songs concerning cops, his presence as a law-and-order chief executive and his impact on law enforcement practices across the country cannot be ignored. Punk bands might not have been raging against him directly in these moments, but they were against the militarization of policing that increased under his watch. In cities and towns throughout America, confrontations between well-armed police and punks inspired the latter to write with an incomparable courage and honesty. Years before N.W.A's "Fuck tha Police" sent shockwaves across the nation, arguably the most famous artistic assertion about police brutality, punk bands were leading the way. Though loud, fast, obnoxious, and at times morbid, they deserve attention as legitimate cultural artifacts regarding the impact of Reagan-Era law enforcement policies and the resultant practices, no matter how hard it is to both hear and listen to what they had to say. And while punks throughout the country engaged in the lyrical lashing of the law, there is no better place to begin than with bands from the Lone Star State, many of which made pummeling the police *the* central aspect of their music.

Dicks Hate the Police

Punk bands from Texas more than anywhere else took aim at the police with unparalleled force as cities across the state witnessed in the early '80s an explosion of creativity unmatched by most scenes. Described by Steven Blush as "crazier and more adventurous artists," the bands that emerged there were definitely unique. The capital city of Austin in particular had two whose places of primacy in punk history are secure, both with multiple songs about police. The Dicks, led by the openly gay, Marxist, and 300-pound singer Gary Floyd, and the Dave Dictor–fronted M.D.C. (Millions of Dead Cops) put Austin on the map in terms of its punk legacy and contribution to the cultural outpourings concerning cops from that era.[10]

The Dicks were a band whose raw power, honesty, and shock approach when performing gained them the respect and admiration of fellow punks everywhere. Their first release was a 7" aptly titled *Dicks Hate the Police*, with the title track, mostly sung from the perspective of a young policeman, one of the most harrowing from the era. Speaking to his parents, Floyd-as-officer implores them to be proud of what he is doing while boasting of his gun-wielding authority and power gained. As the second verse distressingly states, "Daddy, daddy, daddy, proud of your son / He got him a good job, killing ni**ers and Mexicans." Lyrics such as these, illuminating the excessive violence inflected upon members of minority communities, became a consistent theme across many of the recordings at that time, but particularly those coming from Texas bands. The Floyd-led crew did not stop with their first release, and three years later released *Kill from the Heart*, a twelve-song, full-length album including three tracks drawing attention to the violence and racism associated with policing. "Anti-Klan (Part 1)," the first song on the record, insinuates what many others did, that some members of the police force were also members of the KKK. As Floyd continuously announced throughout its nearly two minutes, "I see that you're a policeman / And I know you're in the Ku Klux Klan" and "You're blue by day, but white by night." This is followed later on the album with "Pigs Run Wild," a testimony to the unlimited power of the police, even to kill without penalty. Reiterating the violence done particularly against African Americans and limited legal recourse available to those subjected to police brutality, the second verse states, "We're the ni**ers, kill us fast / We're dying to shoot some white man's ass / 'Cause they can kill us / And they'll be free in a couple of days." Although none of the members of the band were Black, this didn't stop them from writing about the excessive force used by the police on members of minority communities in cities across the country.[11]

One other thing the Dicks did in their songs about police was suggest, similar to the Crucifucks, that violence was an acceptable form of retaliation on the part of those being brutalized because of their race and background. As the third song on *Kill*, titled "No Nazi's Friend," warned, "Just stop your racist slurs / Or your friends might find you dead." Threatening and promoting retributive violence against oppressive police would become a common thread in punk as bands, not only in Texas, became more confident and assertive in their lyrics. While Floyd moved the band to and gathered a new lineup in San Francisco before the release of *Kill*, his former state and the forceful techniques of the police there were still clearly on his mind. As he announced at the beginning of the above verse, "I don't wear no uniform / Or I'd join the Houston pigs." Like Austin, the Bayou City afforded punks plenty to write about concerning the brutal actions of law enforcement officials.[12]

Dead Cops

Austin's M.D.C., like their Floyd-fronted city mates, would firmly establish itself during the era as a leading group in the musical onslaught against Reagan and everything associated with him. They took particular aim at the abuses of police and allegedly changed their name from the Stains to Millions of Dead Cops after witnessing an episode of police brutality during a show at the legendary Cuckoo's Nest in Costa Mesa, California. The Nest was well known as a hotbed for hostile interactions between punks and cops, as were the shows of that evening's headliner, Black Flag. According to Steven Blush, what happened that evening was enough to get Buxf Parrot, bassist for the Dicks, to convince the group to adopt the new name. Over time the band would use various interpretations of their iconic three-letter moniker (Millions of Dead Christians, Multi-Death Corporation, Millions of Delusional Citizens), but the one expressing their distaste for law enforcement stands out among the rest. One reason for this has to be the imagery used on their first full-length album to clearly emphasize the serious concerns they had for policing in America.[13]

Like the artwork on Wasted Youth's *Reagan's In* and Dead Kennedys' *In God We Trust, Inc.*, the album cover for M.D.C.'s 1982 eponymous release is one of the most recognizable and iconic from the era. On the front is a full-sleeve image of a line of police officers in riot gear with batons clenched and ready to strike, a skull and crossbones insignia patch visible on the shoulder of one. It was an adaptation of a work at Austin's Mexican American Cultural Center by Raul Valdez, a muralist whose art adorned building walls and spaces throughout the city for over fifty years. The solid black of the truncheon-wielding fists, the white faceless shields of the riot helmets, the left arms bent slightly backward as they appear to be reaching to the hips where a police pistol might be, the distinct and recognizable blue color of the uniform, the blood red background framing their line—the entire front cover reads like a warning to anyone, punks especially, who would come into contact with such a formidable force. On the back of the sleeve was a Buxf Parrot drawing of a half cop/half Klansman pointing a gun directly at the viewer, an image with a clear racial connotation. M.D.C., like many of their Texas counterparts, was well aware of the often fatal violence used by police against members of the Black community and would not hesitate to use both album imagery and lyrics to drive this point home.

With the song "Dead Cops," the band added to a growing number that were violently suggestive toward police. Repeating the two words of the title over twenty times in less than a minute, its message is evident. In Dictor's sharp, aggressive growl, the lyrics accuse their target of being mafia-like, tools of the upper class, and as the Dicks claimed, members of the Klan. Recorded in Houston, a city whose police department during the late '70s was infamous for being violent and abusive, it mentions what the band felt was becoming an all-too-common pastime among cops, "Huntin' for queers, ni**ers, and you." "Dead Cops" would be followed later on the album by "I Remember," a personal recounting of Dictor's painful memories of interactions with police, including his first arrest at age thirteen, a friend shot in the back during an attempted burglary, kids being shot and killed "'cause they were the wrong color," and the cops bringing drug dogs into his school. Before the spoken intro ends and the tempo quickens to a usual M.D.C. near-frantic pace, Dictor makes the listener aware of the group's perceptions about law enforcement in America. "The police is the klan, is the mafia / And they're all the police state and they're out for me / And soon they're going to be out to get you / So you better get going if you know what's good for you / And take your stand." Coupled with "Dead Cops" and the album's artwork, "I Remember" makes M.D.C. a standard-bearer in the punk community for lyrical contributions concerning police abuses during the Age of Reagan. Though clearly leaders, along with the Dicks, they would not be alone. And Texas would keep them coming.[14]

Teaching You the Fear

While Austin saw the rise of M.D.C. and the Dicks, Houston was developing a scene described by Blush as "the most violent" among those that emerged in Texas at that time. Although he attributes this to the "hostile redneck environment" of the Bayou City, the local police provided plenty of ammunition for punk aggressiveness as well. The infamy of the city's department, which according to Blush made its counterpart in Los Angeles seem almost complaisant, was the result of numerous tragic and appalling episodes in the 1970s. As an article in a 1977 issue of the magazine *Texas Monthly* poignantly asked, "Are the Houston police out of control?" The punk bands forming in the city at the end of that decade clearly thought so, and the lyrics they wrote were inspired by the horrific events that took place.[15]

One of the earliest bands to emerge in Houston that drew attention to police violence in song was Really Red, described by Kevin Mattson as a "politically charged band" from a state that clearly "boiled with punk" in spite of its conservativism. Fronted by Ronnie "U-Ron" Bond, their 1981 album on his C.I.A. label titled *Teaching You the Fear* included the title track, an account of murderous violence on the part of the city's police force. As Bond later reflected on the situation in the city, "The police were always a total pain in the ass. . . . You always had to be looking over your shoulder for the cops. It was worse for blacks, Latinos, and gays." It was these groups that "Teaching You the Fear" sought to bring attention to, particularly the experiences of three Houston residents killed by police in the decade prior to the song and album's release. While the names of Carl Hampton, José Campos Torres, and Fred Paez are not mentioned in "Teaching," their stories are lyrically recounted in the first three verses. All three, an African American, a Latino, and a gay man, were killed by Houston police between 1970 and 1977, with none of the officers involved facing serious sentencing. Hampton, the founder and head of the local People's Party, was gunned down by police snipers from the roof of a church across the street from the group's local office. Torres, a Vietnam War veteran, was beaten nearly to death after being arrested for disorderly conduct in a bar, his body eventually dumped in the bayou and left for dead. Paez, a local activist and member of the city's Gay Political Caucus, was "accidently" shot in the back of the head by an officer he allegedly propositioned sexually. In the wake of his killing, one resident, speaking candidly about what was happening in the city, stated, "Houston cops—by many standards, are the worst cops in the nation: They are disorganized, corrupt, poorly trained and most pertinent to your fears, over armed and brutal." Really Red assertively agreed.[16]

"Teaching You the Fear" reflects the above statement about the Houston police, particularly the part concerning pertinency. Law enforcement throughout the city was described as both armed and dangerous, and citizens from all backgrounds, especially members of minority communities, needed to listen to the lessons clearly being taught. The brutal treatment of persons from these groups was about instilling fear. And at the center of it all was hatred. After recounting what happened to Hampton, Torres, and Paez, the lyrics of the last verse illuminated the underpinning intention. "Divide and conquer, well that's an old game / Divide and conquer, being used again and again" is followed by a listing of all the groups a fear-oriented society would pit against one another—African Americans, Chinese, Jews, upper class, lower class, middle class, punks, hippies, cops. All would hate and be hated when police brutality becomes the norm and residents are subjected to violent and murderous treatment by those who are supposed to protect their communities. Ironically, while it was accused of having one of the most violent departments in the nation, the city's police adopted a new slogan: The Badge Means You Care.[17]

The Badge Means You Suck

The campaign to change the public's perception was too much for punks to ignore, and out of this emerged another Houston band, AK-47. Released in 1980, the group's only recording was a 7″ that specifically aimed at the ridiculousness and hypocrisy of the department's attempt to improve its image. Titled "The Badge Means You Suck," the cover art included a photo of a line of rifle-wielding cops in riot helmets and gas masks, a Houston police badge, and the slogan with the word "care" crossed out and "suck" written above it. Unbeknownst to the police, the group was fronted by journalist Tim Fleck, aka Tim Phlegm, who covered the department for a local radio station. The song became so controversial locally that at one point during a routine meeting with the press, B. K. Johnson, the Houston chief of police, angrily brought it up as something that needed to be dealt with, not knowing that the lead singer and writer of the lyrics was there in the room with him. "The Badge" retells the story surrounding the death of another Houstonian at the hands of the police. Milton Glover, a Vietnam veteran like Torres, was an African American violently gunned down while out walking. Suffering from war-related mental illness, he was stopped by a patrol car because he appeared to be "wild-eyed" at the time. Two officers shot him eight times, seven bullets from one gun alone. According to the police, their cause for firing was Glover allegedly pulling a gun out of his pocket. It was actually a Bible. This was horridly recounted in the song with "Well a black man running in the evening / To a cop is a ni**er crook / They had two loaded revolvers / Milton had just one book." In a clear assessment of police violence in Houston, Phlegm told listeners the macabre truth that Glover and many others personally witnessed. "Murder doesn't bother to whisper / In this fucking town it roars."[18]

The power behind songs like "The Badge Means You Suck" is the brutal honesty with which the affairs of police are lyrically retold, something only punk bands appeared to be doing at that time. Confirming its message, one historian stated, "by 1979, the HPD [Houston Police Department] had become the national poster child for aberrant police behavior." The city, when bands like Really Red and AK-47 were forming, was characterized by a justice system that was one-sided, corrupt, and utterly vile in terms of violence perpetrated against persons, particularly from minority communities. And according to AK-47, a "fascist mindfuck" could only describe how citizens must have felt hearing about the constant abuses of local law enforcement officials, few of which were met with any serious punishment or consequence. According to Phlegm, the badge wearer "sucked," and you, the listener, if unlucky to come across one, were fucked. It would not only be in Texas where this message was shared by punks.[19]

Police Story

While the Lone Star State had its share of bands fueled by episodes of police brutality, law enforcement officials in the state Reagan formerly ran as governor provided as much motivation for punks. Los Angeles saw a number of bands throughout the 1980s use its police department as subject matter in their songwriting. Black Flag in particular had so many interactions with the cops that nothing is written about them without acknowledging this. From show shutdowns to surveillance outside their studio offices, their relationship with the police was tense and legendary. As original frontman Keith Morris noted about these confrontations, "[The police] were Nazis, like your stereotypical uncool Gestapo SS; they'd just as soon bust you over the head with a baton as give you the time of day . . . they were constantly on our tip." Although first recorded with Morris, "Police Story" was included on the band's first full-length album *Damaged*, released in 1981 with Henry Rollins on vocals. A little more than ninety seconds, it opens with feedback from Greg Ginn's guitar sounding almost like a police siren, followed immediately by Rollins's gruff observations of the present state of affairs in L.A. "Fucking city is run by pigs / They take the rights away from all the kids" leads immediately into a declamation of what little can be done about this. Expressing a feeling of dejection that other bands would emulate, Rollins candidly sang, "Understand that we're fighting a war we can't win / They hate us, we hate them / We can't win." With moments like the Elks Lodge Riot fresh in the minds of punks across the city, songs like "Police Story" became commonplace on albums released at that time, many sharing the same message of despair.[20]

A year before *Damaged*, the group released their five-song *Jealous Again* EP, which included the track "Revenge." Less than a minute in length, it is a quick statement of frustration but also of optimism in terms of the possibility of attaining recourse for wrongs inflicted by those in power. Although less descriptive than the retribution-oriented lyrics penned by their Texas counterparts, it still retains a feeling of forcefulness, with lines like "I'll watch you bleed" and "I won't cry if you die." Beginning with the spoken statement, "It's not my imagination / I've got a gun in my back," the next sixty seconds are a chaotic blend of Ginn's lead guitar riffs and the spastic vocals of Ron Reyes, lead singer at the time of the EP's recording. While the song never mentions the police directly, it is clear who the band is referring to. And if anyone was left confused, Reyes's opening to a live performance for the film *Decline of Western Civilization* is enough confirmation. Retelling the story of the band's most recent run-in with cops and their arrest at a show for disturbing the public, Reyes opened his brief pre-song soliloquy with, "Okay, this next song is for the LAPD."[21]

Beyond their lyrics, Black Flag, similar to M.D.C., used visual imagery to express disaffection with the cops. One piece in particular, a flier promoting "Police Story" produced a year after its release, deserves brief mentioning. Created by Raymond Pettibon, Greg Ginn's brother and the artist whose work adorned nearly every one of the band's promotional pieces and album covers between 1978 and 1986, it depicts a visibly distressed police officer with beads of sweat dripping down his forehead. The cause of this distress is the handgun that has been shoved into his mouth, his eyes worriedly peering down at it, and the command being issued. "Make me come, fa**ot!" is written in bold capital letters in a pointed bubble directly above the gun, making it rather than its holder the author of the order. Pettibon's works, including "Police Story" and like the song it promotes, offer what one author has called a "candid and potent narrative" about the experiences of punks. Concerning interactions with the LAPD, few artists outside of the scene were using imagery or lyrics this suggestive to express frustration.[22]

Highway Patrolman . . . Fuck Off!

One of the more hardened songs about police came from Circle One, another L.A.-area band fronted by the near-legendary and immense-in-size John Macias. Their 1981 demo cassette included "Highway Patrolman," which began with Macias's deep voice over a simple drumbeat. For a little over a minute, he spoke to his listeners, preaching more than singing about who cops are, what they do, and how punks should respond to their tactics. A rare song to express a divide between law enforcement officials who actually serve the public and those engaged in the brutality, Macias makes listeners aware in the opening line that "There's a difference between cops and pigs / Cops do their job, pigs think they're god." For punks facing constant harassment from the latter, the only solution, according to Circle One, was to band together and "give them a fight," a common theme across songs but often coupled with a sense of dejection concerning actual effectiveness. The latter feeling is absent in "Highway Patrolman," a testament to the intimidating persona of the band's frontman. As the spoken word intro concludes after eight enunciations of "Unite!" and a harrowing "Highway patrolman . . . fuck off!," the song takes off with a rapid pace and Macias shouting a series of one-word orders to his listeners. "Kick. Stomp. Stab. Cut. Slice. Rip. Churn. Strangle" are followed by "Pigs. Choke. Pigs," as Macias's emphatic decree to listeners. This is added to later with "Watch out. Rip up. Destroy. Bushwhack. Slaughter. Burn. Ambush" as well as "Assassinate," "Castrate," and "Scalp them" in the song's concluding moments. Not alone in this regard, it was one of the most suggestively violent songs about how punks should engage their badged nemeses.[23]

In a strange and sadly ironic twist of fate, Macias was shot and killed by a Santa Monica police officer in 1991, three days after his last performance with Circle One. According to an article in the *LA Times*, he was "yelling something about God" as he pushed a pedestrian into the street before throwing an unarmed security guard who came at him over a railing, thirty feet to the ground below. Chased by the police, he stopped to face them, continuing his religious ramblings. His coat was wrapped around his hand, which they perceived to be a weapon. They took aim and shot. He moved toward them and they fired three more times, but not before he was able to reach for and grab one. Taken to a nearby hospital, he was pronounced dead of wounds to his neck and chest. To those who knew him, John Macias was an intimidating and larger-than-life figure who never backed down, even when confronted by the police. He was also known as someone who cared deeply about those in the punk scene. Both sides can be seen in the story later told by Circle One drummer Jody Hill about when Macias beat a cop with his own baton, having snatched it away while being used on a young punk. Those closest to him also knew what many others might not have, that he suffered from mental illness—clinical depression and schizophrenia—which he was seeking help for at the time of his death. A tragic punk and police story, for sure.[24]

Nightstick Justice

Although police in California and Texas received most of the musical attention from punk bands, they definitely weren't alone. Out east in Boston, more than one group wrote about the overly aggressive practices of law enforcement officials there. Negative FX, one of the earliest (and most short-lived) bands to emerge in the city's scene, used a posthumous 1984 self-titled album to share their resentment on the track "Nightstick Justice." A rapid twenty seconds that ends before one has the chance to even know what hit them, it is a strong assertion about police abuse of power, and justice being whatever the cops want it to be. Similar to what other bands wrote, it begins with "No action here, pig on his beat / Standing around with tired feet / See a kid, whip out the club / Beat his head to a pulp." According to Negative FX, the laws didn't matter to those who were supposed to enforce it, and "nightstick justice" was what punks should assume they would receive when confronted.[25]

Also included on the *Negative FX* album was the song "Citizens Arrest." Although it does not directly reference the police in the manner of "Nightstick Justice," its lyrics are as insightful regarding concerns about justice in America. With the opening lines "Take away rights / Citizens arrest / From blacks and whites / Citizens arrest," it is a powerful pronouncement on the importance of people across the country staying strong and united in the face of oppression. After a rapid-fire intro, singer Jack "Choke" Kelly slows things down to a guttural chant, declaring "They want to stop us, to split us apart / Strip us of our power, make us submit," and ending with a question many in the Boston scene likely had on their minds — "How much longer can we take it?" Returning the tempo to breakneck speed, the final verse clarifies the group's position on who might be responsible for fostering an environment across the country where oppression and injustice continue to be witnessed by punks and members of minority communities — "Reagan pushes too much hate / Together we can fight the state."[26]

With Negative FX, Boston's SSD, also known as SS Decontrol or Society System Decontrol, got in on the lyrical bashing of the city's cops as well on their 1982 debut album *The Kids Will Have Their Say*. "Police Beat," like so many other songs, suggests that unwarranted physical and violent attention was being paid to punks solely because they looked and acted different from members of mainstream society. A little less than two minutes, its power rests not only in the honesty and clarity of the lyrics, but in its slow tempo as well, something only a few bands could pull off. Its title is a witty play on the words used to traditionally describe the territory an individual officer would patrol, and the lyrics waste no time in asserting the real meaning behind their usage. After a bass and drum intro that almost feels like it could accompany a cop walking the beat, frontman David "Springa" Spring's gruff voice spells things out clearly. "Police pick me out of a crowd / 'Cause I dress different, act very loud" are followed in the second verse by "There's no questions asked / They just wanna kick my ass." According to Springa, the abuse received will come in many forms—beat, kick, chase, mase, ruff, and cuff—all for the police to show just how tough they are. And what was likely a question on the minds of so many punks at that time, not just in Boston, he angrily pleads in one of the last lines, "Why won't they just let me be?"[27]

Pressure's On

Not to be outdone by their East Coast neighbors to the north, bands in the nation's capital turned their lyrical attention toward cops as well, although interestingly, they constitute some of the milder denunciations produced by groups during the era. Where their L.A. and Texas counterparts often used macabre imagery and retributive posturing in their lyrics, DC bands appeared to avoid this. That being said, their songs, still intense and aggressive, express the same sense of disaffection toward law enforcement that clearly resonated across hardcore scenes. Not long before joining Black Flag and belting out about L.A. cops in "Police Story," Henry Rollins was fronting the DC band State of Alert (S.O.A.). On their 1981 Dischord-released *No Policy* EP was the song "Public Defender," which mirrored in tone the lyrics from the Flag tune, particularly in terms of the pointlessness of fighting back against brutal police practices. "Give the people a load of shit / He doesn't care a fucking bit / Justice for all but not for you / There's not a fucking thing to do" is another clear expression of a careless pestering attitude on the part of police as well as the futility of fighting back against it. And like so many other songs from the era, Rollins makes it a point to emphasize that the harassment being engaged in is unwarranted and unprovoked, punk personal appearance aside. "It doesn't matter what you've done / You're gonna suffer for his fun," and "Doesn't like you, everybody knows / Don't like your hair, don't like your clothes" explained the experiences of many punks well enough.[28]

S.O.A.'s label mates Red C released an even more poignant expression of police harassment with their track "Pressure's On." Included on the compilation album *Flex Your Head*, it's a one-minute-and-forty-second pronouncement of the emotional pain felt by punks being constantly badgered because of how they looked and acted compared to mainstream Americans. Much of this feeling stems from the passion in lead singer Eric Lagdameo's voice as he belts out each lyric with a clarity oftentimes absent from hardcore songs. The first ten seconds includes what appears to be a heavy-breathing individual running away from someone, their panting heard over a subtle pulsating drum. An attentive listener can also hear this same individual say in between deep breaths, "Why is that man looking at me / He's looking through his thing," before the lyrics kick in with an assertive "Law's on my back / Pressure's always on / Never able to do things on my own." As in "Public Defender," punk personal appearance is at the center of things, Lagdameo reaffirming for listeners who likely already knew that "The way we dress, disturbs them all / They push us against the wall." A similar sentiment could be heard in Scream's "American Justice" from their 1983 *Still Screaming* album. Interestingly, the open verse begins with the lines "I'm walking down the street, just minding my own / In a strange town, a thousand miles from home," situating the described interaction elsewhere than DC. American justice, where singer Peter Stahl has witnessed it, has been of the typical unprovoked type. "When I'm searched by the man and he says to me / That 'I am the law' and that's the way it's gonna be" is followed in a later verse with the usual punk pronouncement of hopelessness: "No matter what's the truth, they're gonna put you away / Push you around no matter what you say." This is doubled down in the chorus and final words where Stahl asks, "It's called American justice / But what can we do?" Like their Dischord label mates S.O.A. and Red C, Scream's lyrics concerning interactions with police are limited to what might best be described as a lament rather than forceful and action-oriented assertion.[29]

Of the DC bands that did sing about cops, one that actually suggested violence be used against them was Government Issue on its song "No Rights." Included on their 1981 EP *Legless Bull*, one of the four leading hardcore releases from Dischord that year, it is a quick lyrical lashing, with frontman John Stabb's words being barely decipherable. After an opening a cappella salvo of "We ain't got no rights!," the first verse interestingly begins with the lines "You say we're guilty of being white / You tell me we're gonna hafta fight," one of many ambiguous pronouncements concerning race that will be assessed in a later chapter. Regarding the band's interactions with the police, it is in the second verse that Stabb, with his intense and clamoring vocals, lets it all hang out. "Cops say shut-up, or you'll get hit / I'm sick and tired of taking their shit / Somebody better kill 'em quick / Somebody hit 'em with their stick" blends the frustration expressed by Red C and S.O.A. with the retributive tendencies of groups like Circle One, though far less descriptive.[30]

Why bands in the nation's capital may not have been as assertive as their counterparts across the country in terms of lyrics concerning police might have had to do with the philosophy behind the formation of the scene there. Ian MacKaye, lead singer of Minor Threat, cofounder of Dischord, and a clearly acknowledged leader of the DC punk movement, stated in a 2009 interview, "So what drove me nuts is that punk rock for me was, at the beginning, kids writing their own songs, forming their own bands, making their own music, putting on their own shows and creating their own scene completely off the radar. . . . So the idea was to stay off the radar and stay out of the view of the police. I didn't want the police to come to our shows. I wanted the shows!" While the lyrics of songs like "Pressure's On," "No Rights," and "Public Defender" prove that staying off the radar and out of view of the Metropolitan Police Department was a challenge for punks in the city, the scene there, if MacKaye describes it accurately, was less confrontational than L.A.'s, where bands like Black Flag appeared to welcome the brutality and harassment they witnessed more often at shows and wrote about in songs. Lyrically speaking, it appears that in the capital, with Ronald Reagan seated not far away in the White House, the relationship between punks and the police was rather tame compared to their counterparts in other major cities across the country. This is not to say there weren't oppressive interactions, but rather to acknowledge that of all the major urban punk scenes, if their limited outpourings are evidence enough, DC punks either witnessed less police violence or were less inclined to sing about it.[31]

Conclusion

Of all the things that punks sang about, interactions with and mistreatment by the police were among the most common. Like the other themes discussed in this book, there are plenty more songs beyond those mentioned. "Police Truck" by Dead Kennedys; "Fascist Pig" by Suicidal Tendencies; "Riot Squad" by Cleveland's Toxic Reasons; "Police Brutality" by New York's Urban Waste; and "Nightstick Justice" by the Tulsa band None of the Above (N.O.T.A.), whose 1985 self-titled LP included other anti-cop anthems like "Ultra Violent," "Taking Away Your Rights," and "Police Front." Anti Scrunti Faction (A.S.F.), one of the earliest queercore bands, lyrically fought the law as well, with "Protect and Serve" from 1985's *A Sure Fuck 7"*. While the preceding song on the record was about the war in Lebanon, one lyric from it could just as easily been in every cop song written at that time: "Reagan's policies create atrocities." Any song from the 1984 Mystic Records *Copulation* album could have been assessed as well, a compilation of bands singing about the brutal tendencies of the L.A.P.D. One of its most simply titled, "I Hate Cops" by the well-named group the Authorities, reflected in straightforward language the growing sense of concern among punks about that state of policing in the Age of Reagan. In the historical discourse concerning police brutality that continues to be critical today, they deserve attention as some of the first and most assertive grassroots reflections.[32]

To be fair, when these bands wrote about police they weren't aiming directly at Ronald Reagan. But they were drawing attention to the practices of law enforcement officials that seemed to become more aggressive and militant during the years surrounding his political ascendancy. Reagan was a law-and-order governor in California, and he took that mentality with him to the Oval Office. As he said in his 1981 speech to the International Association of Police Chiefs, "I believe that this focusing of public attention on crime, its causes, *and those trying to fight it* [italics mine], is one of the most important things that we can do." To punk bands, those entrusted to protect and serve seemed to take Reagan's words at face value, and fighting seemed to become fundamental to the philosophy of justice being administered. And like the other areas of concern during his presidency, they made sure to sing about it, as loudly and aggressively as they could.[33]

CHAPTER SEVEN
Guilty of Being White

> To see those, those monkeys from those African countries—
> damn them, they're still uncomfortable wearing shoes!
> —RONALD REAGAN

> I'm a convict (Guilty!) / Of a racist crime (Guilty!).
> —MINOR THREAT

I Believe in States' Rights

Not long after Reagan was in Detroit's Joe Louis Arena to accept his party's nomination for the 1980 election, he found himself in Mississippi at the Neshoba County fairgrounds. Interestingly, this was the site he agreed to for a first chance to speak to the American people as a formal candidate for president. He was the first from either party to attend the fair since its 1889 opening and had already been endorsed by the Ku Klux Klan prior to taking the stage, endearing him even before he spoke to those in attendance proudly waving their Confederate flags. His remarks that day have been referred to as the "States' Rights" speech, telling listeners he was on their side in getting the federal government off their backs and out of their lives. "I believe in states' rights," he announced. "And if I get the job I'm looking for, I'm going . . . to restore to the states and local communities those functions which properly belong there." According to historian Daniel Lucks, author of *Reconsidering Reagan: Racism, Republicans, and the Road to Trump*, while he had for most of his political career railed against the increasing size and scope of federal authority at the expense of local government, Neshoba was the first time he used the phrase historically associated with preserving segregation and racist Southern customs. It would definitely not go unnoticed.[1]

Reagan's comments were examples of the "dog whistle" racism increasingly connected to the Southern strategy of the Republican Party. Shrouded in coded words and phrases, it appealed to voters in the former states of the Confederacy since the mid-'60s, when Reagan was an emerging force within the New Right. While his language alone was problematic, more so was the historical significance of the location. Only sixteen years earlier, three civil rights activists—James Chaney, Andrew Goodman, and Michael Schwerner—had been violently murdered in Philadelphia, the seat of Neshoba County, by members of the Klan with help from the sheriff's office and local police. After being shot at close range, their bodies were buried in an earthen dam just a few miles up the road from where Reagan stood. It was one of the most tragic happenings of the entire civil rights era, but he mentioned nothing about it in his remarks that day. As Lucks mentioned, "Even worse [than the 'states' rights' quip], Reagan never acknowledged in his speech the murders . . . and it is not possible that Reagan and his campaign staff were unaware of the proximity of the site of the murders to the fair." To some, the meaning of it all resonated loud and clear even while his campaign continuously denied there was any racist intent behind the Neshoba event.[2]

For African Americans, Reagan's choice of Neshoba as the location to kick off his campaign was a sign of things to come. According to Toby Glenn Bates in his work *The Reagan Rhetoric: History and Memory in 1980s America*, Reagan's words that day "echoed far beyond the Mississippi fairground." "His choice of words," Bates continued, "worried millions," many of whom would vote against him in the 1980 election. African Americans in particular would suffer the most during Reagan's tenure, his economic policies disproportionately affecting them as the country's largest impoverished minority group. Reagan launched, according to Lucks, "a counterrevolution in civil rights" and an "assault on the social safety net," having a profound impact on the Black community in America. The Republican Party under his leadership would embrace a "color-blind conservativism" that actually, according to those in the opposition, was better described as "laissez-faire racism," ignoring the systemic and structural realities of the country's racist past. Race relations between White and Black Americans worsened as the nation became increasingly polarized under Reagan's watch. Punks, clearly part of the opposing forces to the Reagan Revolution, could not ignore this. And while few would expressly denounce Reagan as a racist, some tackled lyrically the racism that appeared to be given new energy during his time in office.[3]

Racism Sucks

In his introductory essay to *The Enduring Reagan*, presidential scholar Charles W. Dunn wrote, "Reagan had several shortcomings, including his record on civil rights." With no group is this more evident than African

Americans. Looking back on his first term, the Center on Budget and Policy Priorities published a report in 1986 highlighting this. Titled "Falling Behind: A Report on How Blacks Have Fared under Reagan," it found that Reaganomics resulted in poverty among Blacks worsening significantly since his election in 1980. This was evidence of the "yuppie racism" that Richard Lowy, an ethnic studies scholar, saw as prevalent in the Reagan Era. Writing in a 1991 assessment of race relations in the 1980s, Lowy stated, "Yuppie racism conceptually recognizes the interaction of individual prejudice, institutional and cultural practices, and structural inequality . . . [which] has increased during the Reagan years at the very time when civil rights legislation and social programs have been eroded." Concerning overall impact, Black history scholar Alphine Jefferson summed things up candidly. "From bare human necessities to basic civil rights," he wrote the same year as the "Falling Behind" report was published, "the status of Black America is worse in the 1980s than it was in the 1960s." What these and other scholars writing about the experiences of African Americans during the Reagan Revolution seem to agree on is that things were worse than they were before he entered the White House. Punks, the vast majority of whom were White, were not ignorant of this. They seemed to recognize that the gains made during the civil rights movement were being diminished and that African Americans were suffering in a number of ways under Reagan's rule. Never ones to let injustices happen without a musical response, they wrote about this regularly, making listeners aware that racism was still a major issue facing the nation.[4]

In their opening essay to the edited work *White Riot: Punk Rock and the Politics of Race*, Stephen Duncombe and Maxwell Tremblay claimed, "From its inception punk rock has tried, in myriad ways, to 'solve' the problems of racial identity in a multicultural world. But punk didn't deliver, it couldn't deliver." While it may have ultimately failed, this didn't stop bands across the country from writing songs about the racial tension that seemed to be escalating as the Reagan presidency was taking off. One of the first was the Necros, whose *I.Q. 32* included "Race Riot," a title used by more than the Maumee group to express frustration about the escalating violence between White and Black Americans. Recorded for their original demo cassette with other early punk classics "I Hate My School" and "Police Brutality," it was misinterpreted by some listeners, a point the band took to correcting in a 1982 interview for *Forced Exposure*. Having received numerous letters from fans celebrating their alleged racist attitudes, they came up with a rather simple yet assertive response to send in return—"fuck off." "Race Riot" castigated all Americans for racially motivated riotous behavior while acknowledging that for Blacks, actions were driven more by the need to defend themselves rather than hostility directed toward Whites. While the second chorus announced, "Race Riot! Black man fighting against White," likely what prompted the confused praise of some overly zealous and racially hostile listeners, the final refrain clarified the group's take on what really lay at the heart of things. "Whites call 'em names directly to their faces / They say 'hey ni**er go back to your own places'" illuminated the hostility African Americans had been experiencing for generations. Less than two decades before the Necros drew attention to this with their lyrics, Congress had passed the Fair Housing Act as an effort to end discrimination in housing. Ronald Reagan, running for governor of California at the time, proffered a rather telling response. "If an individual wants to discriminate against Negroes or others in selling or renting his house," he emphatically proclaimed, "he has the right to do so." Thankfully, most punk bands writing about racism during his presidency thought differently.[5]

A year after *I.Q. 32* was released, San Jose's the Unaware recorded "Race War" for the *Not So Quiet on the Western Front* compilation, with its own iteration about living circumstances in America cities. ("This town's divided that's clear / The whites stay on one side / Everyone else is over there.") That same year the *No Core* cassette came out, a compilation of Raleigh, North Carolina bands that included "Race Riot" by the eventual metal crossover group Corrosion of Conformity. With a burning Southern Cross flag on the cover, little was left to the imagination regarding the bands' take on racism in one of the former states of the Confederacy. (Also on the cassette was the track "Friend in D.C.," C.O.C.'s anti-Reagan salvo about the "Jellybean man" who was, according to the final line, "fucking all the people forcefully" because of his tax cuts and program reductions.) In Fresno, the hardcore quartet Capitol Punishment, whose body of work included "El Salvador" from the *Not So Quiet* LP as well as "Killer Cop," "Two-Party System," and "Everyday My Life's a Living Hell," released the assuredly themed "Racism Is Ignorance" on their 1985 album *When "Putsch" Comes to Shove*. ("Racism is ignorance, you redneck Nazi / Racism is ignorance, it's modern day slavery . . . You're so fucked up you declare supremacy . . . Your weaknesses come shining through / There's no one I despise more than you.") Also in '85, The Sarcastic Assholes (T.S.A.) out of Marion, Virginia, included "Racism Sucks" as well as "White Supremacy" on their *Menthol Man* cassette, which also listed tracks titled "Let's Die," "Marion Town Police," and "Kill the Rich." New Jersey's Violent

Image had one of their few recordings, "Racist," included on the *Message for America — Hardcore Has Come of Age* compilation that was released in 1985 as well. And a few bands, Stark Raving Mad from Texas and 5 Balls of Power out of Laconia, New Hampshire, respectively, expressed concerns about discriminatory law enforcement practices with their "Racist Pig" and "Lazy Racist Pig" releases. The former, recorded for their *Amerika* album, also from 1985, cut straight to the point in the final verse with "Call me what you want / You fucking racist pig / You don't have a brain / You're a stupid dick." Interestingly, the first song on the next side of the album, titled "S.O.S.," asked listeners, "Four more years of Ronald Reagan / Are you happy with friendly fascism?"[6]

One band that got seriously straight to the point on issues concerning race was Reno's 7 Seconds on their 1982 Alternative Tentacles EP *Skins, Brains & Guts*. Described by Jeff Bale in an *MRR* review as "Great songs, great band, great people!," their "primitively produced" release was filled with an "enthusiasm and intelligence" that definitely came through in their lyrics. "Anti-Klan," one of innumerable tunes from the era to make reference to the KKK, which, according to a 1980 *Washington Post* piece, was the strongest it had been in a decade, was "destined to become one of the great punk anthems of the '80s." Lines expressing the band's opposition to any racial groups that espoused hatred for others sandwiched a chorus of clear meaning. "I don't want a fuckin' race war (No way!) / I don't want no segregated schools (No way!) / I wanna have the right to choose my friends (Fuck you!) / I don't want your narrowminded ways" offered plenty about the rising tide of racial hostility in America. They reiterated this on "Redneck Society" while bringing Reagan and his support network indirectly into the picture. "The fools with age old morals" that "Believe in old time standards, like guns and bigotry" and only want "Money, war, and racism," have it made in 1980s America, according to frontman Kevin Seconds. "They just sit back and see / Their power's in the White House and the Moral Majority." The EP also included their straightforwardly titled track "Racism Sucks." The six declarations of "Racism sucks" followed by an emphatic "Racism fucking sucks!" in the first chorus resonated loud and clear. While its opening line might make modern listeners concerned due to a racially hostile and insensitive epithet, its closing one put blame squarely on the shoulders of the Oval Office's occupant, suggesting "Kill, kill the K.K.K. Destroy Ronald Reagan!" For 7 Seconds and the many other punk bands that wrote about racism in America at that time, there was clearly cause for concern, and Reagan was somehow connected to what was happening in this regard.[7]

I Hate the Ku Klux Klan

On November 2, 1983, a ceremony was held in the White House Rose Garden where, with Coretta Scott King looking over his shoulder, President Reagan signed a bill that made Martin Luther King Jr. Day a national holiday. The efforts to make this happen had been going on for fifteen years and had faced significant opposition. By the time of the Rose Garden ceremony, some 6 million Americans had signed a petition and public support for the holiday was great. Passed in the House of Representatives by a 338 to 90 vote, it was challenged in the Senate by Jesse Helms, a Republican from North Carolina whose filibuster included accusations that King was a Marxist with ideas "not compatible with the concepts of this country." (Helms was the chair of Reagan's North Carolina campaign during the 1976 election and, according to John Dodd, twenty-five-year president of the Jesse Helms Center, made the Reagan Revolution possible.) Just a few months earlier, at a dinner held in the senator's honor at the Washington Sheraton Hotel, Reagan, who spoke at the event, opened his remarks with a rather telling quip regarding his brashness and oppositional personality, stating, "Now I know why people say, 'Let Helms be Helms.'" When asked during a press conference whether he agreed with the North Carolinian's assessment of King as a communist sympathizer, Reagan unflinchingly responded, "We'll know in about thirty-five years," a reference to when the FBI's files on King would be opened. Less than a month later, recognizing the groundswell of support that the holiday was gaining, Reagan signed the bill that would make Martin Luther King Jr. Day a federal holiday. One group that appeared disappointed by Reagan's flip-flop was the Ku Klux Klan, who up to that time had seen little difference between their stance and his on a number of issues.[8]

By the late 1970s, according to Rick Perlstein in his thorough investigation of Reagan's rise to power, "White supremacist organizations like the KKK had been making increasingly frequent appearances in the news," including one in Helms's backyard, where members of the Klan and American Nazi Party killed five protestors in 1979 during a "Death to the Klan" march in Greensboro. Just ten months before signing the holiday law and during his radio address to the nation on the anniversary of King's birthday, Reagan had called out the Klan as antithetical to the great civil rights leader's message of love, peace, and justice. "[Let] us all make this a time," he pleaded to listeners, "when we rededicate ourselves, young and old, black and white to carry on the work of justice and to totally reject the words and actions of hate embodied in groups like the Ku Klux Klan." Three years earlier, Reagan had followed his own advice when during the election of 1980 he immediately rejected their public endorsement of his candidacy. "I have no tolerance whatsoever for what the Klan represents," he announced. "Indeed, I resent their even using my name." Four years later, Reagan would be less attentive to things when on April 4, 1984, the group would again support Reagan during his reelection run, Imperial Wizard Bill Wilkinson issuing a candid affirmation of the president's first term in the White House. "Anytime you see all the blacks and minorities in this country opposing, strongly, one man, you know he has got to be doing something good for the white race." This preceded a symbolic cross burning and was followed up with "[Republicans] said we're opposed to affirmative action, we're opposed to forced busing and we're for states' rights. For those reasons we supported President Reagan and for those reasons we're going to support President Reagan this year." Whereas Reagan rejected the endorsement without hesitation in 1980, in the days following the 1984 approval there was silence from his office, White House spokesman Larry Speakes even referring questions to the president's reelection campaign. As Dorothy Gilliam, the first African American reporter for the *Washington Post*, wrote at that time, "President Reagan should kick these strange bedfellows out of his life or run the very real risk of being considered a hypocrite at best, a racist at worst." Punks would agree and, like Reagan, they made his hate-oriented, hood-wearing supporters a target of their rage and disgust.[9]

As mentioned above, an early powerful pronouncement concerning the KKK came from 7 Seconds, a band whose body of work included multiple songs addressing racism and discrimination in America. With its opening salvo, "Prejudice throughout the land / Don't look at us we're anti-Klan," they took an early stance against not just the organization, but one of the main issues of support it expressed regarding the Reagan presidency. In the chorus, singer Kevin Seconds proudly proclaimed, "I don't want no segregated schools," an interesting statement in light of the fact that the heralded *Brown v. Board of Education* decision had been made in 1954, nearly three decades prior to the band's musings. According to David Cunningham, author of *Klansville U.S.A.: The Rise and Fall of the Civil Rights-Era Ku Klux Klan*, Klan activity increased significantly in the years following the school desegregation case, and the issue of forced integration became a key aspect of the group's message in the years that followed. Reagan, who would sweep the South in both 1980 and 1984—except Carter's home state of Georgia in the first of these—took a stance on school desegregation that resonated well with his supporters there. Regarding forced busing, which the

Supreme Court had ruled in favor of in 1971, Reagan had long been an advocate of a constitutional amendment outlawing the practice. Concerning private, religious schools engaged in discriminatory admission practices, he had been firm in supporting their tax-exempt status until 1982 and flipped only when advisers warned him that his policies were being perceived by some Americans as racist. Bands like 7 Seconds weren't fooled by Reagan's change of heart, nor were they hesitant to express this. Announcing in the final verse, "Racial groups, they plan attack / I guess they think we won't fight back," the song ends with four emphatic "We're anti-Klan!" pronouncements, expressing the band's strong oppositional stance against the organization that seemed to increasingly favor what was coming from the Reagan White House.[10]

One band that lyrically encouraged listeners to do exactly what 7 Seconds had been—taking a stand—was Seattle's The Fartz. On their 1982 12" *World Full of Hate* . . . was "Take a Stand (against the Klan)," one of many that, according to Jeff Bale in his *MRR* review of the album, "could strip the paint off walls" with the same "sneering vocals," "raging instrumental power," and "perceptive lyrics" that had made their EP titled *Because This Fuckin' World Stinks* . . . , an instant hardcore favorite. On the '82 release were such classic Reagan-Era critiques as "Heroes (Cum Home in Boxes)," "Bible Stories," and "Happy Apathy," as well as "Battle Hymn of Ronald Reagan." The first reference to the Klan on the album was actually in a song called "When Will It End?," an expression of frustration regarding a world going to hell and with an opening line asking, "All the killing Nazi Klan, when will it end?" When coupled with the lyrics of "Take a Stand" ("See those fuckers destroying man / As they carry out their Nazi plan / No such thing as the master race / It's time we put them in their place") as well as the images of Reagan and various Klansmen on both the album cover and insert, and the message is evident. For The Fartz, Reagan and the KKK were no different. While a number of civil rights leaders at the time were expressing concern that Reagan's presidency was engaged in what Daniel Lucks described as "racially regressive policies under the shroud of color-blindness," bands like The Fartz went a step further and called it like they saw it. It's possible they were more in agreement with the family of the fallen civil rights hero Reagan had fought hard against commemorating with a national day of honor. As if writing the opening lyric to his own punk song, Martin Luther King Sr. uttered in 1980, "I'm scared to death of Ronald Reagan." The Fartz, like so many punk bands, turned such fear into ire-infused lyrics, as much in songs about racism in Reagan's America as anything else.[11]

As Reagan prepared for a run at the White House, the Ku Klux Klan, according to a reporter for the *Washington Post*, was "at its most vocal and at its greatest strength in more than a decade." Increased recruitment efforts as well as an escalation of racially motivated episodes of harassment and violence were being reported on more frequently. With the Klan publicly professing the same position as the Reaganauts on issues like affirmative action, forced school busing, and the need for more law and order, it was only natural for punks to go after them with as much fury. Beyond 7 Seconds and The Fartz, bands in every corner of the country lyrically lashed out against the resurgent force with fury. The Dicks, having moved from Austin to San Francisco, released a two-part song titled "Anti-Klan" on 1983's *Kill from the Heart*, one of many to associate law enforcement officials with the hate-spewing group. In his unique and soulful voice, frontman Gary Floyd announced in the song's opening line, "I see that you're a policeman / I know you're in the Ku Klux Klan." Described in a later *Houston Press* piece as "A Band That Actually Scared People," they made targeting Nazis, the Klan, and racist police central to their songwriting throughout their career. Other songs drawing a connection with police were "Cops and Klan" by Annapolis, Maryland's Spastic Rats and "Cops Are the KKK" by a group called UpTight. While *MRR* reviewed the former's '85 *Spread the Disease* cassette as "Some thoughtful reflection . . . showing lots of potential," little can be found on the latter beyond their self-released 1987 cassette with what appears to be a jovial Reagan on the cover and songs like "Die Pig," "Suppressed Aggression," "Red Neck Hick," and "War Is Great" included. Two different tunes titled "Klan Man" were included on essential hardcore compilations from the first half of the decade. The first, joined with Corrosion of Conformity's "Race Riot" on the *No Core* album, was by fellow Raleigh band No Labels. The second was by the New Haven group Fatal Vision and was included on 1985's *Connecticut Fun* alongside songs by groups such as the Vatican Commandos, Lost Generation, and straight edge legends Youth of Today. Even the Ramones got in on the action with 1981's "The KKK Took My Baby Away," a 1950s-sounding pop tune with Joey humorously singing in the bridge, "Ring me, ring me, ring me, up the President / And find out where my baby went," as if Reagan, not far removed from the Neshoba episode when the song was released, might actually come to their aid.[12]

While the Klan did not find its way into a title of any of their songs, Stockton, California's Surrogate Brains, one of the bands from the famed Gilman Street club in Berkeley, targeted it in 1988 with "Extreme Racial Pride," a track included on Lookout! Records' *The Thing That Ate Floyd* compilation.

A powerful denunciation of White supremacy, the candid lyrics about the resurgent hate group take on new meaning once the listener becomes aware that the brazen voice behind them is that of frontman Kendon Smith, an African American. Lines like "The KKK, how can they get away / With all the things they do and say" as well as "And the KKK, they teach their children to hate / And now they're stupid rednecks and belligerent skins" are capped in the song's closing moments with Martin Luther King, Malcolm X, Nat Turner, and the murdered anti-apartheid South African Steve Biko mentioned as falling victim to discriminatory governments that didn't want them interfering with White rule. While Reagan's name does not make it into the song, the mention of Biko as well as apartheid in the opening refrain is interesting in light of his support for the oppressive South African regime. Reagan had maintained close ties to the government there and labeled opposition groups like the African National Congress as communist. His position was described by Archbishop Desmond Tutu, who had visited with Reagan in 1984 after being awarded the Nobel Peace Prize, as "immoral, evil, and totally unChristian." A few years before the Surrogate Brains' release, he even vetoed legislation passed by both houses of Congress to impose economic sanctions on the country, evidence of what Lucks labeled as "his appeasement of the brutal, racist apartheid government." For the band and so many other punks, many of whom got involved with the Free South Africa Movement, this was Reagan being Reagan. Describing the impact of what this usually meant, Smith frustratingly asked in their song "In These Troubled Times," "Why should we have to suffer for Reagan's dirty deeds?"[13]

In a 1981 op-ed piece for the *Wall Street Journal*, Hodding Carter, one of the president's most consistent critics, wrote while reflecting on Reagan and race, "The Klan's resurgence demonstrates that a familiar beast stirs again in the darkest recesses of the nation's psyche." According to Carter, many White Americans were tired of talking about race and being asked to come to terms with the nation's past regarding it, and groups like the KKK, as well as the Reagan-led Republican Party, benefited from this. The two, at that time, seemed well in line with one another, so much so that in the election of 1980 the latter's platform, according to a statement released by the former, "reads as if it was written by a Klansman." While Reagan repudiated their endorsement, his initial silence on the same matter four years later was deafening. What was also deafening was the punk rock response to the resurgence of an organization whose past was filled with violence. As much as anyone, they took it head on with uncompromisingly assertive and candid lyrics about the Klan's hate- and terror-oriented existence.

Reagan, all the while professing to be anti-racist and raised by parents who abhorred discrimination, was enacting policies that were giving racists, like those in the KKK, reason to celebrate. Punks, like a song by the rather childishly named Oxford, Mississippi, band Nightmare on Sesame Street, were screaming "Let's Smash the Klan!" Had Reagan needed help figuring out just what to say to make Americans understand his abhorrence of them, he could well have found help in the lyrics written by punks. One group from Milwaukee, the provocatively named Clitboys, offered a rather simple declaration he could just as easily have uttered had he wanted to: "I hate the Ku Klux Klan."[14]

White Minority

During the 1980 primaries and on his bus while in New Hampshire, Reagan told a joke that would put him in a momentary pickle. Speaking to members of his staff, the presidential hopeful quipped, "How do you tell the Pole at a cock fight? He's the one with the duck. How do you tell the Italian? He's the one who bets on the duck. How do you know the Mafia's there? The duck wins." Hearing him repeat this to reporters, his campaign chief of staff Edwin Meese, who had been with him since his days as governor of California, supposedly scoffed, "There goes Connecticut." Poles and Italians, two of the largest White ethnic groups in the Nutmeg State, became incensed upon reading about it in the papers as reporters dutifully informed the public about the off-color joke. In the wake of the public response, Reagan was forced to apologize, but also suggested he had been duped by the press for printing what should have been clearly understood as an off-the-record moment. While his remarks about the intelligence levels of the two White immigrant groups were disparaging enough, especially coming from a presidential hopeful, it was an even more belittling comment from Nancy Reagan that was cause for serious concern, particularly as it pertained to African Americans. While Reagan was stuck in New Hampshire during a snowstorm, his wife was in Chicago at a fundraising event, connecting him to attendees via telephone. With Reagan on the other end, Nancy spoke to him through the microphone, propitiously saying, "Oh Ronnie, I wish you could be here to see all these beautiful white people," only to correct herself after an awkward pause with, "Beautiful black and white people, I mean." She too would issue a public apology, and like her husband, attempts were made to deflect the insensitivity of her comments with an excuse that she actually was thinking about the snow that had kept him away. Amazingly, neither gaffe hurt Reagan in the election. He would win all three states by a relatively sizable majority, although in Cook County (Chicago) he wasn't even close.[15]

Whether or not Reagan was actually racist in his personal life is a topic in need of definite further historical inquiry. Daniel Lucks states very clearly that, "While Reagan never resorted to the overt racism of a George Wallace, his racially-coded dog whistles on 'law and order,' 'states' rights,' and 'welfare queens' resonated with white Americans." In *On Reagan: The Man and His Presidency*, in his chapter titled "All These Beautiful White People," Ronnie Dugger assessed policy in areas like civil rights and affirmative action during the first two years of Reagan's presidency and stated candidly, "All these events, the substantial and circumstantial, have locked the Republicans into their traditional modern-era stereotype as the white man's party." Regardless of whether one thinks Reagan was racist or held views in line with White supremacist groups like the Ku Klux Klan and American Nazi Party, both of which grew in number during the rise of Reaganland, it cannot be denied that during his presidential tenure, White Americans made gains beyond their Black counterparts, fueling the continued sense of superiority in the former. Like the songs about racism and the Klan, punks too took on the color-blind conservativism of the Reagan Era with songs that directly drew attention to the notion of "whiteness" and all that this entailed. In their eyes, the country was truly struggling with the idea of being, as the title of one United Mutation song announced, a "White Amerika," and a few bands made it a point to let listeners know the concerns they had.[16]

One of the more interesting bands from the era was Boston's Marxist-inspired foursome The Proletariat. Described in a 2016 *Vice* piece as "one of the most incendiary bands in Reagan's America," they ironically left the president's name out of their songs, aspiring instead to be intentionally vague in their musings about the political, social, and economic issues of the day. As frontman Richard Brown revealed in a later interview, "Every other punk band in America at the time mentioned Ronald Reagan in their lyrics. Well, we wouldn't give him that honor." Instead, the group opted to write more about the policies than the person, which can be heard on every song they recorded, included 1982's "White Hands." Targeting the area of the country that had, by the time of Reagan's election, been thoroughly flipped from Democrat to Republican, Brown announced in the opening lines, "White hands across the sunbelt, deny wrong doings," a rather pointed stab at the apathetic tendency of most in the region to ignore or flat out deny any responsibility for the violence and discrimination persons of color were subjected to. A later line, "White hands hold the gavels," read for anyone aware of Reagan's judicial appointments as an insightful barb, even if not mentioning him by name. During his tenure, Reagan would appoint 346 federal judges, African Americans making up only 2 percent of these. One of the many White appointees was William Rehnquist, elevated by Reagan to chief justice and who, according to Lucks, "was an unreconstructed states' rights conservative deeply distrusted by African Americans and the civil rights community." Nominated but rejected by the Senate was the controversial Robert Bork, who, as Lucks continued, "Like Reagan . . . was indifferent to the Supreme Court's historic role in making the nation a more tolerable place for African Americans." With appointments to the hallowed halls of justice that not only put more "white hands on the gavels" but also seemed to move the country backward in terms of civil rights gains for Black Americans, the last line of "White Hands" was rather pointed: "Racist ignorance knows no boundaries."[17]

While groups like The Proletariat confronted things with uncompromisingly clear lyrics, arguably the most important band to come out of the DC Metro area save the Bad Brains, Minor Threat appeared to be looking through a different lens. Godfathers of hardcore punk and one of the earliest straight edge bands whose songs denouncing drug and alcohol usage as well as promiscuous sex became anthemic among adherents, they apparently touched a nerve on their 1982 EP *In My Eyes* with the track "Guilty of Being White." With lyrics like "You blame me for slavery / One hundred years before I was born" as well as "I'm a convict (Guilty!) of a racist crime (Guilty!) / I've only served (Guilty!) nineteen years of time," the song was interpreted by some to be less than sensitive in terms of White/Black relations in America at that time. Written by iconic frontman Ian MacKaye, it was a reflection of his experiences as a White kid attending predominantly Black schools, particularly the heckling he got along with the preponderance of the curriculum being connected to the historical experiences of African Americans. As he stated in a discussion segment between him, Dave Dictor (M.D.C.), and Vic Bondi (Articles of Faith) from the September '83 issue of *MRR*, "I've been brought up in this whole thing where the white man was shit because of slavery. . . . To me, racism is never going to end until people get off this whole thing." Though not in the song, at a critical point in the discussion, MacKaye used the term "ni**er," claiming to have no problem with it and associating it with "bitch" and "jock" as a term that described "assholes" rather than something hate-oriented and derogatory. Challenged by both Bondi and Dictor, MacKaye clarified the meaning of the song as a political statement about the value of the individual over the group. "I am not white people," he asserted. "I am me, and I don't appreciate my schooling, my life being threatened, I don't like being beat up for white people." Reaganites arguably would have concurred with this statement, particularly in light of their position on affirmative action. For them, being Black in America was apparently no reason for special treatment. As Lucks noted, this idea of "reverse discrimination" would be "the cornerstone of [the Reagan] administration's civil rights policy." Although MacKaye clearly did not intend it, "Guilty of Being White" and his interview comments sounded an awful lot like the rhetoric of Reaganism that drew support from groups like the Klan, who, as the now-legendary singer appeared, were tired of race being at the forefront of the nation's concerns and the notion of White guilt connected to it.[18]

On the other side of the country, another legendary group found itself victim of lyrical misinterpretation similar to Minor Threat. Black Flag released in 1980 their *Jealous Again* EP, which included "White Minority." Like "Guilty," its lyrics caused untrained and uninformed listeners to think the group harbored sentiments similar to the growing numbers in support of white supremacy during the years running up to Reagan's election. In the opening lines, Chavo Pederast, listed as the singer on the release, belted out, "We're gonna be a white minority / We won't listen to the majority / We're gonna feel inferiority / We're gonna be a white minority," an apparent call to arms for the many White Americans who by the time Reagan entered the White House felt they were on the cusp of becoming strangers in their own country. Interestingly, according to US census data, White Americans made up 80 percent of the population the year the song was released, with 56 percent of eligible White voters choosing Reagan at the polls. Four years later this number would jump to 66 percent, giving Reagan the largest majority of White voters ever among presidential candidates. There clearly not being a "white minority" at the time of the song's release, its refrain should have made any intelligent listener aware of the band's real intentions. "White pride, you're an American / I'm gonna hide anywhere I can," sung by then-frontman Ron Reyes (Chavo Pederast or "Kid Pedophile" was put on the album sleeve as a joke), a Puerto Rican backed by a drummer from Colombia, makes the band's and songwriter Greg Ginn's stance on White supremacy rather clear. As Ginn would state in a 1981 interview with the zine *Ripper*, "The idea behind it is to take somebody who thinks in terms of 'White Minority' as being afraid of that, and make them look as outrageously stupid as possible. . . . I don't know how they could consider that racist, but people took it that way." If anything, what the circumstances surrounding both Black Flag and Minor Threat show is that racial tension during the rise of Reagan was high, and the lyrics of punk bands from the era were way more nuanced and intellectual than they were given credit for then and now.[19]

Nazi Punks, Fuck Off

In a 1980 editorial for the *Philadelphia Tribune*, African American journalist Julius Nicholas described the personal fear he experienced upon hearing that Reagan had won the presidency. In terms no one could misinterpret, Nicholas said he felt like "a Jew on the eve of Adolf Hitler's chancellorship." Ironically, just three years earlier, members of the National Socialist Party of America (NSPA), a neo-Nazi group with leadership formerly connected to the American Nazi Party, received a favorable ruling from the Supreme Court in a case concerning their right to march. The group even gained support from the American Civil Liberties Union (ACLU) in successfully challenging the Illinois village of Skokie's injunction against the march, although they would ultimately decide to move the event to Chicago. According to historian Kathleen Belew, groups like the NSPA were part of a White power movement gaining momentum in America around the time of the Skokie affair, which also included the Klan among other neo-Nazi organizations. While not directly connected to Reagan, adherents were part of the rising swell of far-right-wing conservativism that also helped bring on the revolution that bears his name. Included in this movement were skinheads, a subcultural group within punk that had begun in England in the 1970s. American skinheads would emerge as the decades changed hands, some of whom embraced White power. (Some would even start their own bands whose racist tropes deserve analysis but are not included here.) In terms of punk rock response, they would also cause those already critical of the Reagan Revolution to add another target to their musical onslaught.[20]

The most likely well-known verbal assault on the rise of a Nazi mentality emerging within punk was by Dead Kennedys. Released along with "Moral Majority" in 1981, it would become one of the iconic songs of the genre. When Jello Biafra had written the lyrics to "Nazi Punks, Fuck Off," punk was being inundated with gangs of White youths, almost entirely male, whose sole purpose seemed to be to enact violence wherever they went, especially during live performances. This was in the early days of hardcore that would contribute to the rise of neo-Nazism within the movement. As Biafra said in a later interview with the *L.A. Times*, "The initial premise of the song was 'You violent people at shows are acting like a bunch of Nazis,' and that was as far as it went." Illuminating the ignorant group-minded mentality of adherents, Biafra bellowed out in the opening verse, "Punk ain't no religious cult / Punk means thinking for yourself / You ain't hardcore cuz you spike your hair / When a jock still lives inside your brain." Never missing a moment to critique establishment America, Biafra, also confronting the prevalence of fascist regalia and imagery within punk, blasted the prevalent symbols of authority in the Age of Reagan with the final verse's "You still think swastikas are cool / The real nazis run your school / They're coaches, businessmen, and cops / In the real fourth Reich you'll be the first to go." For the group, something was happening within punk as Reagan's presidency began. Violence at shows was escalating as more shaved heads emerged in the crowd, and the macho bravado that seemed to inform Reaganism was steadily becoming more commonplace. With "Fuck Off," Biafra and his bandmates would provide a rallying cry for those concerned to definitely emulate.[21]

Between Dead Kennedys' release and the end of Reagan's presidency, bands across America recorded songs that drew attention to this phenomenon. A year after the DK single, Boston's F.U.'s put out their *Kill for Christ* EP, with one song listed on the sleeve simply as "T.N.H." Its cover adorned with a Pushead drawing of a machine gun wielding Jesus, stogie hanging out the side of his mouth and ripped Rambo-like muscles, the lyric sheet revealed the song's title to actually be "Trendy Nazi Hypocrites." Coming in at under a minute, it is a rapid denunciation of the many hardcore adherents who were quick to embrace without thought the rising tide of skinhead, neo-Nazism, and the violence connected to it. ("Hey 'Hardcore Joe' / Eat shit and die, you blow / You think you're on top / You oughta be a cop.") Ironically, the group would find itself the next year labeled by Tim Yohannan in an *MRR* review of their *My America* album as having "a regressive mentality better suited for fraternity jocks than so-called punks" because of its perceived pro-America, love-it-or-leave-it vibe, a sentiment Reaganauts would have been totally in support of. Singer Bob Noxious would even at one point wear a T-shirt with the words "White Power" on the front and on the back, a swastika with "Ni**ers Beware." Talking about their song "White Boy" in an '83 interview with *MRR*, which had a theme similar to Black Flag's "White Minority," Noxious dismissed the shirt as his being ignorant, the imagery and words not actually characterizing how he actually felt. Concerning the Nazi theme, their fellow Bay Staters The Freeze would also take on its punk infiltration with "Nazi Fun," included on *Land of the Lost* alongside insightful sing-alongs like "American Town" and "Days of Desperation." Like many punk bands tired of the violence that had crept in as hardcore became more prevalent,

The Freeze wrote, "The days seem gone when people cared / And punks tried to unite / Blinded by the punch-trash / That primary urge to fight." For them, this was just part of the "Nazi fun" that was appearing more often at shows as well as the "aggression and stupidity" that was starting to dominate the scene.[22]

Similar to Dead Kennedys, another renowned recorder of Reagan-regime rebukes, brought Nazis into their music, but in a different way from their eventual Golden City neighbors. Still operating in Austin as the Stains, the soon-to-be San Franciscans, who would soon be using their law enforcement–inspired M.D.C. moniker, released a 1981 debut single humorously titled "John Wayne Was a Nazi," targeting the film icon in the wake of his death. Having painfully succumbed to stomach cancer in 1979, the Hollywood film star was fresh on the minds of many Americans, including his friend Ronald Reagan, when the Dave Dictor–led Stains were forming in Texas. Like Reagan, Wayne was a conservative Republican, although his alliance with the right began a few decades earlier. At the start of the 1960s, Wayne had joined the John Birch Society, one of the country's most radical right-wing groups that some saw as playing a critical role in Reagan's rise to power in California. After backing Reagan in the gubernatorial elections of '66 and '70, he gave an interview in 1971 for *Playboy* that spelled out clearly where he stood on race relations in America. "I believe in white supremacy," he stated while discussing the circumstances of African and Native Americans. Comments like this, defended by some as having been taken out of context, explain why Dictor, in the opening moments of the song, asserted, "John Wayne was a Nazi / Who liked to play SS / Had a picture of Adolph / Tucked in his cowboy vest." Released shortly after Wayne's passing, Dictor reminded listeners in the chorus, "He was a Nazi / Not anymore / He was a Nazi / Life evens the score." While Reagan proudly boasted his friend was administered no painkillers in the final moments of life, Dictor closed out his punching panegyric with "Well John we have no regrets / As long as you died a long and painful death." For those who bought the single, a quick flip on the record player and listening to "Born To Die" would bring it all together. "A racist dream / A life of hate / With no regret / A Nazi state" was followed up by a chant that resonated with and was used often by many who opposed the Reagan regime throughout the decade: "NO WAR / NO KKK / NO FASCIST USA." Interestingly, this chant would find itself rebooted in 2016, when another Republican presidential candidate promised to restore America to its former glory.[23]

"Nazi Snotzy," "Nazi Youth," "Nazi Threat," "Nazi Skins," "Nazi Dreams," "Tyrant Nazi"—the list of punk songs drawing attention to the rise of neo-Nazism in America and within punk is long. Was Reagan directly responsible for this? No. Did White power advocates feel empowered by his election and the policies associated with the revolution that bears his name? Yes. One group out of Philadelphia would make it clear how they felt as Reagan was leaving office. On the cover of a 1989 7" would be a drawing of the band wielding weapons while riding a piece of heavy machinery, clearly bent on doing some damage to the various White supremacy advocates waiting in their way. Named Dare to Defy, they would spell out their intentions in clear bold black letters at the bottom of the cover: *Steamrolling Neo-Nazis in the '90s*. The legacy of battling against bigots seemed as strong in the music at the end of Reagan's rule as it was at the beginning.[24]

Ah Come On Ma, It's Only a . . .

One thing seems sure concerning Ronald Reagan, and that is there is no record of him ever using the N-word to describe Black persons. "Monkeys," yes, as the opening quote of this chapter reveals from a comment he made to Nixon about African delegates to the United Nations in 1971. This moment offers, according to Lucks, "a revealing glimpse into Reagan's soul." "Strapping young bucks" and "welfare queens" as well were both racially loaded descriptions he used regarding those he felt were taking advantage of government assistance programs. These primarily benefited impoverished African Americans, and he would propose making drastic cuts to many as president. While Reagan might not have used the heinous word, some around him did. Talking about the Southern strategy while working in the Reagan White House, political operative Lee Atwater callously said in 1981, "You start out by saying, 'Ni**er, ni**er, ni**er.' By 1968, you can't say 'ni**er'—that hurts you, backfires. So you say stuff like uh, forced busing, states' rights and all that stuff." Whether he knew it or not, Reagan's usage of the latter phrases in the years leading up to his presidency and during it was to some really not much different than using the N-word before. For some, this was evidence enough of who Reagan actually was, although he would consistently express frustration regarding this perception. Contradicting how he felt about himself, Archbishop Desmond Tutu once uttered with unwavering candor, "I think I should say now that [Reagan] is a racist, pure and simple."[25]

While Reagan might never have used the N-word, punks did, which can be problematic when looking at lyrics forty years after they were written. In the wake of moments such as the George Floyd murder and Black Lives Matter protests, any usage of the term, regardless of historical circumstances, is rightfully considered through a critical lens. Punks in the 1980s singing about the Reagan Revolution should not get a pass when using it, although Ian MacKaye's interview in MRR is fairly informative in terms of how blasé usage of it might have become. Although it can be discomforting, a review of punk songs that used the N-word is critical to understanding just how far they were willing to go to get a point across, particularly their opposition to racism in America in its many forms. Yes, some neo-Nazi, White power bands used it derogatorily as they pushed their message of White supremacy out into the willing ears of many disaffected youths searching for something even beyond what punk offered to identify with and belong to. Their lyrics are not dealt with here as they were less about raging against Reaganism and more about just rage, ignorant and unadulterated. What are considered are those songs where the N-word is used to make a point, not in a racially derogatory way but rather to provide emphasis when challenging wrongdoing in Reagan's America. In many ways, punk usage of the term enunciated its heinousness, bringing it in to elucidate certain matters where racism, in their opinions, was embedded in the very fabric of the country. Using it, as they did homophobic epithets, did afford them the chance to speak truth to power when considering racial issues during the Age of Reagan. Without doing so, some of their most critical assessments would lose the force of thought that make them the illuminating cultural sources they are. Their passion for change informed their decision to use a word that speaks volumes in terms of the nation's contentious past regarding hatred and violence against people of African descent.

Most punks who used the term did so as a pronouncement of anti-racism, a way to metaphorically punch their listeners in the face when shedding light on the experiences of Black Americans. One example was the housing situation and discriminatory practices concerning community living opportunities, an issue more than one punk band wrote about. In the Necros' "Race Riot," singer Barry Hennsler concluded the last verse speaking as a racist White American who might have seen firsthand the result of the Fair Housing Act of 1968, which Reagan had publicly opposed, with "They say 'Hey ni**er go back to your own places.'" A similar message came through in Chronic Sick's "There Goes the Neighborhood." Released in 1983 on their *Cutest Band in Hardcore* EP, it encapsulated the frustration of many whose traditional all-White neighborhoods (the title of a similarly themed song by the DC area band Void who also wrote "Black, Jewish, and Poor") were becoming more diverse by the beginning of the 1980s. In it frontman Greg Gory, who on the cover of the record can be seen with a backward swastika marked on his forehead, tells the story of a young White resident responding violently to the arrival of his new Black neighbors. With his mom pleading, "Wait a minute sonny don't you dare pull that trigger," the youngster's response sadly reflected the callousness of some, stating "Ah come on Ma—It's only a ni**er." Like so many bands addressing issues concerning race, their lyrics too were misinterpreted. As one newspaper report announcing the release mentioned, "The E.P. opens, regretfully, with 'There Goes the Neighborhood,' a tongue-in-cheek song which, nevertheless, will easily be misinterpreted as racist." As Gory (Greg Macolino) would frustratingly iterate in a 2011 *Vice* interview, "The fact that someone would read the lyrics to something like 'There Goes the Neighborhood' and say 'They're racist!' is just retarded." Like so many punk bands then and still, lyrics like these, taken without critical thought, were and still can be perceived as racist rather than critical responses to the racism many saw woven into the fabric of American society. Of all the songs written by Chronic Sick, including their sarcastic sally against the profusion of Reagan-raging at the beginning of the 1980s aptly titled "Reagan Bands," "There Goes the Neighborhood" was by far their most serious in terms of lyrical revelation. Racism was apparently the one thing the New Jersey natives would not joke about.[26]

Where Reagan engaged in what Lucks called "racially freighted caricatures" to "foster hostility and resentment toward nonwhites," punks used the real thing as a mechanism for enunciation of what they perceived to be hostile and at times violent resentment of Whites against Blacks. Some, like Virginia's The Landlords, whose Charlottesville hometown would become the scene of the 2017 Unite the Right rally where neo-Nazis, Klansmen, and other alt-righters gathered under the auspices of White supremacy, poked fun at swastika-scrawling simpletons whose work adorned toilet stall walls across the country. On 1984's *Hey! It's a Teenage House Party* was included "Bathroom Bigot," a hysterical first-person rant about a pen-wielding, chickenshit racist whose written rantings are only produced in the privacy of the privy. Described by renowned punk graphic artist Pushead in an *MRR* review as "One of the better US releases of late from a new, an up-coming band," the "sometimes hilarious and uproarious laughter" caused by the lyrics was accompanied by a "serious side." Both could be heard in "Bathroom Bigot" as vocalist John Beers, announcing in the open that "I'm a bathroom bigot / I hide behind my pen / I write my hate on walls / Don't want my face beat in," pronounced his ersatz emotions with such scornful scripts in the closing verse as "kill fa**ots" and "castrate all ni**ers." While toilet stall scribblings were far from extreme, for many Black Americans in 1984, the year Reagan proclaimed it to be "Morning in America," their lives truly did feel threatened. For many, it seemed more like midnight, as African American novelist and poet Alice Walker wrote that year: "We do not admire their President. We know why the White House is white." For bands like The Landlords, using the N-word in their lyrics was an attempt to express solidarity, albeit an unsettling one when listened to with contemporary ears.[27]

As has already been discussed, the punk assault on policing in America was as thorough as anything they did, and while many of the songs shed light on the ill treatment personally witnessed by punks, a fair share interpreted actions of American law enforcement officers as strongly connected to a resurgence of racial hostility. The bands that sprang up in Texas paid particular attention to this with lyrics that were uncompromisingly frank, and while clearly not racist, groups like the Dicks and M.D.C. would both use the N-word in their songs about police brutality. In his tale of a young officer hoping to make his father proud of his new line of work, Gary Floyd harrowingly stated in the second verse that "He got him a good job / Killing ni**ers and Mexicans." His fellow Austinite Dave Dictor, in M.D.C.'s disparaging death-driven ditty, announced similarly what the "Mafia in blue" were doing at that time—"Huntin' for queers, ni**ers, and you." Houston's Really Red would use the term as well in "Teaching You the Fear," concerning how those in positions of power and authority, particularly the police, use violence and fear to divide the people. ("Hate the ni**ers, hate the ch**ks, hate the jews.") Their Bayou City compatriots AK-47 would do so as well in their retelling of the tragedy of Milton Glover. ("Well a black man running in the evening / To a cop is a ni**er crook.") Originally from Houston but moving eventually to Brooklyn was Stark Raving Mad, whose 1985 album *Amerika* included "Racist Pig," which cut to the chase in the first verse with singer Spunge Oid's (Jeff Tunches) critique of the aspersions often made by police. ("Call him a white boy / Call me a sp*c / Call him a ni**er / Call us all fa**ots.") These bands used the N-word in a manner that must not be misjudged in terms of intent. They clearly were concerned for the well-being and safety of Black Americans, and although doing so from a position of privilege, they took risks in using such a derogatory and heinous term to prove their point regarding police. Like the many other bands that did so for similar reasons, they don't deserve a pass for this, as listening to their lyrics today can cause one to cringe. What they do deserve, to reiterate the point, is critical consideration as candid sources of concern regarding race in Reagan's America.[28]

Conclusion

The question of whether or not Reagan was racist is something historians need to continue to explore but might never get a clear answer on. What is clear is that many leading African Americans during his tenure of office felt he was. As Texas representative and member of the Congressional Black Caucus Mickey Leland noted in 1982, "Black people in this country believe, whether he denies the allegation or not, that [Reagan] is a racist." Be they about the Klan, neo-Nazism, White pride, or racism in general, the lyrics written by punks concerning race relations in America during the Age of Reagan are profoundly insightful. "[The] depth of African American grievances," as Lucks described the impact of Reagan's civil rights policies, was interestingly expressed by a bunch of relatively well-off White kids. Their secondhand awareness and comprehension of the historical injustices witnessed by Blacks across the country resulted in some of the most meaningful criticisms of the era.[29]

Outro

> Make America Great Again!
> —Donald Trump

> No Trump. No KKK. No Fascist U.S.A.
> —M.D.C.

Let's Make America Great . . . Again

While I was writing this book, Donald Trump was gearing up for another run at the presidency, during which a lone gunman named Thomas Matthew Crooks attempted to kill the former president at a campaign rally in Pennsylvania, grazing his ear as he spoke to the crowd. In the days following, John Hinckley Jr., freed in 2022 after forty-one years in custody for Reagan's attempted assassination, wrote on X, "Violence is not the way to go. Give peace a chance." This prompted a user to comment, "Dude you literally shot the 40th president of the United States." While punks might have hated Reagan and Trump (which this chapter discusses), their actions concerning both were limited to lyrical pronouncements, often hyperbolic in terms of violent propositions. Hinckley shot Reagan, not Mike Muir of Suicidal Tendencies. Crooks shot Trump, not one of the contemporary lyricists whose words are as strongly oppositional in tone as their 1980s punk forebears. Punks are artists, not assassins.[1]

Donald Trump, like Ronald Reagan, is a polarizing political figure, and the latter, described by Michael Azerrad as "the figurehead for so much of the discontent in America's underground culture," appears to have been replaced by the former, who inspires as much angst-laden artistic outpourings, especially from punks. For those living under a rock the past decade, the billionaire businessman and public personality burst onto the political scene during *birther-gate*, the dispute concerning President Obama's citizenship. He jockeyed for position in a field of Republicans that would seek the party's nomination in 2016, and after months of unforgettable rallies, speeches, debates, and campaign commercials, would be rewarded in July at the Republican National Convention. Ironically, Trump's name was formally put forward for approval by Alabama Senator Jeff Sessions, the first member of that august body to endorse him months before. Thirty years prior, Sessions had been nominated by Reagan for a federal judgeship but was rejected by the Senate amid charges of racism. He would soon head up Trump's Department of Justice, which at one point during the writing of this book was determining whether or not to indict him. A supporter of both Reagan and Trump, the nomination of Sessions to federal office by both was just one of many similarities between the fortieth and forty-fifth presidents.[2]

Back in 2016, with, as described by Daniel Lucks, an "angry ethnonationalist populism, framed by the Reagan slogan 'Make America Great Again,'" Trump coasted into the White House on a whopping 46 percent of the popular vote. In the days leading up to the election, over 200 former Reaganauts led by Ed Meese, "the keeper of the Reagan flame" according to the *Washington Examiner*, joined together to support the Republican ticket as the "Reagan Alumni Advisory Council for Trump-Pence." Long story short, Reagan, more than a decade after his passing, was alive and well as a political force in the lead-up to Trump's presidency. And while a number of former Reagan supporters vehemently argue that there is no similarity between the two—former Reagan speechwriter Peggy Noonan providing the most thorough refutation of the comparison in her 2016 *Wall Street Journal* piece "Donald Trump Is No Ronald Reagan"—there is enough there to suggest that 2016 and the subsequent Trump administration were as much a Reagan replay as a presidency could be. Beyond the stealing of a slogan, alignment with the Religious Right, a fascination for Andrew Jackson paintings, a grassroots American followership, support from the Klan, Ed Meese, and Republican Senator Tom Cotton of Arkansas saying, "there's a deeper continuity in the beliefs of our 40th and 45th presidents," we have the pronouncements of punks to support this claim. If Trump was no Reagan, as James Capretta of the American Enterprise Institute has claimed, then why a replay of the raging of the '80s, some of which was performed by the same bands? To many punks who witnessed the Reagan Revolution, and some who weren't even born yet, the Donald was very simply the new Ronald. And they weren't going to pass up another chance to riotously rant the way they knew how, in song.[3]

O'Bummer

It's important to note before getting into the myriad songs about the man who sports what Jello Biafra called "Satan's Combover" that the other presidents between him and Reagan also received attention from punk artists, though not to the same degree. While Stacy Thompson accurately assessed the post-Reagan landscape, stating "it is a punk truism that punk music of the '90s suffered without the conspicuous target that Ronald Reagan provided," this didn't stop bands from haranguing the next in line leaders of America. George Bush I, Reagan's vice president and heir apparent to the revolution, had his life threatened on wax similar to his predecessor with a 1990 track by the Seattle trio Coffin Break, a group stuck like many bands founded in the late '80s in a weird musical place between punk and grunge. "Kill the President," recorded for their *Rupture* album, would be released the following year as a single, its bright red cover adorned with a gesticulating Bush and bold yellow letters enumerating the band's titular suggestion. Before making listeners aware of his desire to "Kill that whacky, cooky, funky, whacky, cooky, funky guy in the White House," vocalist Peter Litwin sarcastically confessed, "I'm so happy, we elected Bush today / I'm so happy, another criminal / I'm so happy, we elected another criminal / I'm so happy, wanna kill the president." Sounding similar to punks writing a decade earlier in their protestations about Reagan, Litwin stated concerning his motivation for the song, "I was fuckin' pissed—honestly—that Bush got elected. I could not believe it." Having come together in 1987, the year of the Iran-Contra hearings, Litwin was amazed the country would elect someone not only connected to Reagan, but implicated in the scandal as Bush had been. The man described by historian Greg Grandin as "a wimp and ineffectual, living in the shadow of Reagan . . . Reagan's lapdog" would pardon many involved in the affair. To bands like Coffin Break, whose start came during the Reagan presidency, it seemed like business as usual under his puppet then in power, clearly compelling them, like those that had the previous decade, to critically sound off about it in their lyrics.[4]

Unlike Reagan, Bush the Elder served only one term, defeated in the election of 1992 by Bill Clinton. By then, punk, according to a documentary released that year, had snuck into mainstream American culture. Directed by Dave Markey, cofounder of the early '80s fanzine *We Got Power!* and drummer for the Reagan-Era Santa Monica hardcore band SIN 34, *1991: The Year Punk Broke* followed Sonic Youth and their yet-to-be world famous opening act from the Pacific Northwest on a two-week tour. By the time the film was released, Nirvana's *Nevermind*, with the hit song "Smells Like Teen Spirit" being replayed steadily on MTV, was well on its way to becoming one of the top-selling albums ever. Whether or not he benefited from punk's newfound popularity and near-complete and corporatized metamorphosis into grunge, alternative, or the soon-arriving pop punk of the later '90s, or maybe because he was a Democrat after twelve years of Reagan Republicanism, Clinton received little lyrical attention from the punk community. While during Reagan's tenure punks were screaming "MTV Get Off the Air," during Clinton's they could catch both him and a video from their favorite group on the once-reviled station. While Reagan-Era bands took aim at him directly, those during Clinton's time in the White House focused more on making listeners aware of more systemic problems in the country. One band from the East Bay did use the forty-second president's name in a song, but not to express the same personal anguish that previous groups shared regarding Reagan. Knowledge, a ska/punk/hardcore outfit lead by Nick Traina, son of famed author Danielle Steel, would record a single demo toward the end of Clinton's reign that included the track "Clinton Youth." Released to the public in 1998 on the album *A Gift Before I Go*, after Traina's tragic heroin overdose, its lyrics tell a clear tale of frustration for the apathy of punks-turned-professionals as the angst of the '80s gave way to the acceptance of the '90s. "Once a revolutionary fighting for a cause / Now a successful businessman who'd never break law" seemed to nicely sum up the changes in alternative culture between the decades. But for Traina and a few others, the spirit of punk would live on. As he proudly pronounced in the last verse, "I won't bow down to authority / I won't compromise, I'm gonna stay angry." With Clinton soon out, more opportunities to express this anger, which had been so central to punk in its early stages, were just an election away.[5]

Between Reagan and Trump, the one other president who inspired a significantly sized punk-style assault was George W. Bush, son of Bush I, who some perceived to be the first Republican replay of Reagan. Tax cuts and terrorism (Islamic extremists this go-around rather than communist cabalists), support from Christian fundamentalists, a foreign policy doctrine attached to his name that too vowed to make the world safe for democracy — similarities such as these help explain why Michael Deaver, Reagan's White House deputy chief of staff, once stated about Bush II, "I think he's the most Reagan-like politician we have seen, certainly in the White House." While other Reaganites disagreed, as they would over the Trump comparison, it was clear to some that George W. Bush was "Reaganesque," "Reagan Jr.," and "Reagan's son," as journalist Bill Keller wrote in 2003. Also thinking this way were punk bands who made bashing Bush a prominent practice in the early 2000s. If Bush was the presidential offspring of Reagan, Bush bands appeared to be the proud inheritors of the punk tradition of presidential pummeling. Not since Reagan had punks seemed to be this excited about the prospect of some pouncing on the White House occupant. And they would get another eight years again to do it. Like Reagan before him, Bush II found his likeness used often on the cover of albums, an early one coming from the Orange County band U.S. Bombs. Their 2001 single *Tora! Tora! Tora!* included a waving Bush with a you-know-who's toothbrush mustache, just like Reagan on a Fartz album cover two decades earlier. An Appleton, Wisconsin, group called Wartorn would include another mustachioed Bush, this time in full fascist uniform and Nazi salute, on the cover of their 2005 *Adolf Bushler, War Bastard* EP. Like Reagan, Bush would have his share of Hitler comparisons, with songs like "Bush Is Hitler" and "Heil to Bush," the latter included on a 2003 demo called *Propaganda U$A* by a band that, like Reagan Youth years before, found its naming inspiration from the Oval Office occupant — Death to W.[6]

Beyond cover art and band names, Bush was so inspirational to some bands that entire albums were written with him in mind. Punk godfathers Bad Religion, still around and releasing work as they had been in the early days of Reagan, apparently found the possibility of a second Bush administration too distressing to ignore. Just months after the invasion of Iraq, the group got back into the studio to record *The Empire Strikes First*, described by guitarist Brett Gurewitz as "a polemical record and most definitely inspired by the US preemptively, and needlessly, striking Iraq." While his name doesn't make it onto the lyric sheet, songs like "Let Them Eat War," "Boot Stamping on a Human Face Forever," and the title track express clearly enough the group's oppositional concern regarding another four years of Bush. As Jim Ruland noted in his biography of the band, "With another election coming up in 2004 . . . the band were determined to do their part to make sure Bush wasn't reelected." While Ronald Reagan had talked to Americans about the presence of an evil empire that threatened world peace, to Bad Religion and many punks in the 2000s, America had become exactly that. Like those that came before them and faced off against the Reagan regime, they would join with others to express a shared sense of anger and disaffection through music. The same year they released *Empire*, the group's "Sorrow" would be included on a CD/DVD compilation appropriately titled *Rock Against Bush*. The brainchild of Fat Mike, vocalist/bassist of the long-running band NOFX, it took its cue from the Rock against Reagan movement twenty years earlier. It was accompanied by his Punkvoter.com website, an attempt to get punks politically active in the upcoming election, as well as a second volume that included "Let Them Eat War." With the many other songs from that period like "Fuck Bush!," "Burning Bush," "Kill George Bush," "George W. Shitbag," and "Naming a Library after George Bush Is Like Naming a Delicatessen after Dahmer," it is clear that the forty-third occupant of the White

House was more than inspiring to punks. It was as if they were waiting for another Reagan, and when he apparently arrived they didn't disappoint.[7]

For the bands that wrote these songs and the many others not mentioned, the party wouldn't last, as 2009 brought an end to the reign of Bush and welcomed the country's first and only African American president. Even more than Clinton before him, Barrack Obama appeared to get a pass from punks. Dan Ozzi, author of *Sellout: The Major-Label Feeding Frenzy That Swept Punk, Emo, and Hardcore*, explained in a piece for *Vice* from the last days of the Obama presidency, "[during the Bush years], punks flew the 'Not My President' flag and the spirit of resistance lived on, with no shortage of things to oppose. . . . But then Barack Obama came along and the line blurred." Why this happened, Ozzi continued, was because, "Given the choice between [Obama] and yet another decrepit white man who popped a Viagra every time he thought about bombing brown people, punk made its choice." As Ozzi pointed out, punks appeared to "sit this one out" for a variety of reasons, the president's race likely being the most significant. As America's first minority president, did punks, many of whom had been raging against racial injustice for decades, really want to be in attack mode this go around? Could they really scream "fuck the government!" when this government and its leader seemed to be what they had always been hoping for? One punk who saw past all of this, to the surprise of no one, was Jello Biafra. The former Dead Kennedys frontman stayed true to his roots during the Obama administration, penning an emotionally charged open letter to the president after he won the election that pleaded for him to follow through on his promises of hope and change. Nope. That same year he would form his first full band in nearly a decade, Jello Biafra and the Guantanamo School of Medicine, whose freshman effort, *The Audacity of Hype*, jabbed at the title of Obama's pre-presidential biography as well as his campaign pledge to America. They would put out four records during his two terms, including 2012's *Shock-U-Py!* release, which included "Barackstar O'Bummer," an expression of Biafra's concerns about four more years of politics as usual. As he had regarding Reagan years before, Biafra let loose lyrically, but this time with a strong sense of disappointment rather than disgust. As he dispiritedly pined in the second verse, "Who would have guessed / Our hero on the stage / Would have no spine at all / To lead in any way." Obama, as Ozzi stated, in so many ways was just a continuation of Bush. While a few others cautiously expressed concern in song, it was Biafra who kept the flame of punk's presidential pyre burning. As Obama's administration came to an end, plenty more fuel for the fire was on its way.[8]

Fucked Up Donald

In 2016, out of a field of seventeen initial Republican candidates, nearly all of whom reached back to Reagan for ideological buttressing, Donald Trump emerged as the party's nominee. He won, to quote op-ed columnist Frank Rich, the "quadrennial tug-of-war to seize the mantle of Ronald Reagan," even going so far as to say concerning their relationship in his monosyllabic way, "I helped him. I knew him. He liked me and I liked him." To the amazement (and horror) of many, Trump won, and as Fox News host Bret Baier said, "Heads were exploding back when Reagan was elected, and heads are exploding now." Appearing on conservative pundit Rush Limbaugh's radio show, Baier would reiterate his opinion. "One thing you can say is," he told listeners, "like Reagan, Trump has changed the paradigm." Punks, who had been waiting patiently, seemed to agree, for obviously different reasons, and were ready to pounce. For sure, their heads were exploding, and with an intensity not seen since Reagan they would express their ire lyrically. As Crisis Man, a group from Santa Rosa, would later write in "Commander in Chief" from the intuitively titled *Asleep in America* album, "all that hate / rubs off on kids." With Trump in office, the kids, as they had been with Reagan, appeared ready to hate again.[9]

Donald Trump was not Ronald Reagan. As historian Marcus Witcher recently wrote in *Getting Right with Reagan: The Struggle for True Conservativism: 1980–2016*, "One of the great ironies of the 2016 election was that after more than six years of arguing about the future of the Republican Party and Ronald Reagan's proper legacy, conservatives failed to nominate one of their own." Donald Trump was also not "the punk rock president America deserves," as put forward in a *New York Post* piece immediately after his victory, a claim based on the incorrect notion that "Just not giving a flying fig is the quintessence of punk." This book argues that "giving a flying fig" is exactly what punk is about in terms of message, and the forty-fifth president of the United States clearly inspired punk bands to do that again. Trump was Trump, and for them this was more than enough. As they did to Reagan, punks let loose a hailstorm of haranguing lyrics, and for a few years it felt like old times. As Reagan had been in the eyes of many punk adherents, Trump too was apparently a Nazi. Where D.I. had sung about "Reagan der Fuhrer" back in '83, the first months of the Trump presidency saw a demo released by the Northern California group Fall Children (actually the solo effort of guitarist/vocalist Sasha Guleff) cheekily titled *Make Punk Rock Great Again* and including the track "Donald

Trump Is Not My Fuhrer." That same year Las Vegas's Candy Warpop released their single "Trump Is a Nazi," with accompanying artwork similar to the catastrophe collages that adorned Reagan-Era albums. In anthemic punk style, vocalist Amy Pate, after proclaiming "Donald Trump's a Nazi / He's not my president," announced the arrival of an oppositional force standing strong in the face of Trumpism. ("We are the new Americans of every race, color, and creed / We are the new Americans, we embrace our diversity.") The song would be included that year on *The World Is Watching* collection alongside other contemporary critiques like "Kill the Job Creators" by Assassination Squad and "Bigot President" by The Damnit Jims. With a cartoon caricature of an angry Trump, phone in hand while mushroom clouds explode in the background, the cover made clear on one of the earliest compilations of the Trump Era that punks were ready to bring it with as much energy as their 1980s counterparts had with Reagan.[10]

The 2016 election inspired songs with titles like "Fuck You Donald Trump," "Trump Card," "Do You Think Donald Trump Is Flammable," and "Make America Hate Again," a nice play on the Reagan-Trump election slogan by the Portland outfit Cliterati, and it was clear that once punks realized he had won the presidency, they got to work. In 2017, Trump saw a lot of lyrical action from not only American punk bands but others across the world, just as Reagan had. Oi Polloi, a Scottish group with roots all the way back to the Reagan-Thatcher era (they had once written in a song clamoring against American interference in Nicaragua: "CIA murderers maim and kill / I think Reagan must be mentally ill / A dangerous nutter crazed with power / He's dragging us all nearer to our final hour") was now calling out in "Donald Trump—Fuck You!" the "billionaire asshole" who proudly proclaimed he could "grab 'em by the pussy" and "build the wall." From the country that would supposedly be paying for that wall, Mexico's Acidez released on a split 7" with the Los Angeles group Total Chaos titled *Revolution Has No Borders*, their "Donald Trump Must Die," interestingly (cautiously?) listed on Spotify as "D.T.M.D." Across the northern border, where no wall of separation was suggested needing built, Canada's SFH (Shit from Hell) recorded "Donald Trump Is an Asshole" for their *Kinda Sucks* album, listing the long litany of things he hated such as Mexicans, women, Muslims, and President Obama, to name just a few. Back across the Atlantic in Sweden, whose 1980s punk bands had a rich history of ripping on Reagan (Straw Dogs' "Reagan," Sötlimpa's "Ronald Reagan," Snobbslakt's "Reagan," The Past's "Reagan," Dom Intelligens Befriade's "Cowboy Reagan"), the Reagan reboot received as much attention, with Isotope Soap's Leni Riefenstahl–inspired "Trump des Willens," Giftigt Avfall's "Trampa Ihjäl Trump," translated as "Trample to Death Trump," and The Sensitives' "Trump." In the last of these, the trio from Falun cut right to the chase with "There goes another sexist, racist, sorry excuse for a man" and a plea that likely resonated with many across the world—"Oh Mr. President, don't be such a fucking dick."[11]

Accompanying Shit from Hell in Canada as they tore into Trump was none other than D.O.A., the Vancouver trio whose hardcore punk history went back to the beginning. Although the group had taken some breaks after forming in 1978, they had been consistently recording, with nearly twenty studio albums released since 1980's *Something Better Change*. In '81 they recorded their tribute to Reagan with "Fucked Up Ronnie." Thirty-five years later they would repackage it as "Fucked Up Donald," with only slight changes to the lyrics and an opening that pined, "You're fucked up Donald / You're not gonna last / You've spent your life / Just talking out your ass." Released as a single during the election of 2016, its jet-black cover included an image of an irate Trump, gun in hand pointed right at the listener. They would include the song on *Treason*, an album released in the months leading up to the 2020 election, along with "All the President's Men." The accompanying video for the latter would prominently display Vladimir Putin, Mitch McConnell, Kim Jong Un, and Rudy Giuliani, all of whom adorn the LP's cover surrounding a cocksure, smirking Trump, with "Treason" labeled across his eyes. When asked about the song, singer Joey Shithead said, "When lies and corruption rule the land, it's been a time honored tradition that artists become one of the last lines of defense, that's the tradition of folk, punk, and rap, we have to stand up against the racist, divisive bullshit that's coming from the Whitehouse [sic]." This fairly well summed up how many non-American punks felt about Donald Trump and the responsibility they had to bring it during his presidency. D.O.A., who had stood tall in opposition to Ronald Reagan, refused to sit on the sidelines for Donald Trump. They would be joined by many others. While they and other international punk bands took Trump to task in ways that had to have made their Reagan-Era comrades proud, their American counterparts would not disappoint.[12]

Mein Trumpf

With Trump in office, 2017 looked an awful lot like 1981 in terms of punk outpourings. Fall Children and Candy Warpop would not be alone as groups across the country critically castigated in song the man whose election to the presidency so many thought was improbable. Sharptooth, a feminist hardcore band from Baltimore with uncompromising musical power, would include their "Fuck You Donald Trump" on *Clever Girl*, described in a *Metal Injection* review as "a record that we need," "a truly significant work for our times," "an educational experience: for the things happening around us," and "a call to arms." While Trump's name is never mentioned in the lyrics, it's clear who vocalist Lauren Kashan is angrily screaming about in lines like "Through their lips they spit their hateful rhetoric" and "Red, red, red, red, ties / Black, black, black, black, black hearts." In Buffalo, New York, Trump's election would inspire the formation of the band Social Divorce, similar to Reagan Youth's start in 1980. They would be together for one year only, but in that short time released the *New York State Politics* EP, which included "Message to You Rudy (Giuliani)," "No PENCE Law," and "Trump University." Crutch, a trio out of Oklahoma City, would record "Trump Hunter" on a split, no-label cassette with Dallas's *Star Trek*-inspired Pavel Chekov, lyrically labeling the newly elected leader of the free world a "cheeto dusted fascist," "hopeless fucking coward," and "mindless monster." Battle Pussy, self-described as a "Denver Political Girl Punk Band," released *Revolution* in November, an album chock-full of anti-Trump tracks. Along with "You're Fired" and "Tweety Tweet," tributes to Trump's famous TV catch phrase and favorite mode of communication, the album included "No Trump," taking for its chorus M.D.C.'s "No Trump / No KKK / No Fascist USA" call to arms, as well as the childish and chidingly titled "Trumpty Dumpty." Far from being the last of that year's lashings, one northwest Indiana band took a page from the Suicidal Tendencies with their cacophonous claim about the demise of the Donald. Sounding musically a lot like the Reagan bands of the early '80s, the Liquids unabashedly proclaimed in their near-minute mangling, "I Killed Donald Trump."[13]

To the delight of many "old school" punks, the Reagan-Era bands, some of whom had never gone away, embraced the chance to lambaste the newly inaugurated president and got busy writing. It was as if it was the 1980s all over again, with some of the originals back in the fight. Jello Biafra and the Guantanamo School of Medicine was one of these, with "Satan's Combover" on their *Tea Party Revenge Porn* LP, going well beyond being a humorous hack on Trump's follicle fallacy. An "epic six-and-a-half-minute punk salvo," it was, according to *Rolling Stone*, "a biting anti-Trump screed" from Biafra, "one of punk's most consistently political voices over the decades." "Combover" and other tracks like "Taliban U.S.A." and "We Created Putin" make *Tea Party* "the band's most timeless album, with its frontman "as fierce, as cranked up, and as zealous as ever." Bad Religion, who like Biafra had been recording

Outro 177

pretty much nonstop since their formation, got back into the studio as well to record *Age of Unreason*, an album that, according to Jim Ruland, "effectively got its start on November 8, 2016, when Donald Trump was elected the forty-fifth president of the United States." Even before its release fans were given an indication of its Trump-inspired origins with the single "The Kids Are Alt-Right," described by Ruland as "a scathing rebuke" of Trump and the xenophobic, White supremacist worldview that his administration projected and supporters embraced. As a *Loudwire* review reminded listeners, "With a discography of political punk anthems from the days of Reagan to Obama, it's no surprise Bad Religion would put today's political climate under a microscope for new material." The album would include songs like "End of History," which had Greg Graffin announcing, "I don't believe in golden ages / Or presidents who put kids in cages," a clear jab at the president's MAGA mantra and family separation policy. For Biafra and Bad Religion, Trump was a definite inspiration to write and record as they had years before. Among the progenitors of punk, they would not be alone.[14]

"Punk rock leviathans," as described in 2022 by the alternative music blog *ALT77*, Chicago's Naked Raygun, to the excitement of their fans (including me), got back into the game to record an album during the Trump presidency. Chock-full of songs about American culture and the political climate at that time, it was the group's first full-length release since 1990. Apparently, enough was going on in the country and the world to get the band back in the studio for another go at it after three decades. While not released until after his 2020 defeat, it seems evident that much of the songs' inspiration stems from what was going on during the presidency of a man singer Jeff Pezzati described in 2016 as "pretty incredible . . . a rabble rouser," and in a moment of poor prognostication continued, "I can't see him actually being President, although weirder things have happened. I don't see him going all the way—I think he's too selfish." Naked Raygun had never been a band to be overt regarding lyrical politics, a point Pezzati made in the same 2016 interview. "With the political process, we'll just generalize and poke fun at it and cause people to think a little, maybe," he stated. "We don't point out specifics." So with no mention of Donald Trump in 2021's *Over the Overlords*, it would be easy to assume the group was not interested in joining their fellow '80s icons. But taken with Pezzati's comment about generalizing and getting listeners to think, the album becomes a candid critique of contemporary affairs. "[P]ent-up feelings and emotions about what is going on in our world now that is fucked up and bastardized" is how he described the influences for the songwriting process on the album, and one song in particular appears to express this best. The third track and first single released, "Living in the Good Times," offers an illuminating response to the key question Pezzati said informed the album's lyrics — "What is this fuckery?" With lines like "Living in the house of trained desperation," "Wasting my time looking for the crucial justice," "Dream of a day when we're finally gonna fuck the bastards," and "All I fear is that I'm walking in a sightline / And I'm caught on the wrong side of the police line," and the sources of fuckery become clear. Coupled with the others, including "Farewell to Arms," the final lyrical song on the album and a strong criticism of the American culture of gun ownership, *Overlords* stands well among the Trump-Age releases offered by the again-aroused Reagan-Era bands.[15]

While Naked Raygun would avoid overtness in their lyrics, one band that got their start berating Reaganism would continue its unconcealed and abrasive musical assault on America as harshly as ever now that Trump was in the White House. In the final words of his memoir, ironically published the same year Trump was elected, famed hardcore frontman Dave Dictor proudly pronounced, "I believe punk rock will never die as long as the kids find passion, cause, and voice." Clearly, for Dictor and his still-running band M.D.C., always passionate and never lacking in voice, Donald Trump was cause célèbre enough to not only write some new songs, but also to reboot a few older favorites. Like Jello Biafra and his Guantanamo crew, they would cut straight to the point in their 2017 release, *Mein Trumpf*, their first full-length album in thirteen years. An obvious take on Adolf Hitler's *Mein Kampf*, it was described by one reviewer as "a searing indictment of current US politics that is true to the band's radical left-wing self, and one that represents a musical call to equality and a wake up call against intolerance and hatred." The title track, one of the group's new tunes, begins with a "Build that wall!" chant laid over a Hitler speech recording, a juxtaposition that leaves little to the imagination of any listener. Thus begins the nearly six-minute condemnation that continuously asks, "What the Trump is going on?" as Dictor lets loose a torrent of lyrical abuse upon the forty-fifth president. The first song on the album, it is followed by such other insightful cultural critiques as "Working for Satan," "Drones," and "Don't Open the Door," another in the long list of songs by the group expressing concern for police practices in America, only to be wrapped up with a redo of one of their most well-known tunes, "Born to Die." Included on their 1982 first full-length album alongside the hardcore classics "Dead Cops," "John Wayne Was a Nazi," and

"American Achievements," it included a slight tweak in the original lyrics, with "No Trump, No KKK, No Fascist U.S.A." First chanted during the 2016 American Music Awards by Green Day, it would become a rallying cry for many disaffected during the Trump administration. As D.O.A. had done, Dictor and the group would even reboot another Reagan-Era release a few years later, with "Bye Bye Ronnie" updated as a farewell to "Donny." One reviewer of *Mein Trumpf* summed things up well in terms of the band's continued work: "In their 38 years of existence, hardcore punk legends M.D.C. have seen some of the worst presidencies in US history, forming at the start of the Reagan administration and remaining in the fight to see the dreaded Trump era." Theirs, like that of so many punk bands, is a body of work that should no longer be ignored in terms of critical contribution to the protest-oriented cultural discourse of the late twentieth and early twenty-first centuries.[16]

Punk's Dead—Long Live Punk!

This book did not attempt to prove anything, but rather to show that the lyrics written by punk bands, commonly ignored by scholars of the Reagan Era, deserve attention as rich sources of cultural criticism. If "punk lyrics are punks' collective consciousness," and "are, on some level, always intended to make a difference," as Gerfried Ambrosch concludes, to understand punk one must dig into the songs. In so many ways, during the ages of Reagan and Trump (and even Bush II), these expressed an uncompromising and unfiltered sense of disaffection that oftentimes is drowned out by the loud and obnoxious nature of the genre in general. Punk is often violent, macabre, and absurd, none of which should take away from the candor and clarity of cause in lyrics from bands across the country, many trudging along for the past five decades. As evidenced by the outpourings of bands (young and old) during the first Trump administration, punk is not dead. Nor will it likely be in the future. Punk has died a number of deaths only to be reborn time and time again. Presidents will continue to be elected and punks will continue to express anger and concern in song, at certain moments—Republican administrations apparently—more so than others. Ronald Reagan, in many ways the first modern Republican president, was clearly a big target for punks to take aim at. Trump was as well. Now that he is back for a second go at the presidency, will we witness more of what we got from punks during his first term? We'll just have to wait and see. If punk bands take to song, which I expect they will, we should really listen. Our ears may ring and we will likely get offended, but we will definitely be enlightened if we do. In the form of presidential pummeling and haranguing the American head of state, punk will never die. For those interested in understanding presidential politics, particularly grassroots oppositional forces, punks' lyrics offer a treasure trove of cultural commentary that should never be ignored. With four more years of Donald Trump to target, fans of punk should strap in and get ready for the ride. To quote the founding fathers, "Hey! Ho! Let's Go!"[17]

Acknowledgments

Never in a million years did I think I would write a book, especially one about punk music. As the title of Youth of Today's 1988 album *We're Not in This Alone* suggests, this didn't happen without the support and assistance of a number of people. I am thrilled to have this book published by the University of North Carolina Press and could not have asked for two better guides along the way, my editors Lucas Church and Thomas Bedenbaugh. Both were interested and engaged in the project from day one, and their suggestions throughout the writing process were warmly received and appreciated. They and the excellent reviewers they secured strengthened the manuscript, and what follows would not have come to print without their constructive criticism and support.

In many ways the seeds of this book were planted during my Fulbright experience at University College London's Institute of Education. Living in W10 a stone's throw from the Westway, it was the music of local legends The Clash, godfathers of punk, that rang in my ears daily on my walk to White City station to catch the Central Line to Russell Square or while waiting for the 220 bus to Harlesden. At the IOE, it was working with Robin Whitburn and Abdul Mohamud that I was introduced to the idea of "doing justice to history," an approach that suggests teachers dig into the past to uncover forgotten and marginalized stories. While I didn't know it at the time, this would get me thinking critically about punk lyrics as primary sources, and I would wonder why they were rarely if ever mentioned in the historical record surrounding the Reagan Revolution. At St. Claudine's Catholic School for Girls, it was Sharon Aninakwa, Ciára McCombe, and Nebiat Michael—three of the most brilliant teachers I've ever worked with—who not only welcomed me into their classrooms, but made me feel part of something special during my time there. All of them—Robin, Abdul, Sharon, Ciára, and Nebiat—inspired me and gave me the confidence to start digging into the punk past.

The immediate beginnings of this book can be traced to Mount Coe in Baxter State Park, Maine, during a hiking trip with Andrew Hartman and Keith Pluymers, both professors in the History Department at Illinois State University. I had just finished reading Kevin Mattson's book—to which I owe a debt of inspirational gratitude as well—and mentioned that while I loved it, I wanted more, especially something lyrical in nature. Andrew and Keith, after I made them listen to a Spotify playlist I put together of Reagan-related punk songs from the 1980s while driving deep into Katahdin Woods and Waters National Monument, suggested I write the book I wanted to read. Both have been continuously encouraging since that 2020 trip, and I've been blessed to have them around for support. Andrew in particular has been a constant source of intellectual stimulation, critically reading passages texted to him and offering advice when applicable. His friendship gave me the confidence I needed to believe I could actually write and get a book published.

The true birth of this book goes back a long way, to 1986 when I moved to Normal, Illinois. It was through my older brother Mike, a freshman in high school at the time, that I was introduced to punk music. Tapes of the Misfits, Minor Threat, Black Flag, M.D.C., Angry Samoans, Dead Kennedys, and many others were shared with me, and trips to Appletree Records on Saturday afternoons to thumb through the endless rows of cassettes are remembered fondly. It was my brother who first let me tag along to the Gallery for the all-ages shows held upstairs, to see local groups Naked Hippy and the Semicids, as well as Chicago's Naked Raygun, my favorite then and still. Some of the most fun I had during the writing was not only sending him passages to read, but songs we had listened to years before, sparking in both of us a memory of youthful days gone by. Mike was and is a great older brother who brought punk music into my life, without which this book wouldn't exist.

I lived in England from 1975 to 1977, the birth of punk, and just outside of Washington, DC, from 1984 to 1986, during Revolution Summer. Sadly, I was too young to witness either moment. I also lived in Alabama, Kansas, Maryland, and Korea before finally settling in the middle of corn and bean fields in central Illinois. My dad was in the army and we had an interesting experience growing up, uprooting every few years, with all the challenges that come with that. While you hate it as a kid, you come to appreciate and understand the uniqueness of it all as you get older. My mom and dad—Laura and Mike—have been very loving parents, giving my brother and me good lives and upbringings. While both will be proud of me for writing a book, neither should likely read it, good Reagan Republicans that they are. That being said, they have supported me and my adventurous nature since bringing me into the world, which I will always be grateful for.

I especially want to acknowledge the love and support of my immediate family. This is for Patrick, who hates punk music but whose attitude is more punk than he'll ever admit it to be. This is also for Delaney, whose heart is warm, mind is critical, and spirit is courageous—a punk in many ways. This is for Devin as well, who has only begun to understand his potential but who has a punk-oriented do-it-yourself mindset, for sure. Most importantly, this is for Teresa, who is not a big fan of the music I love but tolerated it playing constantly for the four years I've been writing this book, as well as turning a blind eye (sort of) to all the records I purchased for "research" as I wrote it. Three decades after telling her, to quote the Ramones, "I want to be your boyfriend," she is still by my side and I by hers. From her strength I draw my own.

Lastly, this is for the bands. Without them, there is no book.

Appendix

The following is a list of songs written between 1981 and 1989, the years of Reagan's presidency, that include his name (i.e., Reagan or Ronnie), some form of variation of it (i.e., Reaganomix or Reaganites), or something that directly connects to him (i.e., Libyan Hit Squad or Jodie Foster's Army) in the title. It is not complete, as I am sure there are more out there to be found. As well, there are plenty of songs from the time frame that mentioned Reagan in the lyrics but not in the title that aren't included. Thank you not only to the bands that wrote them but also to the individuals who posted them on either YouTube or Discogs for me to find. Thank you especially to those groups that included lyric sheets, which came in very helpful during the writing of this book.

Song Title	Band	Album	State or Country	Year
Reagan & The Reaganites	Ovenmen	Rock Against Racism E.P.	Williamsburg, NY	1981
Reagan Country	Shattered Faith	I Love America/ Reagan Country	Huntington Beach, CA	1981
Reagan's In	Wasted Youth	Reagan's In	Los Angeles, CA	1981
Ronnie's Song	LAX	Ronnie's Song	Redondo Beach, CA	1981
JFA (Jodie Foster's Army)	JFA	Blatant Localism EP	Phoenix, AZ	1981
R. Reagan	Idiootti	Demo 25.10.1980 + Practices	Finland	1981
Fucked Up Ronnie	D.O.A.	Positively D.O.A.	Vancouver, BC	1981
Impeach Reagan	The Lunatics	Various — Segments		1981
If Reagan Played Disco	Minutemen	Bean-Spill E.P.	San Pedro, CA	1982
Hey, Ronnie	Government Issue	Flex Your Head	Washington, DC	1982

(continued)

Song Title	Band	Album	State or Country	Year
Reagum	Lennonburger	Not So Quiet On the Western Front	San Francisco, CA	1982
Assassination Attempt	Demented Youth	Not So Quiet On the Western Front	San Francisco, CA	1982
Reagan's War	Demented Youth	Better Homes Demo Tape	San Francisco, CA	1982
Reagan Youth	Rebel Truth	Various — Charred Remains	Sacramento, CA	1982
On Your Head	No Crisis	She's Into the Scene	Huntington Beach, CA	1982
Battle Hymn of Ronald Reagan	The Fartz	World Full of Hate . . .	Seattle, WA	1982
Reagan's War Puppets	The Accüsed	22 Song Demo	Seattle, WA	1982
Ronald Reagan	Youth in Action	Your Nothing	Wisconsin	1982
Mister Reagan	The Silent Age	The Silent Age	New York, NY	1982
Ode to . . .	Beastie Boys	Polly Wog Stew EP	New York, NY	1982
Friend in D.C.	Corrosion of Conformity	No Core Compilation	Raleigh, NC	1982
Libyan Hit Squad	Tongue Avulsion	Not So Quiet On the Western Front		1982
Reagan	Daily Terror	Schmutzige Zeiten	W. Germany	1982
R. Reagan	Wutstock	Various — Korn Live — Ab Geht Er	W. Germany	1982
Hey Ronald	UsOpaRaus	Zieh Leine Ronald!	W. Germany	1982
Guten Morgen Mr. Reagan	UsOpaRaus	Zieh Leine Ronald!	W. Germany	1982
Ronald Reagan	NUF	NRW — Lärmträgersampler No. 1	W. Germany	1982
Ronald Reagan Nuklearer Cowboy	Torpedo	Schöne Neue Welt	W. Germany	1982

Song Title	Band	Album	State or Country	Year
Reagan Boggie	Destruktiva Liv	Destruktive Liv/Slam/Zeke Varg	Sweden	1982
What's Going On Inside Ronald Reagan's Brain?!	Deformed	Gas Attack! Without Warning!	Denmark	1982
Reagan & Oswald	Massagraf	Hatelijke Groenten	Netherlands	1982
Ronald Reagan Sucks	D.D.T.		Netherlands	1982
Red Ronnie Is a Bitch	Fallout	Various—Punk's Not Dead	Italy	1982
Ronald Reagan	4 Minute Warning	Ability Stinks	UK	1982
Reaganomics	D.R.I.	Dirty Rotten EP	Houston, TX	1983
Reagan Der Fuhrer	D.I.	D.I.	Fullerton, CA	1983
Reagan's Agenda	Target of Demand		Long Beach, CA	1983
Reagan Sucks	Bum Kon		Denver, CO	1983
Mummy From Hollywood	Angry Red Planet	The Angry Red Planet E.P./Too Much Knowledge Can Be Dangerous	Detroit, MI	1983
Ballad of Ronnie Raygun	White Trash	Trash Is Truth/Wake Up! E.P.	Denver, CO	1983
Fuck You Ronnie	The Abortion Squad	Demo 1983	Manchester, NH	1983
John Hinkley Jr. (What Has Jodie Foster Done To You?)	ISM	A Diet for Worms	New York, NY	1983
Reagan Bands	Chronic Sick	Reagan Bands	New Jersey	1983

(*continued*)

Song Title	Band	Album	State or Country	Year
I Shot Reagan	Suicidal Tendencies	Suicidal Tendencies	Venice, CA	1983
Reagan	Wards	The World Ain't Pretty and Neither Are We	Burlington, VT	1983
Reaganomics	No Direction	No Direction	Sioux Falls, SD	1983
Kill The President	Menstrual Cycles	Retirement Home	Hialeah, FL	1983
Reagan's Theme (Shut Up)	The Other Side	Reagan's Theme (Shut Up)		1983
Ronald Reagan	Inferno	Tod & Wahnsinn	W. Germany	1983
Ronald Raeggy	Agen 53	Agen 53 + A.V. Blox	W. Germany	1983
Ronald Reagan	The Past	7 Låtars EP	Sweden	1983
Reagan	Straw Dogs		Sweden	1983
Ronald Reagan	Sötlimpa (S.L.A.)	On the Streets Again	Sweden	1983
(ev'ry day's a) Reagan Day	Cheetah Chrome Motherfuckers	We Are the Juvenile Delinquency	Italy	1983
Isterismo di Reagan	Fallout	EP	Italy	1983
Reagan	Stanx	Holland Hardcore	Netherlands	1983
Reagan Ditty	Yollow Swollows	Various—6 Scandals	Netherlands	1983
Mr Reagan No Future	More Action	Various—Second Time Around	Belgium	1983
Reagan Sucks	Red Tide	Rundown	Victoria, BC	1983
Reagan Youth	Reagan Youth	Youth Anthems for the New Order	New York, NY	1984
Up With Reagan	The Stisism Band	Introducing . . . Stisism	New York, NY	1984
Reaganomics Fuck	Accelerators	Various—I'm Buck Naked!	Union, NJ	1984

Song Title	Band	Album	State or Country	Year
Reagan's Gestapo	Teenage Depression	Skank or Die	Providence, RI	1984
A Political Song	Pop-O-Pies	Joe's Second Record	San Francisco, CA	1984
Ronald Reagan	Harsh Reality	Various—Hardcore 84 Fresno Comp.	Fresno, CA	1984
President	Ill Repute	Various—Nardcore	Oxnard, CA	1984
Hinkley Had a Vision	The Crucifucks	The Crucifucks	Lansing, MI	1984
Young Ron	The Gynecologists	A Goat . . . You Geek	Bloomington, IN	1984
Ron and Nancy	The Gynecologists	A Goat . . . You Geek	Bloomington, IN	1984
Keppia Ronaldille	Rattus	Rattus	Finland	1984
Reagan Hijo de Puta	Delirium Femens	Que Se Vayan Ya!!	Spain	1984
Reagan	Kauneus and Terveys	Various—Belse Bop	Finland	1984
Ronald on Sika	Kauneus and Terveys	Various—Belse Bop	Finland	1984
Not Yet Ron	Verbal Assault	Bullshit Detector Three	Portsmouth, UK	1984
Guns of Reagan	Riff-O-Matics	Various—Independent World Vo. 1	Germany	1984
Bonzo Goes To Bitburg	Ramones	Bonzo Goes to Bitburg	New York, NY	1985
Reaganomix	Beefeater	Plays for Lovers	Washington, DC	1985
Fuck Reagan	White 'N' Hairy	Various—I Love Pomona	Pomona, CA	1985
Raygunomics	Agent 86	Scary Action	Arcata, CA	1985

(continued)

Song Title	Band	Album	State or Country	Year
Reagan is Your Lord	F	11 Song Demo Cassette	Lake Worth, FL	1985
Fuck, Shit, I Hate Reagan	Pagan Faith	Pagan Faith	St. Petersburg, FL	1985
Reagan Again (Battle Cry)	Plasma Alliance	We Can't Wait	Cleveland, OH	1985
Ronnie's a Dick	Khadafy Youth	Allah Fall Down	Maryland	1985
Reagan Had Skin Cancer	Wake Up Screaming	Aaargh! No! I Can't Stand It! . . .	Wales	1985
Ronald Reagan	Dis-Organized Bunch of Fuckers	Nebenwirkung/ D.B.F.	W. Germany	1985
Reagan	Resistance	Various—Hideous Headchop'n	W. Germany	1985
Reagen	Fluchtversuch	Fluchtversuch	Germany?	1985
Song About Little Reagan	Deformacja	Various—Jarocin' 85	Poland	1985
Resident President	The Depraved	Come On Down	UK	1985
Ronald Reagan	Delirium	Various—The Raw Power Of Life . . . 2	Netherlands	1985
Ronnie Is Dead	Crisis-C	Nihil Obstat	Netherlands	1985
Ronnie	Gøtefix	Living Suitcase on Core	Netherlands	1985
Rockabilly Reagan	Rattus	Ihmiset on Sairaita	Finland	1985
Ronald & Tsernenko	Mielenhäiriö	Various—Aivokuolema 2	Finland	1985
Reagan Cowboy	Dom Intelligens Befriade	Dom Intelligens Befriade	Sweden	1985
Reagan	Snobbslakt	Various—Furir Kurir Vol. 1	Sweden	1985

Song Title	Band	Album	State or Country	Year
Reaganomics	Dog Killer	Last Act of a Desperate Band	Chico, CA	1986
I'm Your President	Caustic Notions	Never Look Back	Saratoga, CA	1986
Reagan Spawn	Vivisect	Vivisect	Boston, MA	1986
California Pipeline	Murphy's Law	Murphy's Law	New York, NY	1986
Bonzo Fucked Reagan	Psycho Sin	Evil Seeks Sanctuary	Hoboken, NJ	1986
Reagan's War	Spoiled Brats	Various—Quest For The Corn Girl		1986
Ronald McRaygun	Dayglo Abortions	Feed Us A Fetus	Victoria, BC	1986
Ronnie And Maggie	Attic 22	Various—Support Your Local Underdogs	Belgium	1986
Rockin' Ronald	Krapotkin	Kosacker	Sweden	1986
Ronnie Wants War	Strebers	Ur Led Är . . .	Sweden	1986
Hullu Reagan	Brutal	Various—Vapautus!	Finland	1986
Reagan	Terveykeskus	Various—Despotism 1986—Reaganin Joululhjat 2	Finland	1986
Ronnie's Still Acting	Anti Hierarchy	Various—Stone the Flamin' Crows!!	Australia	1986
The Jellybean Man	Fear and Loathing	A Box of Fluffy Ducks	Australia	1986
Ronald Reagan	Criminal Sex	Various—Bloodsucker	UK	1986
Bye Bye Ronnie	M.D.C.	This Blood's for You	San Francisco, CA	1987
Reagan Gun Club	Social Spit	Psycho Ward	San Diego, CA	1987

(*continued*)

Song Title	Band	Album	State or Country	Year
Scrawny Little Bitch (Love Song for Ronald Reagan to Sing)	The Rub	Bikini Gospel	Los Angeles, CA	1987
Reagan	Naked Hippy	I Thought Woodstock Was Over Demo	Normal, IL	1987
Who's President	The Ozzfish Experience	Liberty and Justice for All	South Holland, IL	1987
Mr. President	Solid Waste	1987 Demo		1987
Gunning For The President	G.B.H.	No Need to Panic	UK	1987
What Do You Want Ronald Reagan	Spermbirds	Memento Mori/ Spermbirds	W. Germany	1987
Reagan	The Nuts	26 Hours	Sweden	1987
The President of the U.S.A.	Strong Concentration Of Anger	Strong Concentration of Anger	Netherlands	1987
Hitler-Ronnie	Death Sentence		Vancouver, BC	1987
Mate Reagan	Tropa Suicida	Agora É Nossa Vez . . . Vingança ! / Lutar Ou Morrer	Brazil	1987
Ronald Reagan Must Die	Psycho Sin	88 Blasts from the Tribals of 1988	Hoboken, NJ	1988
Reagan Is a Poseur	Stikky	3 and a Half Demo	Santa Clara, CA	1988
A Reagan	The Crime Gang Bang	Figli Della Rabbia, Figli Del Dolore	Italy	1988
Fuck Reagan	Social Disease	Poki's Dead	San Francisco, CA	1988
Reagan Was A Hippy	Degeneration	Degeneration	Minneapolis, MN	1988

Song Title	Band	Album	State or Country	Year
Impeach Reagan	A.P.P.L.E.	Plutocracy=Tyranny & Exploitation	New York, NY	1988
Anti-Reagan	M.I.S.	Donations for Broken Glass	Longview, WA	1988
Monarch Reagan	Complicated Bone Marrow Transplant	Speak	Bennington, VT	1988
Cowboy Ronnie	Youth Crew	Doodt Illegal/Youth Crew Split Tape	Belgium	1988
Cowboy Ronnie	Genossen	Kein Chance	W. Germany	1988
Die For Ronnie Part 1	Memento Mori	Memento Mori	W. Germany	1988
Die For Ronnie Part 2	Memento Mori	Memento Mori	W. Germany	1988
Ronnie Reagan	Anstifter	Anstifter	W. Germany	1988
Run Ronald	Electro Hippies	The Only Good Punk . . . Is a Dead One	UK	1988
Ronaldo Hitler	Dizintria	Various—Ódio Mortal	Brazil	1988
Obrigado Reagan	W.C.H.C.	Various—Ódio Mortal	Brazil	1988
Day With Reagan	The Stains	The Stains	Portland, ME	1989
Kill the President	The Offspring	The Offspring	Garden Grove, CA	1989
Ronnie Rotten	Drugstore	Eggshell	Sweden	1989

Notes

Introduction

1. "Reagan's Letter Announcing His Alzheimer's Diagnosis."
2. "Remarks by Former British Prime Minister Margaret Thatcher," *New York Times*, June 11, 2004.
3. "Remarks by Senator John Danforth," *New York Times*, June 11, 2004.
4. "Dead Reagan Special," *MRR Radio*, June 6, 2004.
5. *MRR*, #255, 2004.
6. *MRR*, #255, 2004.
7. Mattson, *We're Not Here to Entertain*, 40, 291.
8. Artificial Peace, "Suburban Wasteland," recorded November 1981, track 3 on *Complete Session '81*, Dischord; Government Issue, "Bored to Death," released September 1981, track 7 on *Legless Bull*, Dischord; Black Flag, "Depression," released November 1981, track 9 on *Damaged*, Unicorn.
9. Ambrosch, *The Poetry of Punk*, 29.
10. N.O.T.A., "Nightstick Justice," released 1985, track 13 on *N.O.T.A.*, Rabid Cat; Dicks, "No Fuckin' War," released 1984, track 1 on *Peace?*, R Radica; D.R.I., "God Is Broke," released 1985, track 10 on *Dealing with It*, Death.
11. Hurchalla, *Going Underground*, 103.
12. O'Hara, *The Philosophy of Punk*, 11.
13. Dunn, *Global Punk*, 53, 55.
14. Ratner-Rosenhagen, *The Ideas That Made America*, 2–3.

Chapter One

1. "Inaugural Address 1981"; Lou Cannon, "Reagan Leaving a Legacy of Surprises," *Washington Post*, January 15, 1989.
2. Troy, *The Reagan Revolution*, 21.
3. "Inaugural Address 1981."
4. Maskell, *Politics as Sound*, 75.
5. Shayna Maskell, "'There Is No Hope for the USA': Bad Brains and the Sounds of Race in DC Hardcore," in Butz and Winkler, *Hardcore Research*, 132; "How Henry Rollins Helped Bad Brains," *Double J*, July 18, 2014; Greg Tate, "Bad Brains: Hardcore of Darkness," *Village Voice*, April 27, 1982.
6. Ogg, *Dead Kennedys*, 4.
7. *MRR*, #442, 2020; Mattson, *We're Not Here to Entertain*, 83.
8. Wasted Youth, "Fuck Authority," released 1981, track 6 on *Reagan's In*, ICI Sanoblast.

9. Maskell, *Politics as Sound*, 95; Minor Threat, "Minor Threat," released 1981, track 7 on *Filler*, Dischord.

10. Ogg, *Dead Kennedys*, 116.

11. Ensminger, *Left of the Dial*, 225–26.

12. Caroline Covington, "Austin's Rule Breaking 80s Punk Scene on Full Display in 'Texas Is the Reason,'" KUT 90.5, October 23, 2020.

13. *MRR #3*, 1981; quoted in Paul Rachman, *American Hardcore*, 2006.

14. D.O.A., "Smash the State," released 1981, track 11 on *Hardcore 81*, Friends.

15. Wasted Youth, "Reagan's In"; NOFX, "Reagan Sucks," released 1996, track 4 on *Fuck the Kids*, Fat Wreck.

16. Shattered Faith, "Reagan in '81," released 1981, track 2 on *I Love America/Reagan in '81*, Posh Boy.

17. Shattered Faith, "I Love America," released 1981, track 1 on *I Love America/Reagan in '81*, Posh Boy.

18. Cannon, *President Reagan*, 587; Ramones, "Bonzo Goes to Bitburg," released 1985, track 1 on *Bonzo Goes to Bitburg*, Beggars Banquet.

19. "Nobody's Perfect: An Interview with Joey and Richie of the Ramones," *East Coast Rocker*, no. 4, 1986; Ramones, "Bonzo Goes to Bitburg."

20. Reagan Youth, "New Aryans," released 1984, track 1 on *Youth Anthems for the New Order*, R Radical; Reagan Youth, "Reagan Youth," released 1984, track 2 on *Youth Anthems for the New Order*, R. Radical; "History," *Reagan Youth*, https://www.reagan-youth.com/history, accessed May 2, 2002.

21. D.I., "Reagan der Fuhrer," released 1983, track 4 on *D.I.*, Revenge.

22. JFA, "JFA," released 1981, track 2 on *Blatant Localism*, Placebo.

23. Ism, "John Hinckley Jr. (What Has Jodie Foster Done to You?)," released 1983, track 6 on *A Diet for the Worms*, S.I.N.

24. Sam McPheeters, "The Troublemaker," *Vice* 16, no. 1, January 1, 2009; Crucifucks, "Hinckley Had a Vision," released 1984, track 8 on *The Crucifucks*, Alternative Tentacles.

25. Tongue Avulsion, "Libyan Hit Squad," released 1982, track 35 on *Not So Quiet on the Western Front*, Alternative Tentacles; "A Plot Thickens," *Time*, December 14, 1981.

26. Demented Youth, "Assassination Attempt," released 1982, track 23 on *Not So Quiet on the Western Front*, Alternative Tentacles; Demented Youth, "Reagan's War," released 1982, track 3 on *Better Homes* demo cassette, not on a label.

27. Suicidal Tendencies, "I Shot the Devil," released 1983, track 3 on *Suicidal Tendencies*, Frontier.

28. *Touch & Go*, #17, 1981.

29. *MRR*, #4, 1983; The Fartz, "Battle Hymn of Ronald Reagan," released 1982, track 8 on *World Full of Hate . . .* , Alternative Tentacles.

30. Blush, *American Hardcore*, 147; Government Issue, "Hey Ronnie," released 1982, track 12 on *Flex Your Head*, Dischord.

31. Lennonburger, "Reagum," released 1982, track 21 on *Not So Quiet on the Western Front*, Alternative Tentacles.

32. James Tobin, "Reaganomics in Retrospect," in Kymlick and Matthews, *The Reagan Revolution?*, 103; Dead Kennedys, "Dear Abby," released 1986, track 3 on *Bedtime for Democracy*, Alternative Tentacles.

33. Rowse, *One Sweet Guy and What He Is Doing to You*, 73.

34. *MRR*, #28, 1985; D.R.I., "Reaganomics," released 1985, track 16 on *Dealing with It!*, Bloody Skull; Beefeater, "Reaganomix," released 1985, track 2 on *Plays for Lovers*, Dischord; Cause for Alarm, "Time to Try," released 1983, track 3 on *Cause for Alarm*, not on a label.

35. No Direction, "Reaganomics," released 1983, track 11 on *No Direction*, No Direction; US Bureau of Labor Statistics, Unemployment Rate in South Dakota [LAUST460000000000003A], retrieved from FRED, Federal Reserve Bank of St. Louis, September 28, 2022.

36. "Dog Killer," *Terminal Escape*, December 10, 2013; Dog Killer, "Reaganomics," released 1986, track 10 on *Last Act of a Desperate Band*, Anal Ranger; Robert Lekachman, "The Economic Consequences of Ronald Reagan," *Washington Post*, October 2, 1988.

37. Accelerators, "Reaganomics Fuck Off," released 1984, track 25 on *I'm Buck Naked!*, Bad Compilation Tapes; Robert Lekachman, "The Economy," in Gartner, Greer, and Riessman, *What Reagan Is Doing to Us*, 202.

38. D.O.A., "Fucked Up Ronnie," released 1981, track 1 on *Positively D.O.A.*, Alternative Tentacles; Dayglo Abortions, "Ronald McRaygun," released 1986, track 11 on *Feed Us a Fetus*, Toxic Shock.

39. The Past, "Ronald Reagan," released 1983, track 1 on *7 Latars EP*, Birdskit.

40. *MRR*, #6, 1983.

Chapter Two

1. LaVoie, "Ronald Reagan's 'To Restore America,'" 362.

2. "Address Accepting the Presidential Nomination at the Republican National Convention in Detroit"; Hoffmann, "Requiem," 26; The Wipers, "Youth of America," released 1981, track 6 on *Youth of America*, Park Avenue Records.

3. Shattered Faith, "I Love America," released 1981, track 1 on *I Love America/Reagan Country*, Posh Boy; Conflict, "America's Right," released 1982, track 1 on *America's Right*, Unjust Tapes; Tom Reardon, "The Most Influential Arizona Punk Records: #6—Conflict, *Last Hour*," *Phoenix New Times*, December 18, 2014; *MRR*, #002, 1982.

4. Money Dogs, "America Is Falling," released 193, track 1 on *America Is Falling*, not on a label; *MRR*, #006, 1983; Money Dogs, "Peace Moscow," track 8 on *America Is Falling*; Money Dogs, "Your Town (X-Town)," track 3 on *America Is Falling*.

5. Whipping Boy, "America Must Die!," released 1983, track 1 on *The Sound of No Hands Clapping*, CFI Records; Whipping Boy, "Hero," released 1983, track 2 on *The Sound of No Hands Clapping*; Pig Children, "America's Dying in Her Sleep," released 1985, track 2 on *Blood for the State*, Savage Beat Records; Pig Children, "Grand Ole Flag," released 1985, track 5 on *Blood for the State*.

6. 7 Seconds, "Fuck Your Amerika," released 1982, track 13 on *Not So Quiet on the Western Front*, Alternative Tentacles; David Ensminger, "The Top 20 Punk Protest Songs for July 4th," *PopMatters*, July 2012.

7. BHT, "Amerika," released 1986, track 1 on *The Prime Directive*, not on a label; Lookouts!, "Fourth Reich (Nazi Amerika)," released 1987, track 19 on *One Planet One People*, Lookout! Records.

8. Stark Raving Mad, "Are You Sleeping?" released 1985, track 1 on *Amerika*, Slob Records; Stark Raving Mad, "Take a Stand," released 1985, track 2 on *Amerika*; *MRR*, #033, 1986; Stark Raving Mad, "S.O.S." released 1985, track 9 on *Amerika*.

9. Foner, "The Contested History of American Freedom," 13; Coe, "The Language of Freedom in the American Presidency, 1933–2006," 376.

10. Regan, "The Reagan Presidency in Perspective," 418; "Inaugural Address"; "Remarks at Memorial Day Ceremonies at Arlington National Cemetery"; "Remarks and a Question-and-Answer Session with the Students and Faculty at Moscow State University."

11. Hüsker Dü, "In a Free Land," released 1982, track 1 on *In a Free Land*, New Alliance Records; Mattson, *We're Not Here to Entertain*, 282–84.

12. The Patriots, "The Land of the Free," released 1983, track 1 on *The Land of the Free*, Another Lousy Record; Warboy, "Land of the Free," released 1983, track 9 on *Futile Living*, Confessional Records; Fearless Iranians from Hell, "Land of the Free," released 1986, track 9 on *Fearless Iranians from Hell*, not on a label; Crash Course, "Land of the Free," released 1986, track 11 on *Pilgrimage to Hell*, Hellcore/Landlubber Records.

13. Unified Field, "Land of the Free," released 1988, track 5 on *Demo 1988*, not on a label; *MRR*, #59, 1988; Angry Red Planet, "Land of the Free," released 1988, track 10 on *Get Me a Shovel*, Angry Red Records; *MRR*, #10, 1983. Angry Red Planet, "Mummy from Hollywood," released 1983, track 2 on *Too Much Knowledge Can Be Dangerous*, Angry Red Records.

14. "The Shuttle Explosion," *New York Times*, January 29, 1986; "Address to the Nation on the Explosion of the Space Shuttle *Challenger*"; "Inaugural Address 1981."

15. Saigon, "America (Home of the Free and the Brave)," released 1981, track 4 on *Annihilation*, WWII Records; Mecht Mensch, "Land of the Brave," released 1983, track 3 on *Acceptance*, Bone Air.

16. "Radio Address to the Nation on Flag Day and Father's Day"; Tom Murphy, "Naked Raygun's Jeff Pezzati on Wax Trax, and Why and How the Band Got Back Together," *Westworld*, September 18, 2013; Naked Raygun, "Home of the Brave," released 1986, track 1 on *All Rise*, Homestead Records.

17. Jim Capaldi, "Pete Seeger Used to Do a Parody of 'This Old Man,'" Google Groups, September 16, 1998, https://groups.google.com/g/rec.music.folk/c/F6tfT VLO8wA?pli=1.

18. "Inaugural Address 1981"; "Labor Day Speech at Liberty State Park, Jersey City, New Jersey."

19. "Remarks at a White House Ceremony Celebrating Hispanic Heritage Week."

20. Bad Religion, "American Dream," released 1982, track 10 on *How Could Hell Be Any Worse?*, Epitaph; quoted in Barrett, *Gambling with History*, 90; Human Therapy, "American Dream," released 1983, track 2 on *Domesticated People*, Doctor Dream Records.

21. Articles of Faith, "American Dreams," released 1984, track 10 on *Give Thanks*, Reflex Records; Econochrist, "Fuck Your American Dreams," released 1988, track 6 on *It Runs Deep*, Truant Records.

22. Corrupted Morals, "American Dream," released 1987, track 4 on *Demo 1987*, not on a label; *MRR*, #41, 1986; Corrupted Morals, "Be All You Can Be," released 1988, track 2 on *Chet*, Lookout! Records.

23. Kate Coleman, "The Roots of Ed Meese," *Los Angeles Times*, May 4, 1986; Lekachman, *Visions and Nightmares*, 149. Corrupted Morals, "The Adventures of Edwin Meese," released 1988, track 5 on *Chet*, Lookout! Records; "Defeated by Pornography," *New York Times*, June 2, 1986; quoted in Alan Sears, "Ed Meese: The Enduring Voice of the Reagan Revolution," *Townhall*, October 8, 2019.

24. "Prouder, Stronger, Better"; Agent 86, *Scary Action*, released 1985 on Arcatones; Social Unrest, *SU-2000*, released 1985 on Libertine Records; Social Unrest, "General Enemy," released 1982, track 1 on *Rat in a Maze*, Libertine Records.

25. Ira Glasser, "The Coming Assault on Civil Liberties," in Gartner, Greer, and Riessman, *What Reagan Is Doing to Us*, 248; Naked Raygun, "Only in America," released 1984, track 11 on *Throb Throb*, Homestead Records.

Chapter Three

1. "Farewell Address to the Nation."

2. Quoted in Mervin, "Ronald Reagan's Place in History," *Journal of American Studies*, 269; Rowse, *One Sweet Guy and What He Is Doing to You*, 1; Gartner, Greer, and Riessman, *What Reagan Is Doing to Us*, vii; Hugh Heclo, "The Mixed Legacies of Ronald Reagan," in Dunn, *The Enduring Reagan*, 13.

3. Spheeris, *Suburbia*; Vincent Canby, "Down-and-Out Youths in 'Suburbia,'" *New York Times*, April 13, 1984.

4. Morris, *It's a Sprawl World After All*, 1–3.

5. McGirr, *Suburban Warriors*, 42, 29; Void, "Suburbs Suck!," released 2011, track 7 on *Sessions 1981–1983*, Dischord Records.

6. Rapport, *Damaged*, 10; Black Flag, "Depression," released 1980, track 2 on *The Decline of Western Civilization*, Slash.

7. Orwell, *Coming Up for Air*; Goulding, "The Sound of the Suburbs"; Government Issue, "Bored to Death," released 1981, track 7 on *Legless Bull* EP, Dischord Records; Teenage PhDs, "Too Bored to Die," released 1980, track 3 on *Teenage PhDs*, Erectile.

8. Jackson, *Crabgrass Frontier*; Suburban Mutilation, *The Opera Ain't Over until the Fat Lady Sings!*, released 1984, Reamed Pork Rex; Bored Suburban Youths, *Red Menace—Farewell Suburbia*, released 1988, Menace Records; Michael L. Miller, "Art Event Tonight at G.R.O.W. Cafe," *Columbia Record*, August 8, 1986; White Suburban Youth, "Suburban Streets," released 2014, track 15 on *White Suburban Youth*, Trouble in River City Records.

9. The Lewd, "Suburban Prodigy," released 1982, track 6 on *American Wino*, ICI Records; B.P., "Suburban Life," released 1986, track 12 on *Draft Beer . . . Not Me*, No Clubs Records; Adrenalin O.D., "Suburbia," released 1983, track 1 on *Let's Barbecue*, Buy Our Records; Artificial Peace, "Suburban Wasteland," released 1985, track 29 on *Flex Your Head*, Dischord Records.

10. Really Red, "Suburban Disease," released 1982, track 3 on *New Strings for Old Puppets*, C.I.A. Records; False Prophets, "Suburbanites Invade," released 1986, track 10 on *False Prophets*, Alternative Tentacles; The Morons, "Suburbanite," released 1981, track 1 on *Suburbanite/Changing Days*, Lark Beat; Heavy Mental, "Suburb IA," released 1985, track 1 on *Heavy Mental*, MMR Publishing; Descendents, "Suburban

Home," released 1982, track 9 on *Milo Goes to College*, New Alliance Records; Ryan Ritchie, "Why Former Descendents' Bass Player Isn't Rushing Out to See the Band's New Documentary," *OC Weekly*, August 23, 2013.

11. "Radio Address to the Nation on Education."

12. National Commission on Excellence in Education, "A Nation at Risk"; Clark and Amiot, "The Impact of the Reagan Administration on Federal Education Policy," 258.

13. The Beach Boys, "Be True to Your School," released 1963, track 1 on *Be True to Your School/In My Room*, Capitol Records; Gary U. S. Bonds, "School Is Out," released 1961, track 1 on *School Is Out/One Million Tears*, Legrand Records; Alice Cooper, "School's Out," released 1972, track 1 on *School's Out*, Warner Bros. Records; Ramones, "Rock 'n' Roll High School," released 1980, track 1 on *Rock 'n' Roll High School*, Sire.

14. Brodinsky, "Something Happened: Education in the Seventies," 238.

15. Necros, "I Hate My School," released 1981, track 6 on *I.Q. 32*, Touch and Go/Dischord Records; *Touch & Go*, #10, 1981.

16. Redd Kross, "I Hate My School," released 1981, track 3 on *Red Cross*, Posh Boy; Clabaugh, "The Educational Legacy of Ronald Reagan," 259.

17. *MRR*, #004, 1983; No Rock Stars, "I Hated School," released 1982, track 27 on *No Core*, No Core Records; *MRR*, #023, 1985; The Landlords, "I Hate School," released 1984, track 17 on *Hey! It's a Teenage House Party*, Catch Trout Records; erinohare, "Fast forward: Punk Band The Landlords' First Album Gets a Slick Reissue," *C-Ville*, June 27, 2018.

18. JFA, "Out of School," released 1981, track 1 on *Blatant Localism*, Placebo Records; The Replacements, "Fuck School," released 1982, track 2 on *Stink*, Twin/Tone Records; Hüsker Dü, "Guns at My School," released 1982, track 4 on *Land Speed Record*, New Alliance Records; Overkill, "Burn the School," released 1982, track 3 on *Overkill*, SST Records; Rights of the Accused, "In School," released 1984, track 3 on *Innocence*, Little Farmer Music.

19. Pedestrian Abuse, "Fuck School," released 1984, track 16 on *This Is the Central Coast*, Bopp n' Skin Records; Chemical Waste, "School Sucks!," released 1987, track 5 on *Life's a Bitch*, not on a label; Sin 34, "Forced Education," released 1983, track 10 on *Life Is Boring So Why Not Steal This Record*, New Underground Records; No, "American School System," released 1983, track 17 on *America's Dairyland*, not on a label; Clabaugh, "The Educational Legacy of Ronald Reagan," 259; Clark and Amiot, "The Impact of the Reagan Administration on Federal Education Policy," 262.

20. Quoted in "13 Reasons Why Jimmy Carter Is America's Greenest President," *More Than Just Parks*, accessed February 23, 2023.

21. Holden, "The Reagan Years," 988; quoted in Thomas H. Harris, "How Many Trees Do You Need to See?" *New York Times*, June 24, 1973; "Reagan, Spare That Tree!" *Washington Post*, August 17, 1980.

22. Quoted in Kevin L. Jones, "Notorious SF Punk Band Flipper Turns 40 with Slightly Happier Birthday," *Datebook: San Francisco Chronicle*, July 10, 2019; quoted in Mark Prindle, "Flipper: A Whale of Band," *Mark's Record Reviews*, http://www.markprindle.com/flipper.htm, accessed February 21, 2023; Maureen Orth, "The Love Canal Saga Comes to TV," *Washington Post*, February 14, 1982.

23. Flipper, "Love Canal," released 1981, track 1 on *Love Canal/Ha Ha Ha*, Subterranean Records; New York State Department of Health, *Love Canal: A Special Report to the Governor and Legislature*, https://www.health.ny.gov/environmental/investigations/love_canal/lcreport.htm; Sun, "Armand Hammer Named to Head Cancer Panel," 311.

24. Armed Citizens, "Toxic Waste," released 1983, track 2 on *Make Sense*, Big City Records; Ultra Violence, "Toxic Waste," released 1987, track 9 on *Ultra Violence*, not on a label; Heart Attack, "Toxic Lullaby," released 1984, track 4 on *Subliminal Seduction*, Rat Cage Records; Rosalind H. Williams, "Solidarism, an Answer to Reagan Darwinism," *New York Times*, July 2, 1981.

25. Agnostic Front, "Toxic Shock," released 1986, track 7 on *Cause for Alarm*, Combat Core; Iver Peterson, "Michigan Residents Seek Investigation of Dioxins," *New York Times*, March 15, 1983; Leslie Maitland, "E.P.A. Aides Charge Superiors Forced Shift in Dow Study," *New York Times*, March 19, 1983; Philip Shabecoff, "House Charges Head of E.P.A. with Contempt," *New York Times*, December 17, 1982.

26. Quoted in Francis X. Clines, "Reagan Makes Counterattack in E.P.A. Fight," *New York Times*, March 12, 1983; Vig and Kraft, *Environmental Policy in the 1980s*, ix; State of Confusion, "Public Lands," released 1986, track 4 on *6.3 Million Acres*, Silence; Wayne R. Flower, "Music History, Part 10: The Early Boise Years 1986–1987," *A Music History*, August 25, 2011.

27. Dead Kennedys, "Cesspool in Eden," released 1986, track 11 on *Bedtime for Democracy*, Alternative Tentacles; Reagan Youth, "Acid Rain," released 1988, track 10 on *Volume 2*, New Red Archives; Corrosion of Conformity, "Poison Planet," released 1986, track 11 on *Eye for an Eye*, Toxic Shock; Capitalist Casualties, "Nuclear National Park," released 1988, track 3 on *26 Songs*, not on a label; Bedlam, "New Jersey; Chemical Dump State," released 1984, track 2 on *(Total) Bedlam*, Buy Our Records; Steven Cohen, "Defusing the Toxic Time Bomb: Federal Hazardous Waste Programs," in Vig and Kraft, *Environmental Policy in the 1980s*, 274, 290.

28. "Radio Address to the Nation on Federal Drug Policy"; Douglas Quenqua, "Nancy Reagan's Most Memorable 'Just Say No' Moments," *PR Week*, March 7, 2016; "Nancy Reagan's 'Just Say No Campaign,'" CNN, September 1982.

29. Haenfler, *Straight Edge*, 10; Minor Threat, "Straight Edge," released 1981, track 4 on *Filler*, Dischord; Minor Threat, "Out of Step," released 1981, track 2 on *In My Eyes*, Dischord.

30. Haenfler, *Straight Edge*, 10; quoted in Lahickey, *All Ages*, xi; Uniform Choice, "Straight and Alert," released 1984, track 6 on demo, not on label; The Abused, "Drug Free Youth, " released 1982, track 8 on demo, not on label; Tony Rettman, "The Abused's Kevin Crowley Looks Back on the Early Days of NYHC," *Vice*, March 5, 2015; *MRR*, #1, 1982; SS Decontrol, "Headed Straight," released 1982, track 11 on *The Kids Will Have Their Say*, Xclaim!

31. 7 Seconds, "Straight On," released 1984, track 5 on *The Crew*, Better Youth Organization; 7 Seconds, "Drug Control," released 1986, track 12 on *Walk Together, Rock Together*, Better Youth Organization; "Address to the Nation on the Campaign against Drug Abuse"; quoted in Lahickey, *All Ages*, 161.

32. "Disaffection," *Oxford English Dictionary*, https://www.oed.com/dictionary/disaffection_n?tl=true, accessed March 23, 2023; Agent Orange, "A Cry for Help in a

World Gone Mad," released 1981, track 6 on *Living in Darkness*, Posh Boy; "Friday, May 15, 1981," *Ronald Reagan Presidential Foundation and Institute*, https://www.reaganfoundation.org/ronald-reagan/white-house-diaries/diary-entry-05151981/?srsltid=AfmBOoq__jPxRX9xzZZQJLvKYluwmi7DYCc3ZTga4OQpCQjRkh5lBYWV; Bad Religion, "Fuck Armageddon . . . This Is Hell," released 1982, track 5 on *How Could Hell Be Any Worse?*, Epitaph.

Chapter Four

1. Perlstein, *Reaganland*, 842; "National Affairs Campaign Address on Religious Liberty"; Hadden and Shupe, *Televangelism*, 28.
2. "National Affairs Campaign Address on Religious Liberty."
3. Johnson and Tamney, "The Christian Right and the 1980 Presidential Election," 123; "National Affairs Campaign Address on Religious Liberty."
4. Daniel K. Williams, "Reagan's Religious Right: The Unlikely Alliance between Southern Evangelicals and a California Conservative," in Hudson and Davies, *Ronald Reagan and the 1980s*, 135–49; quoted in James R. Dickenson, "Religion Is Powerful GOP Theme," *Washington Post*, August 24, 1984.
5. Hartman, *A War for the Soul of America*, 98; M.D.C., "Millions of Damn Christians," released 1987, track 1 on *This Bloods for You*, R Radical.
6. Robert C. Liebman, "Mobilizing the Moral Majority," in Liebman and Wuthnow, *The New Christian Right*, 55.
7. Liebman, "Mobilizing the Moral Majority," 55; Dead Kennedys, "Moral Majority," released 1981, track 2 on *In God We Trust, Inc.*, Alternative Tentacles.
8. Dead Kennedys, "Moral Majority."
9. Dead Kennedys, "Religious Vomit," released in 1981, track 1 on *In God We Trust, Inc.*, Alternative Tentacles; Dead Kennedys, "We've Got a Bigger Problem Now," released 1981, track 8 on *In God We Trust, Inc.*, Alternative Tentacles.
10. Quoted in Bushnell and Turcotte, *The Art of Punk*.
11. John Hall, "Falwell Credited with Voter Influence outside Virginia," *Journal Champion*, 1978; Falwell, *Listen America!*.
12. Williams, *God's Own Party*, 178–79; Really Red, *Despise Moral Majority*, released 1980, C.I.A.; "Moral Majority," *Lost Horizons: A Tribute to Doug Hopkins*, http://www.losthorizons.info/bands/Moral_Majority.html, accessed October 10, 2022; Circle Jerks, "Moral Majority," released 1982, track 11 on *Wild in the Streets*, Faulty Products.
13. "Remarks at the Annual Convention of Religious Broadcasters"; Circle Jerks, "Moral Majority."
14. Youth Brigade, "Moral Majority," released 1982, track 14 on *Flex Your Head*, Dischord; quoted in Williams, *God's Own Party*, 178.
15. White Trash, "Piss on the Moral Majority," released 1982, track 6 on *White Trash*, self-released; ELF, "Moral Majority," released 1983, track 3 on *SF Sound of Music Club Live, Vol. 1*, SOM; Mr. Epp and the Calculations, "Moral Majority," released 1983, track 6 on *Live As All Get Out!*, Deux Ex Machina; *MRR #9*, October/November 1983; Modern Warfare, "Moral Majority," released 1983, track 5 on *Life Is Boring So*

Why Not Steal This Record, New Underground; Sacred Denial, "Moral Majority," released 1986, track 7 on *Extra Strength Tylenol Anyone?*, Forefront.

16. James Mann, "Analysis," *U.S. News & World Report*, December 29, 1980/January 5, 1981, 69.

17. "Letter from Jerry Falwell on Keeping Old Time Gospel Hour on Air," *Portal to Texas History*, https://texashistory.unt.edu/ark:/67531/metadc177440/, accessed July 7, 2023; Cannon, *President Reagan*, 819.

18. Angry Samoans, "Homo-Sexual," released 1982, track 7 on *Back from Samoa*, Bad Trip Records; *Ink Disease*, #14, 1988; "Angry Samoans: Politically Incorrect before Politically Incorrect Was Cool (and a TV show)," https://starlingdb.org/music/temp/samoans.html, accessed July 7, 2023; Florian Braun, "Angry Samoans," *Juice Magazine*, January 1, 2008.

19. Ugly Americans, "Homophobia," released 1985, track 6 on *Who's Been Sleeping . . . in My Bed*, Armageddon; Shannon Mullen, "Anti-Reagan Groups Jam, Speak Out on East," *The Chronicle*, September 17, 1984.

20. Mills, *Clockwork Orange County*; Crawford, *Salad Days*; Losurdo and Tillman, *You Weren't There*; Dead Kennedys, "Night of the Living Rednecks," released 1987, track 17 on *Give Me Convenience or Give Me Death*, Alternative Tentacles.

21. Gay Cowboys in Bondage, "Cowboys Are Gay," released 1986, track on *Live Seriousness*, TPOS; "Sockeye," *Trouser Press*, https://trouserpress.com/reviews/sockeye/, accessed July 7, 2023; Pajama Slave Dancers, "Homo Truck Driving Man," released 1982, track 19 on *All You Can Eat!*, Pajamara; Descendents, "I'm Not a Loser," released 1982, track 3 on *Milo Goes to College*, New Alliance Records; P. J. Kinzer, "The Descendents Have Grown Up, and It's Not So Bad," *Nashville Scene*, May 24, 2018; Naked Hippy, "Conservative F*g," released 1989, track 13 on *Naked Hippy*, Smile or Die! Records; *Threatening Society*, #5, 1988.

22. Patton, *Punk Crisis*, 147; *MRR*, #006, 1983; The Dickies, "Going Homo," released 1989, track 5 on *Second Coming*, Enigma; 7 Seconds, "Regress No Way," released 1986, track 1 on *Walk Together, Rock Together*, Better Youth Organization.

23. "Pat Buchanan's Greatest Hits," *Washington Post*, February 4, 1987; Cannon, *President Reagan*, 814; Wilentz, *The Age of Reagan*, 185.

24. Jack Tragic, "Homo Parade," released 1989, track 1 on *White Ni**er Rising*, Old Nick Productions; M.O.D., "A.I.D.S.," released 1987, track 19 on *U.S.A. for M.O.D.*, Caroline Records; Bedlam, "AIDS Alley," released 1985, track 6 on *Last Train to Hagerstown*, Bona Fide Records; The Left, "Jesus Loves the Left," https://georgebrigman.com/page11.html, accessed October 27, 2023; Bedlam, "A.I.D.S.," released 1984, track 6 on *(Total) Bedlam*, Buy Our Records; Cherri Bird, "INTERVIEW: Bill Milano—M.O.D.," *The Rock-Pit*, June 29, 2017, https://www.therockpit.net/2017/interview-billy-milano-m-o-d/; Sean L. Maloney, "Twenty-Six Years Later, and There's Still No Apologizing for Thrash-Metal Weirdos M.O.D.'s Offensive Debut," *Nashville Scene*, July 3, 2013.

25. Hadden, "The Rise and Fall of American Televangelism," 120; Johnson, *Sleepwalking through History*, 196; The Silent Age, "Video Christians," released 1982, track 1 on *The Silent Age*, Remote Records.

26. Controllers, "Electric Church," released 1979, track 2 on *Tooth and Nail*, Upsetter.

27. "Los Olvidados," Alternative Tentacles Records, https://alternativetentacles.com/pages/artist-page/los-olvidados, accessed April 7, 2023; Los Olvidados, "Pay Salvation," released 1982, track 11 on *Not So Quiet on the Western Front*, Alternative Tentacles; "Bakker Bought Rolls-Royce for Himself and for His Ministry with AM-Fox Bakker," *APNews*, May 21, 1987.

28. Government Issue, "Religious Ripoff," released 1981, track 1 on *Legless Bull*, Dischord; Bob Dyer, "Falling from Grace, Part 5: The Rev. Ernest Angley—Modest House, Big Plane (Boeing 747)," *Akron Beacon Journal*, October 18, 2014; "Pastor to Presidents: Billy Graham and Ronald Reagan," *Billy Graham Library*, November 19, 2020; Bob Dyer, "Ernest Angley Admitted Sexual Encounter," *Akron Beacon Journal*, January 23, 2019.

29. D.R.I., "God Is Broke," released 1985, track 10 on *Dealing with It!*, Bloody Skull; P.T.L. Klub, "Join P.T.L.," released 1985, track 4 on *13 Commandments*, Mystic Records; P.T.L. Klub, "M.X.," released 1985, track 11 on *13 Commandments*, Mystic Records; Sherryl Connelly, "The Story of Televangelists Jim and Tammy Faye Bakker's Fall from Grace," *New York Daily News*, August 5, 2017.

30. Art Harris, "Falwell Takes Control, Bars Bakker from PTL," *Washington Post*, April 29, 1987; Myra McPherson, "The Rise of the Falwell Empire," *Washington Post*, September 26, 1984; Surrogate Brains, "Jim and Tammy," released 1988, track 4 on *Surrogate Brains/I Am the Hamster*, Fascist Food Records; Prevaricators, "Jesus H Falwell," released 1985, track 5 on *Snubculture*, Disrupted.

31. Prevaricators, "Jesus H Falwell"; "Letter from Jerry Falwell on Keeping Old Time Gospel Hour on Air," *UNT Digital Library*, August 13, 1981, accessed October 14, 2022.

32. Hadden and Shupe, *Televangelism*, 29.

33. Lekachman, *Visions and Nightmares*, 214; "Remarks at the St. Ann's Festival in Hoboken, New Jersey."

34. "Remarks to the National Catholic Education Association in Chicago, Illinois"; *MRR*, #006, 1983; Negative Element, "Temples of Corruption," released 1983, track 3 on *Yes, We Have No Bananas!*, Version Sound; Negative Element, "Pay the Lord," released 1983, track 8 on *Yes, We Have No Bananas!*, Version Sound.

35. *MRR*, #002, 1982; Channel 3, "Catholic Boy," released 1982, track 4 on *Fear of Life*, Posh Boy; "Remarks to the National Catholic Education Association in Chicago, Illinois."

36. *MRR*, #032, 1986; Subculture, "Catholic Schools," released 1985, track 14 on *I Heard a Scream*, No Core.

37. McAndrews, *What They Wished For*, 198; Chemotherapy, "Smart, Tough, and Catholic," released 1983, track 7 on *Chemotherapy*, Uprising; Craig Lee, "Pop-O-Pies Put an End to the Search," *Los Angeles Times*, October 21, 1983; Pop-O-Pies, "The Catholics Are Attacking," released 1981, track 2 on *The White EP*, 415.

38. Bad Religion, "Faith in God," released 1982, track 4 on *How Could Hell Be Any Worse?*, Epitaph; Bad Religion, "The Voice of God Is Government," released 1982, track 12 on *How Could Hell Be Any Worse?*, Epitaph; Uniform Choice, "Religion Is Recruiting," released 2015, track 3 on *1982 Orange Peel Sessions*, Dr. Strange; Rights of the Accused, "Faith," released 1984, track 1 on *Innocence*, Little Farmer; Heart Attack, "God Is Dead," released 1981, track 3 on *God Is Dead*, Gun Fun Music; The Fartz, "Bible Stories," released 1982, track 10 on *World Full of Hate . . .*, Alternative Tentacles;

Battalion of Saints, "Second Coming," released 1984, track 7 on *Second Coming*, Nutrons; False Prophets, "7 Deadly Sins," released 1986, track 1 on *False Prophets*, Alternative Tentacles; Poison Idea, "God Not God," released 1986, track 3 on *Kings of Punk*, Pusmort; Minor Threat, "Filler," released 1981, track 1 on *Filler*, Dischord.

39. Crucifix, "Religion Kills," released 1981, track 3 on *Crucifix*, Universal; The Proletariat, "Religion Is the Opium of the Masses," released 1982, track 8 on *This Is Boston, Not L.A.*, Modern Method; (Impatient) Youth, "Praise the Lord and Pass the Ammunition," released 1982, track 21 on *Not So Quiet on the Western Front*, Alternative Tentacles; Really Red, "White Lies," released 1981, track 9 on *Teaching You the Fear*, C.I.A.; Unseen Force, "Jesus Slaves," released 1986, track 11 on *In Search of the Truth*, Turbulent; Social Unrest, "Lord's Prayer," released 1982, track 4 on *Rat in a Maze*, Libertine; The Freeze, "Warped Confessional," released 1981, track 1 on *Rabid Reaction*, Modern Method.

40. Anti-Climex, "Game of the Arseholes," released 1986, track 5 on *What Are You Doing about That Hole in Your Head?*, Rot; Asocial, "Religion Sucks," released 1986, track 4 on *Religion Sucks*, Dissonance; Dayglo Abortions, "Religions Bumfucks," released 1986, track 12 on *Feed Us a Fetus*, Fringe; D.O.A., *Positively D.O.A. (No God No Country No Lies)*, released 1981, Alternative Tentacles; Fear and Loathing, "Moral Majority," released 1986, track 2 on *A Box of Fluffy Ducks*, El Crappo; Death Sentence, "Moral Majority," released 1985, track 3 on *Ryan—Thanks for the Support*, Single Bullet Theory; Porkeria T., "Religion, Esperanza, Desperados," released 1985, track 2 on *Porkeria T.*, no label; Anti-Dogmatikks, "Campos de Cruces," released 1984, track 9 on *La Lucha Continua!!!*, Prod. N.D.F.; Autodefensa, "No Religion—No Poder," released 1984, track 12 on *La Lucha Continua!!!*, Prod. N.D.F.; Karne Krua, "Jesus Is Dead," released 1988, track 6 on *Cenas de Ódio e Revolta*, Lokaos.

41. Chaotic Dischord, "Fuck Religion, Fuck Politics, Fuck the Lot of You," released 1983, track 1 on *Fuck Religion, Fuck Politics, Fuck the Lot of You*, Riot City; Discharge, "Religion Instigates," released 1980, track 5 on *Fight Back*, Clay; Criminal Justice, "Victim of Religion," released 1983, track 2 on *Demo 83*, Justice; Suburban Filth, "Smash Religion," released 1983, track 24 on *Suburban Filth*, no label; Suburban Filth, "Religion Is Shit," released 1983, track 38 on *Suburban Filth*, no label; A.P.F. Brigade, "Man Created God," released 1982, track 14 on *Sick Society*, APF; A.P.F. Brigade, "Jesus Who," released 1982, track 5 on *Sick Society*, APF; Exploited, "Jesus Is Dead," released 1986, track 3 on *Jesus Is Dead*, Rough Justice.

42. Black Market Baby, "Downward Christian Soldiers," released 1983, track 1 on *Senseless Offerings*, Fountain of Youth.

43. Quoted in Rowse, *One Sweet Guy and What He Is Doing to You*, 131.

44. James Davison Hunter, "The Liberal Reaction," in Liebman and Wuthnow, *The New Christian Right*, 149.

Chapter Five

1. Quoted in Hunt, *We Begin Bombing in Five Minutes*, 1.

2. Hunt, *We Begin Bombing in Five Minutes*, 4; quoted in Paul Taylor, "Mondale Says President's Joke Wasn't Funny," *Washington Post*, August 14, 1984; Celestine Bohlen,

"Soviets Formally Denounce Reagan's Joke," *Washington Post*, August 16, 1984; Dad and the Boys, "Reagan," released 1985, track 1 on *Reagan (in the White House)*, Wave Records.

3. "Address to the Veterans of Foreign Wars Convention in Chicago."

4. Charles Krauthammer, "The Reagan Doctrine," *Washington Post*, July 19, 1985; Hugh Heclo, "The Mixed Legacies of Ronald Reagan," in Dunn, *The Enduring Reagan*, 22.

5. Clash, "London Calling," released 1979, track 1 on *London Calling*, CBS; The Weirdos, "We Got the Neutron Bomb," released 1978, track 1 on *We Got the Neutron Bomb*, Dangerhouse; Nena, "99 Red Balloons," released 1983, track 1 on *99 Red Balloons*, Epic; Prince, "Ronnie Talk to Russia," released 1981, track 5 on *Controversy*, Warner Bros.; Genesis, "Land of Confusion," released 1986, track 3 on *Invisible Touch*, Charisma; M.D.C., "Born to Die," released 1982, track 3 on *Millions of Dead Cops*, R Radical.

6. Quoted in Anthony Gregory, "Honor Reagan's Promise and Abolish the Selective Service," *Independent Institute*, June 15, 2004, https://www.independent.org/news/article.asp?id=1317; quoted in Richard Halloran, "Reagan, in a Shift, Plans to Continue Sign-Up for Draft, *New York Times*, January 8, 1982.

7. Quoted in Halloran, "Reagan, in a Shift"; The Sluts, "Draft Song," released 1982, track 13 on *12" Of Sluts*, Spread 'Um.

8. Ogg, *Dead Kennedys*, 1; Dead Kennedys, "When Ya Get Drafted," released 1980, track 3 on *Fresh Fruit for Rotting Vegetables*, Cherry Red.

9. Dicks, "I Hope You Get Drafted," released 1984, track 3 on *Peace?*, R Radical.

10. Dicks, "No Fuckin' War," released 1984, track 1 on *Peace?*, R Radical; Dicks, "Nobody Asked Me," released 1984, track 2 on *Peace?*, R Radical; "The Situation in Grenada," *United Nations Digital Library*, https://digitallibrary.un.org/record/56923?ln=en, accessed November 7, 2022.

11. D.R.I., "Draft Me," released 1983, track 4 on *Dirty Rotten* EP, Dirty Rotten Records; D.R.I., "War Crimes," released 1983, track 1 on *Dirty Rotten* EP, Dirty Rotten Records; D.R.I., "F.D.R.C." released 1983, track 5 on *Dirty Rotten* EP, Dirty Rotten Records; D.R.I., "I Don't Need Society," released 1985, track 13 on *Dealing with It!*, Death Records; D.R.I., "Stupid, Stupid War," released 1985, track 6 on *Dealing with It!*, Death Records; D.R.I., "Argument Then War," released 1985, track 19 on *Dealing with It!*, Death Records.

12. Bum Kon, "The Draft," released 1983, track 4 on *Drunken Sex Sucks*, Local Anesthetic Records; Bum Kon, "Nancy Reagan Fashion Show," released 2008, track 5 on *Drunk Sex Sucks*, Maximumrocknroll; Bum Kon, "Reagan Sucks," released 2008, track 14 on *Drunk Sex Sucks*, Maximumrocknroll; Neon Christ, "Draft Song," released 1984, track 2 on *Parental Suppression*, Social Crisis Records; Neon Christ, "Doom/After," released 1984, track 8 on *Parental Suppression*, Social Crisis Records; Christ on Parade, "Don't Draft Me," released 1985, track 1 on *On the Radio*, E-Ville Tapes; Christ on Parade, "Drop Out," released 1985, track 1 on *Sounds of Nature*, Pusmort; Christ on Parade, "The Plague-Mirror Image," released 1985, track 2 on *Sounds of Nature*, Pusmort; Christ on Parade, "Thoughts of War," released 1985, track 3 on *Sounds of Nature*, Pusmort; Christ on Parade, "America the Myth," released 1985, track 10 on *Sounds of Nature*, Pusmort; Entropy, "Draft or Die," released 1985, track 28 on *Entropy*, not on label; B.P., "There's Gonna Be a War," released 1986, track 1 on *Draft*

Beer . . . *Not Me*, No Clubs Records; B.P., "Better Off Dead," released 1986, track 2 on *Draft Beer . . . Not Me*, No Clubs Records; B.P., "Forget the World," released 1986, track 8 on *Draft Beer . . . Not Me*, No Clubs Records.

13. The Silent Age, "Hey Mister Reagan," released 1982, track 3 on *The Silent Age*, Remote Records.

14. Quoted in Philip Geyelin, "When Reagan Was Being Reagan," *Washington Post*, April 22, 1984; "Address to the Veterans of Foreign Wars Convention in Chicago"; Jerry's Kids, "Vietnam Syndrome," released 1983, track 6 on *Is This My World?*, Xclaim!

15. Circle One, "Vietnam Vets," released 1983, track 10 on *Patterns of Force*, Upstart Records.

16. Quoted in "The Beirut Bombing: Thirty Years Later," *Marines Corps University*, https://www.usmcu.edu/Research/Marine-Corps-History-Division/Brief-Histories/Beirut-Bombing-Thirty-Years-Later/, accessed November 7, 2022; Sex Mutants, "Lebanon," released 1985, track 2 on *Escape from Society*, Rag Records; D.I., "Going to Lebanon," released 1987, track 2 on *Rat Music for Rat People Vol. III*, CD Presents, Ltd.

17. Robert G. Kaiser, "White Paper on El Salvador Is Faulty," *Washington Post*, June 9, 1981; Raymond Bonner, "Time for the U.S. to Apologize to El Salvador," *The Nation*, April 15, 2016.

18. Johnson, *Sleepwalking through History*, 255; Insane, "El Salvador," released 1982, track 1 on *El Salvador*, No Future Records; Capitol Punishment, "El Salvador," released 1982, track 7 on *Not So Quiet on the Western Front*, Alternative Tentacles; MRR, #009, 1983; Fatal Existence, "A Living Hell," released 1983, track 8 on *Life's Adventure Begins Here*, not on label; Fatal Existence, "American Interests," track 15 on *Life's Adventure Begins Here*, not on label.

19. Dr. Know, "El Salvador," released 1987, track 3 on *The Original Group*, Mystic Records; David Klowden, "5051," *The Che Underground* (blog), https://cheunderground.site/related-bands/5051-2/, accessed November 13, 2023; 5.0.5.1., "El Salvador," released 1982, track 1 on *5.0.5.1.*, Biased Music Unlimited; Detention, "El Salvador," released 1983, track 2 on *Dead Rock 'n' Rollers*, Rigor Mortis.

20. Jello Biafra with D.O.A., "Wish I Was in El Salvador," released 1989, track 3 on *Last Scream of the Missing Neighbors*, Alternative Tentacles.

21. Lookouts!, "Don't Cry for Nicaragua," released 1987, track 20 on *One Planet, One People*, Lookout! Records; CBMT, "Ollie North," released 1988, track 3 on *Speak*, Scorch; CBMT, "Monarch Reagan," released 1988, track 5 on *Speak*, Scorch.

22. M.D.C., "Guns for Nicaragua," released 1987, track 8 on *Millions of Damn Christians*, R Radical Records.

23. Sewer Trout, "Wally & the Beaver Go to Nicaragua," released 1987, track 11 on *Turn It Around!*, Maximumrocknroll; quoted in Janet Cawley and Nathaniel Sheppard Jr., "Contributors Tell of 1-2 Punch for Contra Aid," *Chicago Tribune*, May 22, 1987; Sewer Trout, "Coors for Contras," released 1988, track 5 on *Songs about Drinking*, Lookout! Records.

24. Dugger, *On Reagan*, 350–51; Naked Raygun, "Managua," released 1984, track 13 on *Throb Throb*, Homestead Records.

25. Hurchalla, *Going Underground*, 102; "Three Minutes to Midnight," *Bulletin of the Atomic Scientists*, January 1984, https://thebulletin.org/files/1984%20Clock%20Statement.pdf.

26. Uniform Choice, "War Is Here," released 2015, track 4 on *1982 Orange Peel Sessions*, Dr. Strange Records; Agnostic Front, "Final War," released 1983, track 2 on *United Blood*, self-released.

27. Negative FX, "Government War Plans," released 2003, track 1 on *Government War Plans: 1982 Demo Tape Boston*, Distortions Records; The Abused, "War Games," released 1983, track 2 on *Loud and Clear*, Abused Music; Artificial Peace, "War Path," released 2010, track 11 on *Complete Session November 81*, Dischord Records.

28. Suburban Death Trip, "War," released 1985, track 19 on *Mind Shattering Power Blasts Demo*, self-released; Really Red, "War Sucks," released 1985, track 9 on *Rest in Pain*, C.I.A. Records; Musical Suicide, "War Is Bad," released 1984, track 3 on *Little Fish in the Big Sea*, Couch Records; Honor Roll, "War," released 1983, track 9 on *Your Skull Is My Bowl!*, self-released; The Fartz, "War," released 1981, track 8 on *Because This Fuckin' World Stinks*, Fartz Records.

29. T.S.O.L., "Superficial Love," released 1981, track 1 on *T.S.O.L.*, Posh Boy; Bad Religion, "Part III," released 1982, track 3 on *How Could Hell Be Any Worse?*, Epitaph; Marching Plague, "World War 4," released 1983, track 2 on *Rock 'n' Roll Asshole*, C.I.A. Records; Adrenaline O.D., "World War IV," released 1984, track 10 on *The Wacky Hi-Jinks of Adrenaline O.D.*, Buy Our Records; Harsh Reality, "Next World War," released 2021, track 10 on *Face the Harsh Reality*, Centredivider Records.

30. Scheer, *With Enough Shovels*, 2; *Flipside*, #41, 1983; quoted in Scheer, *With Enough Shovels*, 18; Scheer, *With Enough Shovels*, 100.

31. *MRR*, #049, 1987; Christ on a Crutch, "Nuclear Holocaust: A X-Mas Song," released 1988, track 5 on *Spread Your Filth*, Over the Top Records; D.I., "Nuclear Funeral," released 1983, track 2 on *Team Goon*, Revenge Records; Negative FX, "Nuclear Fear," released 1985, track 16 on *Negative FX*, Taang! Records; Decline, "Nuclear Death," released 1986, track 1 on *Decline*, self-released; Diddly Squat, "Nuclear Age," released 1987, track 3 on *No Questions*, self-released; Scheer, *With Enough Shovels*, 120.

32. Quoted in Geoffrey Godsell, "Limited Nuclear Warfare Why Reagan Worries Europe," *Christian Science Monitor*, October 21, 1981; Toxic Reasons, "Limited Nuclear War," released 1984, track 8 on *Kill by Remote Control*, Alternative Tentacles; Toxic Reasons, "Destroyer," released 1984, track 2 on *Kill by Remote Control*, Alternative Tentacles.

33. Schaller, *Reckoning with Reagan*, 122; Azerrad, *Our Band Could Be Your Life*, 68.

34. Lekachman, *Visions and Nightmares*, 126–27.

Chapter Six

1. "Speech before the University of Southern California Law Day Luncheon, Los Angeles"; "First Inaugural Address."

2. "Radio Address to the Nation on Crime and Criminal Justice Reform"; Kraska, *Militarizing the American Criminal Justice System*, 11.

3. Hurchalla, *Going Underground*, 55.

4. Hurchalla, *Going Underground*, 14.

5. Quoted in Spitz and Mullin, *We Got the Neutron Bomb*, 188, 189; quoted in Hurchalla, *Going Underground*, 14–16.

6. Chris Morris, "A New Wave of Police Brutality," Chris Morris's Wasted Space, https://watusichris.tumblr.com/post/106422397202/la-reader-elks-lodge-hall-police-riot-march-1979, accessed May 13, 2022.

7. Afflicted, "Here Comes the Cops," released 1984, track 10 on *International P.E.A.C.E. Compilation*, R Radical; Necros, "Police Brutality," released 1981, track 2 on *Sex Drive*, Touch and Go.

8. Pop-O-Pies, "Fascists Eat Donuts," released 1982, track 6 on *The White*, 415; NOFX, "Cops and Donuts," released 1988, track 6 on *The Album*, Mystic.

9. Crucifucks, "Cops for Fertilizer," released 1984, track 7 on *The Crucifucks*, Alternative Tentacles; Nazi Bitch and the Jews, "Dead Porker," released 1982, track 28 on *Not So Quiet on the Western Front*, Alternative Tentacles.

10. Blush, *American Hardcore*, 263.

11. Dicks, "Dicks Hate the Police," released 1980, track 1 on *The Dicks Hate the Police*, Radical; Dicks, "Anti-Klan (Part 1)," released 1983, track 1 on *Kill from the Heart*, SST Records; Dicks, "Pigs Run Wild," released 1983, track 7 on *Kill from the Heart*, SST Records.

12. Dicks, "No Nazi Friend," released 1983, track 7 on *Kill from the Heart*, SST Records.

13. Blush, *American Hardcore*, 269.

14. M.D.C., "Dead Cops," released 1982, track 2 on *Millions of Dead Cops*, R Radical; M.D.C., "I Remember," released 1982, track 6 on *Millions of Dead Cops*, R Radical.

15. Blush, *American Hardcore*, 273; Tom Curtis, "Support Your Local Police," *Texas Monthly*, September 1977, https://www.texasmonthly.com/news-politics/support-your-local-police/.

16. Mattson, *We're Not Here to Entertain*, 88; U-Ron, interview by David Ensminger, *MRR*, #326, 2010, https://www.maximumrocknroll.com/blast-from-the-past-really-red-part-two-u-ron-speaks/; quoted in Watson, *Race and the Houston Police Department*, 111.

17. Really Red, "Teaching You the Fear," released 1981, track 4 on *Teaching You the Fear*, C.I.A.

18. Susan Elizabeth Shepard, "A Houston Punk Band's Protest Anthem Still Resonates, Forty Years after Its Release," *Texas Monthly*, March 10, 2021, https://www.texasmonthly.com/arts-entertainment/houston-punk-bands-protest-anthem-still-resonates-forty-years-after-release/; AK-47, "The Badge Means You Suck," released 1980, track 1 on *The Badge Means You Suck*, Pineapple.

19. Watson, *Race and the Houston Police Department*, 129.

20. Quoted in Chick, *Spray Paint the Walls*, 66; Black Flag, "Police Story," released 1981, track 7 on *Damaged*, SST Records.

21. Black Flag, "Revenge," released 1980, track 2 on *Jealous Again*, SST Records.

22. Hillary Chapman, "The Work of Raymond Pettibon: Three Decades' of Provocative Imagery, Sardonic Wit, and Brazen Insights," *Artnet*, September 23, 2013, https://news.artnet.com/market/the-work-of-raymond-pettibon-35707.

23. Circle One, "Highway Patrolman," unreleased demo, 1981; Markey, *Slog*.

24. Julio Moran, "Police Kill Man, Wound Another Near 2 Beaches," *Los Angeles Times*, May 31, 1991; quoted in "Punk-Rock Time Capsule: John Macias and Circle One," *There's Something Hard in There*, May 4, 2013, http://theressomethinghardinthere.blogspot.com/2013/05/punk-rock-time-capsule-john-macias-and.html.

25. Negative FX, "Nightstick Justice," released 1985, track 13 on *Negative FX*, Taang!

26. Negative FX, "Citizens Arrest," released 1985, track 6 on *Negative FX*, Taang!

27. SSD, "Police Beat," released 1982, track 16 on *The Kids Will Have Their Say*, Dischord/XClaim!

28. State of Alert, "Public Defender," released 1981, track 9 on *No Police EP*, Dischord.

29. Red C, "Pressure's On," released 1982, track 18 on *Flex Your Head*, Dischord; Scream, "American Justice," released 1983, track 8 on *Still Screaming*, Dischord.

30. Government Issue, "No Rights," released 1981, track 8 on *Legless Bull EP*, Dischord.

31. Quoted in Mark Pringle, "Ian MacKaye—2009," http://www.markprindle.com/mackaye-i.htm, accessed August 26, 2002.

32. Dead Kennedys, "Police Truck," released 1980, track 1 on *Holiday in Cambodia/Police Truck*, Decay; Suicidal Tendencies, "Fascist Pig," released 1983, track 10 on *Suicidal Tendencies*, Frontier; Toxic Reasons, "Riot Squad," released 1982, track 5 on *Independence*, Risky; Urban Waste, "Police Brutality," released 1983, track 1 on *Police Brutality*, Mob-Style; Anti Scrunti Faction, "Protect and Serve," released 1985, track 4 on *A Sure Fuck*, Unclean Records.

33. "Remarks at the Annual Meeting of the International Association of Police Chiefs in New Orleans, Louisiana."

Chapter Seven

1. David M. Halbingfer, "In Lott's Life, Long Shadows of Segregation," *New York Times*, December 15, 2002; "Ronald Reagan's 1980 Neshoba County Fair Speech," *Neshoba Democrat*, accessed May 30, 2023; Lucks, *Reconsidering Reagan*, 144–52.

2. Ben Fountain, "American Crossroads: Reagan, Trump, and the Devil Down South: How the Republican Party's Dog-Whistle Racism, Refined by Richard Nixon and Perfected by Ronald Reagan, Led Inexorably to Donald Trump," *The Guardian*, March 5, 2016; Lucks, *Reconsidering Reagan*, 145–46.

3. Bates, *The Reagan Rhetoric*, 22, 43; Lucks, *Reconsidering Reagan*, 155–75.

4. Dunn, *The Enduring Reagan*, 9; Center on Budget and Policy Priorities, "Falling Behind"; Lowy, "Yuppie Racism," 446; Jefferson, "Black America in the 1980s," 2; Bowser, "Race Relations in the 1980s"; Kinloch, "Black America in the 1980s."

5. Duncombe and Tremblay, *White Riot*, 14; Necros, "Race Riot," released 1981, track 4 on *I.Q. 32*, Touch and Go/Dischord Records; *Forced Exposure*, #2, 1982; quoted in Lucks, *Reconsidering Reagan*, 11.

6. Unaware, "Race War," released 1982, track 14 on *Not So Quiet on the Western Front*, Alternative Tentacles; Corrosion of Conformity, "Race Riot," released 1982, track 42 on *No Core*, No Core Records; Corrosion of Conformity, "Friend in D.C.," released

1982, track 38 on *No Core*, No Core Records; Capitol Punishment, "Racism Is Ignorance," released 1985, track 7 on *When "Putsch" Comes to Shove*, Stage Dive; The Sarcastic Assholes, "Racism Sucks," released 1985, track 2 on *Menthol Man*, CRS Productions; Violent Image, "Racist," released 1985, track 11 on *Message from America—Hardcore Has Come of Age*, Urinal Records; Stark Raving Mad, "Racist Pig," released 1985, track 6 on *Amerika*, Slob Records; 5 Balls of Power, "Lazy Racist Pig," released 1986, track 8 on *Operations in Musical Warfare*, not on label; Stark Raving Mad, "S.O.S." released 1985, track 9 on *Amerika*, Slob Records.

7. *MRR*, #002, 1982; 7 Seconds, "Anti Klan," released 1982, track 7 on *Skins, Brains & Guts*, Alternative Tentacles; Karlyn Barker, "A Resurgence by the Klan," *Washington Post*, June 2, 1980; 7 Seconds, "Redneck Society," released 1982, track 3 on *Skins, Brains & Guts*, Alternative Tentacles; 7 Seconds, "Racism Sucks," released 1982, track 5 on *Skins, Brains & Guts*, Alternative Tentacles.

8. "The 15 Year Battle for Martin Luther King, Jr. Day," *National Museum of African American History and Culture*, https://nmaahc.si.edu/explore/stories/15-year-battle-martin-luther-king-jr-day, accessed May 30, 2023; Steven V. Roberts, "King Holiday Faces a Filibuster," *New York Times*, October 4, 1983; John Dodd, "How Jesse Helms Made the Reagan Revolution Possible," *North Carolina History Project*, https://northcarolinahistory.org/commentary/how-jesse-helms-made-the-reagan-revolution-possible/, accessed May 30, 2023; "President Reagan's Remarks at a Dinner for Senator Jesse Helms of North Carolina"; quoted in Francis X. Clines, "Reagan's Doubts on Dr. King Disclosed," *New York Times*, October 22, 1983.

9. Perlstein, *Reaganland*, 830; "Radio Address to the Nation on the Anniversary of the Birth of Martin Luther King, Jr."; quoted in "Reagan," *Alabama Journal*, September 2, 1980; quoted in "Ku Klux Leader Promotes Reagan as Klan's Candidate," *Alabama Journal*, April 16, 1984; Dorothy Gilliam, "KKK Support," *Washington Post*, April 23, 1984.

10. 7 Seconds, "Anti Klan," released 1982, track 7 on *Skins, Brains & Guts*, Alternative Tentacles; David Cunningham, "The Civil Rights Era and the Rise of the Ku Klux Klan," *OUPblog*, January 13, 2015, https://blog.oup.com/2015/01/north-carolina-ku-klux-klan-civil-rights/.

11. The Fartz, "Take a Stand (against the Klan)," released 1982, track 15 on *World Full of Hate . . .* , Alternative Tentacles; *MRR*, #004, 1983; quoted in Lucks, *Reconsidering Reagan*, 133.

12. Karlyn Barker, "A Resurgence by the Klan," *Washington Post*, June 2, 1980; Dicks, "Anti-Klan," released 1983, track 1 on *Kill from the Heart*, SST Records; David Ensminger, "The Dicks from Texas: A Punk Band That Actually Scared People," *Houston Press*, October 7, 2015; Spastic Rats, "Cops and Klan," released 1984, track 3 on *Spread the Disease*, Vermin Scum Records; Up-Tight, "Cops Are the KKK," released 1987, track 14 on *Up-Tight*, not on label; *MRR*, #023, 1985; No Labels, "Klan Man," released 1982, track 17 on *No Core*, No Core Records; Fatal Vision, "Klan Man," released 1985, track 3 on *Connecticut Fun*, Incas Records; Ramones, "The KKK Took My Baby Away," released 1981, track 3 on *Pleasant Dreams*, Sire.

13. Surrogate Brains, "Extreme Racial Pride," released 1988, track 25 on *The Thing That Ate Floyd*, Lookout! Records; quoted in "Raising Voices against Apartheid," *New*

York Times, December 11, 1984; Lucks, *Reconsidering Reagan*, 13; Surrogate Brains, "In These Troubled Times," released 1988, track 1 on *Surrogate Brains/I Am the Hamster*, Fascist Food Records.

14. Carter, *The Reagan Years*, 64; "Campaign Report: Mrs. Harris Quotes Klan in Its Backing of Reagan," *New York Times*, August 7, 1980; Nightmare on Sesame Street, "Let's Smash the Klan," released 1988, track 1 on *Let's Smash the Klan: 13 Song Demo*, Assault with Intent to Free; Clitboys, "I Hate the Ku Klux Klan," released 1983, track 3 on *We Don't Play the Game*, Detour Records.

15. Wayne King, "Reagan, after Apology, Explains His Recounting of an Ethnic Joke; Request to Repeat Story 'There Goes Connecticut,'" *New York Times*, February 19. 1980; quoted in Dugger, *On Reagan*, 202.

16. Daniel S. Lucks, "Racism Wrapped Up in Sunny, Fatherly Love: Puncturing the Iconic Myth of Reagan in 'The Reagans' Docuseries," *Beacon Broadside*, February 12, 2021, https://www.beaconbroadside.com/broadside/2021/02/racism-packaged-in-sunny-fatherly-love-puncturing-the-iconic-myth-of-reagan-in-the-reagans-docuserie.html; Dugger, *On Reagan*, 217; United Mutation, "White Amerika," released 1983, track 3 on demo tape, not on label.

17. Tim Scott, "How The Proletariat Became One of the Most Incendiary Bands in Reagan's America," *Vice*, September 4, 2016; Carlos Ramirez, "Richard Brown (The Proletariat)," *No Echo: Hardcore, Metal and Everything in Between*, October 17, 2017, https://www.noecho.net/interviews/richard-brown-the-proletariat; The Proletariat, "White Hands," released 1982, track 6 on *Distortion*, not on label; Lucks, *Reconsidering Reagan*, 218, 227.

18. Minor Threat, "Guilty of Being White," released 1981, track 3 on *In My Eyes*, Dischord Records; *MRR*, #008, 1983; Lucks, *Reconsidering Reagan*, 177.

19. Black Flag, "White Minority," released 1980, track 3 on *Jealous Again*, SST Records; "Population Profile of the United States 1984/85," *United States Census Bureau*, https://www2.census.gov/library/publications/1987/demographics/p23-150.pdf, accessed May 31, 2023; *Ripper*, #6, 1981.

20. Quoted in Lucks, *Reconsidering Reagan*, 150; "ACLU History: Taking a Stand for Free Speech In Skokie," ACLU, https://www.aclu.org/other/aclu-history-taking-stand-free-speech-skokie, accessed May 31, 2023; Kathleen Belew, "The History of White Power," *New York Times*, April 18, 2018; "A Timeline of the Racist Skinhead Movement," *Southern Poverty Law Center*, https://www.splcenter.org/fighting-hate/intelligence-report/2015/timeline-racist-skinhead-movement, accessed May 31, 2023.

21. Dead Kennedys, "Nazi Punks—Fuck Off," released 1981, track 1 on *Nazi Punks Fuck Off!/Moral Majority*, Alternative Tentacles; Robert Pursell, "How L.A. Punks of the '80s and '90s Kept Neo-Nazis out of Their Scene," *Los Angeles Magazine*, January 31, 2018; August Brown, "Jello Biafra on 'Nazi Punks' and Hate Speech," *Los Angeles Times*, August 9, 2012.

22. F.U.'s, "T.N.H.," released 1982, track 7 on *Kill for Christ*, Xclaim!; *MRR*, #005, 1983; *MRR*, #008, 1983; The Freeze, "Nazi Fun," released 1983, track 7 on *Land of the Lost*, Modern Method Records.

23. Stains, "John Wayne Was a Nazi," released 1981, track 1 on *John Wayne Was a Nazi*, R Radical Records; Critchlow, *When Hollywood Was Right*, 155–83; Eli Rosen-

berg, "'I Believe in White Supremacy': John Wayne's Notorious 1971 Playboy Interview Goes Viral on Twitter," *Washington Post*, February 20, 2019; Ronald Reagan, "Unforgettable John Wayne," *Readers Digest*, October 1979, 114–19; Stains, "Born to Die," released 1981, track 2 on *John Wayne Was a Nazi*, R Radical Records.

24. Hypnotics, "Nazi Snotzy," released 1982, track 4 on *Indoor Friends*, Enigma; Antidote, "Nazi Youth," released 1983, track 2 on *Thou Shalt Not Kill*, Antidote Records; Krakdown, "Nazi Threat," released 1987, track 2 on *Krakdown*, not on label; Screaming Mailboxes of Destiny, "Nazi Skins," released 1986, track 10 on *Screaming Mailboxes of Destiny*, Gravelvoice Records; The Lookouts!, "Nazi Dreams," released 1987, track 14 on *One Planet One People*, Lookout! Records; Last Round Up, "Tyrant Nazi," released 1989, track 8 on *Wasted Time Demo*, not on label; Dare to Defy, *Steamrolling Neo-Nazis in the 90's*, released 1989, Totally Hot Records.

25. Lucks, *Reconsidering Reagan*, 7; quoted in Rick Perlstein, "Exclusive: Lee Atwater's Infamous 1981 Interview on the Southern Strategy," *The Nation*, November 12, 2012; quoted in Lucks, *Reconsidering Reagan*, 196.

26. Necros, "Race Riot," released 1981, track 4 on *I.Q. 32*, Touch and Go/Dischord Records; Chronic Sick, "There Goes the Neighborhood," released 1983, track 1 on *Cutest Band in Hardcore*, Mutha Records; Kevin Lamastra, "Chronic Sick Live Up to Name on 'Cutest' Hardcore E.P.," https://www.kbdrecords.com/2008/10/27/chronic-sick-cutest-band-in-hardcore-ep-12/, accessed June 5, 2023; "Rettsounds—Chronic Sick," *Vice*, January 14, 2011.

27. Lucks, *Reconsidering Reagan*, 109; The Landlords, "Bathroom Bigot," released 1984, track 4 on *Hey! It's a Teenage House Party!*, Catch Trout Records; MRR, #023, 1985; erinohare, "The Hard Core: Charlottesville Punk's Ongoing Legacy," *C-Ville*, February 13, 2019, https://www.c-ville.com/the-hard-core-charlottesville-punks-ongoing-legacy/; quoted in Lucks, *Reconsidering Reagan*, 176.

28. Dicks, "Dicks Hate the Police," released 1980, track 1 on *The Dicks Hate the Police*, Radical Records; M.D.C., "Dead Cops/America's So Straight," released 1982, track 2 on *Millions of Dead Cops*, R Radical Records; Really Red, "Teaching You the Fear," released 1981, track 4 on *Teaching You the Fear*, C.I.A. Records; AK-47, "The Badge Means You Suck," released 1980, track 1 on *The Badge Means You Suck*, Pineapple Records; Stark Raving Mad, "Racist Pig," released 1985, track 6 on *Amerika*, Slob Records.

29. Quoted in Lucks, *Reconsidering Reagan*, 155; Lucks, *Reconsidering Reagan*, 228.

Outro

1. "Man Who Tried to Assassinate Ronald Reagan Says 'Violence Not the Way' after Donald Trump Shooting," *Sky News*, July 18, 2024.

2. Azerrad, *Our Band Could Be Your Life*, 4; Michael Barbaro, "Donald Trump Clung to 'Birther' Lie for Years, And Still Isn't Apologetic," *New York Times*, September 16, 2016; Nina Totenberg, "Racially Charged Remarks Derailed Trump's Attorney General Nominee 30 Years Ago," NPR, November 18, 2016.

3. Lucks, *Reconsidering Reagan*, 253; Paul Bedard, "Reagan for Trump: Meese Leads over 200 Reaganites to Team Trump," *Washington Examiner*, October 29, 2016; Peggy

Noonan, "Donald Trump Is No Ronald Reagan," *Wall Street Journal*, June 24, 2016; John McCormick, "Tom Cotton Compares Reagan to Trump in Speech on Future of the GOP," *Wall Street Journal*, March 8, 2022; James Capretta, "Why Attempts to Compare Donald Trump to Ronald Reagan Fall Flat," *The Dispatch*, March 30, 2022.

4. Thompson, *Punk Productions*, 49; Coffin Break, "Kill the President," released 1991, track 1 on *Kill the President*, C/Z Records; Greg Grandin, "How George H. W. Bush's Pardons for Iran-Contra Conspirators Set the Stage for Trump's Impunity," *Democracy Now!*, December 4, 2018.

5. Markey, *1991: The Year Punk Broke*; Knowledge, "Clinton Youth," released 1998, track 6 on *A Gift before I Go*, Asian Man Records.

6. Quoted in Bill Keller, "The Radical Presidency of George W. Bush; Reagan's Son," *New York Times*, January 26, 2003; U.S. Bombs, *Tora! Tora! Tora!*, released 2001, TKO Records; Wartorn, *Adolf Bushler War Bastard*, released 2005, Crimes against Humanity Records; Phobia, "Bush Is Hitler," released 2007, track 16 on *They've Taken Everything*, Profane Existence; Death to W, "Heil to Bush," released 2003, track 3 on *Propaganda U$A*, not on label.

7. Bad Religion, *The Empire Strikes First*, released 2004, Epitaph; quoted in Ruland, *Do What You Want*, 251; Ruland, *Do What You Want*, 252. Bad Religion, "Sorrow," released 2004, track 3.2 on DVD *Rock against Bush Vol. 1*, Fat Wreck Chords; Bad Religion, "Let Them Eat War," released 2004, track 2 on *Rock against Bush Vol. 2*, Fat Wreck Chords; Forward, "Fuck Bush!," released 2004, track 1 on *Burn Down the Corrupted Justice*, Partners in Crime; The Pussy Pirates, "Burning Bush," released 2008, track 9 on *Plastic Paradise*, Riot Grrrl Ink; The Brainwashed, "Kill George Bush!!!," released 2002, track 2 on demo, not on label; Environmental Youth Crunch, "George W. Shitbag," released 2008, track 2 on *We Love to Smush the Family of Bush!*, Dead Tank Records; Bantha Fodder, "Naming a Library after George Bush Is Like Naming a Delicatessen after Dahmer," released 2009, track 21 on *Depending on Which Side You Play First*, Arbco.

8. Dan Ozzi, "Barack Obama, the President That Punk Gave a Pass to," *Vice*, January 12, 2017; Josiah Hughes, "Jello Biafra Writes Open Letter to Obama," *exclaim!*@#, December 16, 2008, https://exclaim.ca/music/article/jello_biafra_writes_open_letter_to_obama; Jello Biafra and the Guantanamo School of Medicine, "Barackstar O'Bummer," released 2012, track 2 on *Shock-U-Py!*, Alternative Tentacles.

9. Frank Rich, "What the Donald Shares with the Ronald," *New York*, June 1, 2016; quoted in Susan B. Glasser, "Is Trump the Second Coming of Reagan? Fox News's Bret Baier Wants You to Think He Just Might Be," *New Yorker*, May 18, 2018; Crisis Man, "Commander in Chief," released 2022, track 6 on *Asleep in America*, not on label.

10. Witcher, *Getting Right with Reagan*, 271; Kyle Smith, "Donald Trump Is the Punk-Rock President America Deserves," *New York Post*, November 9, 2016; Fall Children, "Donald Trump Is Not My Fuhrer," released 2017, track 4 on *Make Punk Rock Great Again*, not on label; Candy Warpop, "Trump Is a Nazi," released 2017, track 20 on *The Whole World Is Watching*, SquidHat Records.

11. Bi Tyrant, "Fuck You Donald Trump," released 2016, track 8 on *Bisexual Tyrant*, not on label; The Vatican, "Trump Card," released 2016, track 1 on *The Trump Card*, not on label; Savage World, "Do You Think Donald Trump Is Flammable?," released 2016, track 6 on *Savage World*, not on label; Cliterati, "Make America Hate Again,"

released 1986, track 2 on *Cliterati*, Tankcrimes; Oi Polloi, "Donald Trump—Fuck You," released 2017, track 1 on *Donald Trump—Fuck You!/UK 2017*, Urinal Vinyl Records; Acidez, "Donald Trump Must Die," released 2017, track 3 on *Revolution Has No Borders*, Bambam Records; SFH, "Donald Trump Is an Asshole," released 2017, track 4 on *Kinda Sucks*, Ugly Pop Records; Isotope Soap, "Trump des Willens," released 2017, track 5 on *Piñata Chaos*; Giftigt Avfall, "Trampa Ihjäl Trump," released 2017, track 5 on *Krossa SD*, Anti Ljudkvalité Wreckords; The Sensitives, "Trump," released 2017, track 2 on *Love Songs for Haters*, Sunny Bastards.

12. D.O.A., "Fucked Up Donald," released 2016, track 1 on *Fucked Up Donald*, Sudden Death Records; D.O.A., "All the President's Men," released 2020, track 1 on *Treason*, Sudden Death Records; Bill Pearis, "Watch D.O.A. Rail against Trump in 'All the President's Men' Video," *Brooklyn Vegan*, September 21, 2020, https://www.brooklynvegan.com/watch-d-o-a-rail-against-trump-in-all-the-presidents-men-video/.

13. Sharptooth, "Fuck You Donald Trump," released 2017, track 4 on *Clever Girl*, Pure Noise Records; "Album Review: Sharptooth *Clever Girl*," *Metal Injection*, November 10, 2017, https://metalinjection.net/reviews/sharptooth-clever-girl; Social Divorce, "Trump University," released 2017, track 4 on *New York State Politics*, Bankrupt Studios; Crutch, "Trump Hunter," released 2017, track 10 on *Crutch/Pavel Chekov*, not on label; Battle Pussy, "No Trump," released 2017, track 6 on *Revolution*, not on label; Liquids, "I Killed Donald Trump," released 1987, track 3 on *Hot Liqs*, Hip Kid Records.

14. Jello Biafra and the Guantanamo School of Medicine, "Satan's Combover," released 2020, track 1 on *Tea Party Revenge Porn*, Alternative Tentacles; Jon Blistein, "Jello Biafra Offers Up a Biting Anti-Trump Screed on 'Satan's Combover,'" *Rolling Stone*, November 3, 2020; Ruland, *Do What You Want*, 290; Bad Religion, "The Kids Are Alt-Right," released 2018, track 1 on *The Kids Are Alt-Right*, Epitaph; Ruland, *Do What You Want*, 290–91; Graham Hartmann, "Bad Religion Lampoon Political Extremism with 'The Kids Are Alt-Right,'" *Loudwire*, June 20, 2018, https://loudwire.com/bad-religion-the-kids-are-alt-right/; Bad Religion, "End of History," released 2019, track 6 on *Age of Unreason*, Epitaph.

15. "Interview with Bill Stephens (Naked Raygun)," *ALT77*, January 5, 2022, https://alt77.com/interview-with-bill-stephens-naked-raygun/; Dan Reilly, "Q&A: Naked Raygun's Jeff Pezzati on New Album, Dave Grohl's Fandom, and 'Caustic' Steve Albini," *SPIN*, January 8, 2016; Sean McLennan, "Interview: Naked Raygun's Jeff Pezzati and Fritz Dorea on First Record in 30 Years," *New Noise Magazine*, January 20, 2022; Naked Raygun, "Living in the Good Times," released 2021, track 3 on *Over the Overlords*, Wax Trax! Records.

16. Dictor, *MDC*, 188; "Album Review: MDC—Mein Trumpf," *ThePunkSite.com*, November 29, 2017, https://www.thepunksite.com/reviews/album-review-mdc-mein-trumpf/; M.D.C., "Mein Trumpf," released 2017, track 1 on *Mein Trumpf*, Primordial Records; M.D.C., "Born to Die," released 2017, track 12 on *Mein Trumpf*, Primordial Records; Kory Grow, "No Trump! No KKK! No Fascist USA!: The Punk History," *Rolling Stone*, November 21, 2016; M.D.C., "Bye Bye Donny," released 2022, track 1 on *Bye Bye Donny*, Grimace Records; Max McLaughlin, "Album Review: MDC—Mein Trumpf," *New Noise Magazine*, November 28, 2017.

17. Ambrosch, *The Poetry of Punk*, 47.

Bibliography

Newspapers and Magazines

The following newspapers and magazines were consulted, all online. When used in the book, the accompanying note includes specific bibliographic details including either date of publication or access and web address, when applicable.

Akron Beacon Journal	Juice	Phoenix New Times
Alabama Journal (Montgomery)	Los Angeles Magazine	Politico
	Los Angeles Times	PR Week
APNews	Nashville Scene	Rolling Stone
Atlantic	Nation	San Francisco Chronicle
CNN	Neshoba Democrat	SPIN
Chronicle (Durham, NC)	New Noise Magazine	Time
Columbia Record	New York Daily News	Townhall
C-Ville Weekly	New York Magazine	Vice
Democracy Now!	New York Post	Village Voice
Dispatch	New York Times	Washington Examiner
Guardian	NPR	Washington Post
Houston Press	OC Weekly	Westworld

Zines

The following zines were consulted and quotes taken from each. All were accessed online with the *Internet Archive* except *Touch & Go* and *We've Got the Power!*, their complete editions published by Bazillion Points being used instead. For *Maximum Rocknroll*, which was primarily to find reviews of bands/albums, the search engine at maximumrocknroll.com/reviews/ was very handy as well.

Flipside	Maximum Rocknroll (MRR)	Threatening Society
Forced Exposure		Touch & Go
Ink Disease	Ripper	We Got the Power!

Articles

Ambrosch, Gerfried. "American Punk: The Relations between Punk Rock, Hardcore, and American Culture." *American Studies* 60, nos. 2/3 (2015): 215–33.

Begnal, Martin. "American Punk and the Rhetoric of 'Political Correctness.'" *Popular Music and Society* 46, no. 2 (2023): 172–90.

Bell, Terrel H. "Education Policy Development in the Reagan Administration." *Phi Delta Kappan* 67, no. 7 (1986): 487–93.

Bennett, Andy. "Punk's Not Dead: The Continuing Significance of Punk Rock for an Older Generation of Fans." *Sociology* 40, no. 2 (2006): 219–35.

"Black America Has Overlooked the Racist Policies of Ronald Reagan." *Journal of Blacks in Higher Education* 64 (2009): 13–14.

Bowser, Benjamin P. "Race Relations in the 1980s: The Case of the United States." *Journal of Black Studies* 15, no. 3 (1985): 307–24.

Brodinsky, Ben. "Something Happened: Education in the Seventies." *Phi Delta Kappan* 61, no. 4 (1979): 238–41.

Brown, Peter Robert. "The Center at the Margins: American Exceptionalism in California Punk, ca. 1977–1983." *Popular Music and Society* 44, no. 4 (2021): 357–77.

Center on Budget and Policy Priorities. "Falling Behind: A Report on How Blacks Have Fared Under Reagan." *Journal of Black Studies* 17, no. 2 (1986): 148–71.

Clabaugh, Gary K. "The Educational Legacy of Ronald Reagan." *Educational Horizons* 82, no. 4 (2004): 256–59.

Clark, David L., and Mary Anne Amiot. "The Impact of the Reagan Administration on Federal Education Policy." *Phi Delta Kappan* 63, no. 4 (1981): 258–62.

Coe, Kevin. "The Language of Freedom in the American Presidency, 1933–2006." *Presidential Studies Quarterly* 37, no. 3 (2007): 375–98.

Cullen, Shaun. "White Skin, Black Flag: Hardcore Punk, Racialization, and the Politics of Sound in Southern California." *Criticism* 58, no. 1 (2016): 59–85.

Dallek, Matthew. "Not Ready for Mt. Rushmore: Reconciling the Myth of Ronald Reagan with the Reality." *American Scholar* 78, no. 3 (2009): 13–23.

"Falling Behind: A Report on How Blacks Have Fared Under Reagan." *Journal of Black Studies* 17, no. 2 (1986): 148–71.

Foner, Eric. "The Contested History of American Freedom." *Pennsylvania Magazine of History and Biography* 137, no. 1 (2013): 13–31.

Gayte, Marie. "The Vatican and the Reagan Administration: A Cold War Alliance?" *Catholic Historical Review* 97, no. 4 (2011): 713–36.

Gilbert, Robert E. "The Politics of Presidential Illness: Ronald Reagan and the Iran-Contra Scandal." *Politics and the Life Sciences* 33, no. 2 (2014): 58–76.

Goulding, Simon. "The Sound of the Suburbs: Orwell, Bowling and the Estates in *Coming Up for Air*." *Literary London: Interdisciplinary Studies in the Representation of London* 7, no. 1 (2009).

Grinnell, George C. "Punk Is Dead: Notes toward the Apocalyptic Tone Adopted by Punk Rock." *English Studies in Canada* 45, no. 4 (2019): 53–81.

Hadden, Jeffrey K. "The Rise and Fall of American Televangelism." *Annals of the American Academy of Political Science* 527 (1993): 113–30.

Harrison, Michael M. "Reagan's World." *Foreign Policy* 43 (1981): 3–16.

Heclo, Hugh. "The Mixed Legacies of Ronald Reagan." *Presidential Studies Quarterly* 38, no. 4 (2008): 555–74.

Hoffmann, Stanley. "Requiem." *Foreign Policy* 42 (1981): 3–26.

Holden, Constance. "The Reagan Years: Environmentalists Tremble." *Science* 210, no. 4473 (1980): 988–91.

Jefferson, Alphine W. "Black America in the 1980s: Rhetoric vs. Reality." *Black Scholar* 17, no. 3 (1986): 2–9.

Johnson, Robert H. "Misguided Morality: Ethics and the Reagan Doctrine." *Political Science Quarterly* 103, no. 3 (1988): 509–29.
Johnson, Stephen D., and Joseph B. Tamney. "The Christian Right and the 1980 Presidential Election." *Journal for the Scientific Study of Religion* 21, no. 2 (1982): 123–31.
Kincheloe, Joe L. "Preparing a Place for the Righteous: Reagan, Education, and the New Right." *Journal of Thought* 20, no. 4 (1985): 3–17.
Kinloch, Graham C. "Black America in the 1980s: Theoretical and Practical Implications." *Humboldt Journal of Social Relations* 14, nos. 1/2 (1987): 1–23.
Knott, Stephen F. "Reagan's Critics." *National Interest* 44 (1996): 66–77.
Kraft, Michael E., and Norman J. Vig. "Environmental Policy in the Reagan Presidency." *Political Science Quarterly* 99, no. 3 (1984): 415–39.
Lafeber, Walter. "The Reagan Administration and Revolutions in Central America." *Political Science Quarterly* 99, no. 1 (1984); 1–25.
LaVoie, Mark. "Ronald Reagan's 'To Restore America': Political Lifeline in the 1976 Primary." *Southern Communication Journal* 86, no. 4 (2021): 362–74.
"Looking Back: Ronald Reagan, a Master of Racial Polarization." *Journal of Blacks in Higher Education* 58 (2007/8): 33–36.
Lowy, Richard. "Yuppie Racism: Race Relations in the 1980s." *Journal of Black Studies* 21, no. 4 (1991): 445–64.
Marley, David John. "Ronald Reagan and the Splintering of the Christian Right." *Journal of Church and State* 48, no. 4 (2006): 851–68.
Mattson, Kevin. "Did Punk Matter? Analyzing the Practices of Youth Subculture during the 1980s." *American Studies* 42, no. 1 (2001): 69–97.
Mervin, David. "Ronald Reagan's Place in History." *Journal of American Studies* 23, no. 2 (1989): 269–86.
National Commission on Excellence in Education. "A Nation at Risk: The Imperative for Educational Reform." *Elementary School Journal* 84, no. 2 (1983): 112–30.
Pach, Chester. "The Reagan Doctrine: Principle, Pragmatism, and Policy." *Presidential Studies Quarterly* 36, no. 1 (2006): 75–88.
Primuth, Richard. "Ronald Reagan Use of Race in the 1976 and 1980 Presidential Elections." *Georgia Historical Quarterly* 100, no. 1 (2016): 36–66.
Prinz, Jesse. "The Aesthetics of Punk Rock." *Philosophy Compass* 9, no. 9 (2014): 583–93.
Putnam, Jackson K. "Governor Reagan: A Reappraisal." *California History* 83, no. 4 (2006): 24–45.
Regan, Donald. "The Reagan Presidency in Perspective." *Presidential Studies Quarterly* 16, no. 3 (1986): 414–20.
Rowland, Robert C., and John M. Jones. "'Until Next Week': The Saturday Radio Addresses of Ronald Reagan." *Presidential Studies Quarterly* 32, no. 4 (2002): 84–110.
Scott, James M. "Reagan's Doctrine? The Formulation of an American Foreign Policy Strategy." *Presidential Studies Quarterly* 26, no. 4 (1996): 1047–61.
Stalcup, Scott. "Noise Noise Noise: Punk Rock's History since 1965." *Studies in Popular Culture* 23, no. 3 (2001): 51–64.

Sun, Marjorie. "Armand Hammer Named to Head Cancer Panel." *Science* 214, no. 4158 (1981): 311.

Traber, Daniel S. "L.A.'s 'White Minority': Punk and the Contradictions of Self-Marginalization." *Cultural Critique* no. 48 (2001): 30–64.

Tucker, Robert W. "Reagan's Foreign Policy." *Foreign Affairs* 68, no. 1 (1988/1989): 1–27.

Turrini, Joseph M. "'Well I Don't Care about History': Oral History and the Making of Collective Memory in Punk Rock." *Notes* 70, no. 1 (2013): 59–77.

Weinberg, Philip. "Masquerade for Privilege: Deregulation Undermining Environmental Protection." *Washington and Lee Law Review* 45, no. 4 (1988): 1321–43.

Wildavsky, Aaron. "The Triumph of Ronald Reagan." *The National Interest* no. 14 (1988/89): 3–9.

Books

Ambrosch, Gerfried. *The Poetry of Punk: The Meaning behind Punk Rock and Hardcore Lyrics*. New York: Routledge, 2018.

Andersen, Mark, and Mark Jenkins. *Dance of Days: Two Decades of Punk in the Nation's Capital*. Brooklyn: Akashic Books, 2009.

Azerrad, Michael. *Our Band Could Be Your Life: Scenes from the Indie Underground, 1981–1991*. New York: Back Bay Books, 2001.

Baldassare, Mark. *Trouble in Paradise: The Suburban Transformation in America*. New York: Columbia University Press, 1986.

Barrett, Laurence I. *Gambling with History: Reagan in the White House*. Garden City, NY: Doubleday, 1983.

Bates, Toby Glenn. *The Reagan Rhetoric: History and Memory in 1980s America*. DeKalb: Northern Illinois University Press, 2011.

Blush, Steven. *American Hardcore: A Tribal History*, 2nd ed. Port Townsend, WA: Feral House, 2010.

Boulware, Jack, and Silke Tudor. *Gimme Something Better: The Profound, Progressive, and Occasionally Pointless History of Bay Area Punk from Dead Kennedys to Green Day*. London: Penguin, 2009.

Bunch, Will. *Tear Down This Myth: The Right-Wing Distortion of the Reagan Legacy*. New York: Free Press, 2010.

Butz, Konstantin, and Robert A. Winkler., eds. *Hardcore Research: Punk, Practice, Politics*. Bielefeld, Germany: transcript, 2023.

Callen, Zachary, and Philip Rocco, eds. *American Political Development and the Trump Presidency*. Philadelphia: University of Pennsylvania Press, 2020.

Cannon, Lou. *President Reagan: The Role of a Lifetime*. New York: Simon & Schuster, 1991.

Carter, Hodding. *The Reagan Years*. New York: George Braziller, 1988.

Chick, Stevie. *Spray Paint the Walls: The Story of Black Flag*. Oakland, CA: PM Press.

Chidester, Jeffrey L., and Paul Kengor, eds. *Reagan's Legacy in a World Transformed*. Cambridge, MA: Harvard University Press, 2015.

Collins, Cyn. *Complicated Fun: The Birth of Minneapolis Punk and Indie Rock, 1974–1984*. St. Paul: Minnesota Historical Society Press, 2017.
Critchlow, Donald T. *When Hollywood Was Right: How Movie Stars, Studio Moguls, and Big Business Remade American Politics*. New York: Cambridge University Press, 2013.
Cunningham, David. *Klansville, U.S.A.: The Rise and Fall of the Civil Rights-Era Ku Klux Klan*. New York: Oxford University Press, 2012.
Dictor, Dave. *MDC: Memoir from a Damaged Civilization*. San Francisco: Manic D Press, 2016.
Dugger, Ronnie. *On Reagan: The Man and His Presidency*. New York: McGraw-Hill, 1983.
Duncan, Chris, ed. *My First Time: A Collection of First Punk Show Stories*. Oakland, CA: AK Press, 2007.
Duncombe, Stephen, and Maxwell Tremblay, eds. *White Riot: Punk Rock and the Politics of Race*. New York: Verso, 2011.
Dunn, Charles., ed. *The Enduring Reagan*. Lexington: University Press of Kentucky, 2009.
Dunn, Kevin. *Global Punk: Resistance and Rebellion in Everyday Life*. New York: Bloomsbury Academic, 2016.
Ensminger, David. *Left of the Dial: Conversations with Punk Icons*. Oakland, CA: PM Press, 2013.
———. *The Politics of Punk: Protest and Revolt from the Streets*. Lanham, MD: Rowman & Littlefield, 2016.
Falwell, Jerry. *Listen America*. New York: Doubleday, 1980.
Furness, Zach, ed. *Punkademics: The Basement Show in the Ivory Tower*. Brooklyn: Minor Compositions, 2012.
Gartner, Alan, Colin Greer, and Frank Riessman. *What Reagan Is Doing to Us*. New York: Harper & Row, 1982.
Graffin, Greg. *Punk Paradox: A Memoir*. New York: Hachette Books, 2022.
Hadden, Jeffrey K., and Anson Shupe. *Televangelism: Power and Politics on God's Frontier*. New York: Henry Holt, 1988.
Haenfler, Ross. *Straight Edge: Clean-Living Youth, Hardcore Punk, and Social Change*. New Brunswick, NJ: Rutgers University Press, 2006.
Hartman, Andrew. *A War for the Soul of America: A History of the Culture Wars*. Chicago: University of Chicago Press, 2019.
Hayton, Jeff. *Culture from the Slums: Punk Rock in East and West Germany*. New York: Oxford University Press, 2022.
Hudson, Cheryl, and Gareth Davies. *Ronald Reagan and the 1980s: Perceptions, Policies, Legacies*. New York: Palgrave Macmillan, 2008.
Hunt, Andrew. *We Begin Bombing in Five Minutes: Late Cold War Culture in the Age of Reagan*. Boston: University of Massachusetts Press, 2021.
Hurchalla, George. *Going Underground: American Punk, 1979–1989*. Oakland, CA: PM Press, 2016.
Jackson, Kenneth T. *Crabgrass Frontier: The Suburbanization of the United States*. New York: Oxford University Press, 1985.

Johnson, Haynes. *Sleepwalking through History: America in the Reagan Years*. New York: W. W. Norton, 1991.

Kleinknecht, William. *The Man Who Sold the World: Ronald Reagan and the Betrayal of Main Street America*. New York: Nation Books, 2009.

Knoblauch, William M. *Nuclear Freeze in a Cold War: The Reagan Administration, Cultural Activism, and the End of the Arms Race*. Boston: University of Massachusetts Press, 2017.

Kosar, Kevin R. *Ronald Reagan and Education Policy*. Studies in Governance and Politics, 2011.

Kraska, Peter B. *Militarizing the American Criminal Justice System: The Changing Roles of the Armed Forces and the Police*. Boston: Northeastern University Press, 2001.

Kristiansen, Lars J., Joseph R. Blaney, Philip J. Chidester, and Brent K. Simonds. *Screaming for Change: Articulating a Unifying Philosophy of Punk Rock*. Plymouth, UK: Lexington Books, 2010.

Kurz, Kenneth Franklin. *The Reagan Years A to Z: An Alphabetical History of Ronald Reagan's Presidency*. Los Angeles: Lowell House, 1996.

Kymlicka, B. B., and Jean V. Matthews. *The Reagan Revolution?* Chicago: Dorsey Press, 1988.

Lahickey, Beth. *All Ages: Reflections on Straight Edge*. Huntington Beach, CA: Revelation Books, 1997.

Larson, Jen B. *Hit Girls: Women of Punk in the USA, 1975-1983*. Port Townsend, WA: Feral House, 2023.

Lekachman, Robert. *Greed Is Not Enough: Reaganomics*. New York: Pantheon Books, 1982.

———. *Visions and Nightmares: America after Reagan*. New York: Macmillan, 1987.

Liebman, Robert C., and Robert Wuthnow. *The New Christian Right: Mobilization and Legitimation*. New York: Aldine, 1983.

Lucks, Daniel S. *Reconsidering Reagan: Racism, Republicans, and the Road to Trump*. Boston: Beacon Press, 2020.

MacLeod, Dewar. *Kids of the Black Hole: Punk Rock in Postsuburban California*. Norman: University of Oklahoma Press, 2010.

Malkin, John. *Punk Revolution! An Oral History of Punk Rock Politics and Activism*. Lanham, MD: Rowman & Littlefield, 2023.

Martin, William C. *With God on Our Side: The Rise of the Religious Right in America*. New York: Broadway Books, 1996.

Maskell, Shayna L. *Politics as Sound: The Washington, D.C. Hardcore Scene, 1978-1983*. Urbana: University of Illinois Press, 2021.

Mattson, Kevin. *We're Not Here to Entertain: Punk Rock, Ronald Reagan, and the Real Culture War of 1980s America*. New York: Oxford University Press, 2020.

McAndrews, Lawrence J. *What They Wished For: American Catholics and American Presidents, 1960-2004*. Athens: University of Georgia Press, 2014.

McGirr, Lisa. *Suburban Warriors: The Origins of the New American Right*. Princeton, NJ: Princeton University Press, 2001.

Mohr, Tim. *Burning Down the Haus: Punk Rock, Revolution, and the Fall of the Berlin Wall*. Chapel Hill, NC: Algonquin, 2018.

Morris, Douglas E. *It's a Sprawl World After All: The Human Cost of Unplanned Growth—and Visions of a Better Future*. Gabriola Island, BC: New Society, 2005.

O'Connor, Alan. *Punk Record Labels and the Struggle for Autonomy: The Emergence of DIY*. Lanham, MD: Lexington Books, 2008.

Ogg, Alex. *Dead Kennedys: Fresh Fruit for Rotting Vegetables, the Early Years*. Oakland, CA: PM Press, 2014.

O'Hara, Craig. *The Philosophy of Punk: More Than Noise*. San Francisco: AK Press, 1999.

Orwell, George. *Coming Up for Air*. London: Gollancz, 1939.

Patton, Raymond A. *Punk Crisis: The Global Punk Rock Revolution*. New York: Oxford University Press, 2018.

Perlstein, Rick. *Reaganland: America's Right Turn, 1976–1980*. New York: Simon & Schuster, 2020.

Rapport, Evan. *Damaged: Musicality and Race in Early American Punk*. Jackson: University of Mississippi Press, 2020.

Ratner-Rosenhagen, Jennifer. *The Ideas That Made America: A Brief History*. New York: Oxford University Press, 2019.

Rettman, Tony. *NYHC: New York Hardcore 1980–1990*. Brooklyn: Brazillion Points, 2014.

Ross, Benjamin. *Dead End: Suburban Sprawl and the Rebirth of American Urbanism*. New York: Oxford University Press, 2014.

Rowse, Arthur E. *One Sweet Guy and What He Is Doing to You*. Washington, DC: Consumer News, 1981.

Ruland, Jim. *Do What You Want: The Story of Bad Religion*. New York: Hachette Books, 2020.

Sabin, Roger, ed. *Punk Rock: So What? The Cultural Legacy of Punk*. New York: Routledge, 1999.

Schaller, Michael. *Reckoning with Reagan: America and Its President in the 1980s*. New York: Oxford University Press, 1992.

Scheer, Robert. *With Enough Shovels: Reagan, Bush and Nuclear War*. New York: Random House, 1982.

Sinker, Daniel, ed. *We Owe You Nothing: Punk Planet, the Collected Interviews*. Chicago: Punk Planet Books, 2008.

Smith, Gary S. *Faith and the Presidency: From George Washington to George W. Bush*. New York: Oxford University Press, 2006.

Speth, James Gustave. *They Knew: The Federal Government's Fifty-Year Role in Causing the Climate Crisis*. Cambridge, MA: MIT Press, 2021.

Spitz, Marc, and Brendan Mullen. *We Got the Neutron Bomb: The Untold Story of L.A. Punk*. New York: Three Rivers, 2001.

Street, John. *Music and Politics*. Malden, MA: Polity Press, 2012.

Suren, Bob. *Crate Digger: An Obsession with Punk Records*. Portland, OR: Microcosm, 2015.

Thompson, Stacy. *Punk Productions: Unfinished Business*. Albany: SUNY Press, 2004.

Troy, Gil. *The Reagan Revolution: A Very Short Introduction*. Oxford: Oxford University Press, 2009.

Vig, Norman J., and Michael E. Kraft. *Environmental Policy in the 1980s: Reagan's New Agenda*. Washington, DC: CQ Press, 1984.
Watson, Dwight. *Race and the Houston Police Department, 1930-1990*. College Station: Texas A&M University Press, 2005.
Wilentz, Sean. *The Age of Reagan: A History, 1974-2008*. New York: HarperCollins, 2008.
Williams, Daniel K. *God's Own Party: The Making of the Christian Right*. New York: Oxford University Press, 2010.
Witcher, Marcus M. *Getting Right with Reagan: The Struggle for True Conservativism: 1980-2016*. Lawrence: University Press of Kansas, 2019.
Wright, Jonathan, and Dawson Barrett. *Punks in Peoria: Making a Scene in the American Heartland*. Urbana: University of Illinois Press, 2021.

Speeches and Addresses of Ronald Reagan

These are the main speeches and addresses consulted for the book, all of which were accessed online using the *Ronald Reagan Presidential Library and Museum*, *The American Presidency Project*, or the *Ronald Reagan Presidential Foundation and Institute* websites. They are listed in chronological order.

"Speech before the University of Southern California Law Day Luncheon, Los Angeles." April 29, 1967.
"First Inaugural Address." January 5, 1967.
"Address Accepting the Presidential Nomination at the Republican National Convention in Detroit." July 17, 1980.
"Address to the Veterans of Foreign Wars Convention in Chicago." August 18, 1980.
"National Affairs Campaign Address on Religious Liberty." August 22, 1980.
"Labor Day Speech at Liberty State Park, Jersey City, New Jersey." September 1, 1980.
"Inaugural Address 1981." January 20, 1981.
"Remarks at the Annual Meeting of the International Association of Police Chiefs in New Orleans, Louisiana." September 28, 1981.
"Remarks to the National Catholic Education Association in Chicago." April 15, 1982.
"Remarks at Memorial Day Ceremonies at Arlington National Cemetery." May 31, 1982.
"Radio Address to the Nation on Crime and Criminal Justice Reform." September 11, 1982.
"Remarks at a White House Ceremony Celebrating Hispanic Heritage Week." September 15, 1982.
"Radio Address to the Nation on Federal Drug Policy." October 2, 1982.
"Radio Address to the Nation on the Anniversary of the Birth of Martin Luther King, Jr." January 15, 1983.
"Remarks at the Annual Convention of Religious Broadcasters." January 31, 1983.
"Radio Address to the Nation on Education." March 12, 1983.
"President Reagan's Remarks at a Dinner for Senator Jesse Helms of North Carolina." June 16, 1983.

"Remarks at the St. Ann's Festival in Hoboken, New Jersey." July 26, 1984.
"Prouder, Stronger, Better." Campaign ad, 1984.
"Address to the Nation on the Explosion of the Space Shuttle *Challenger*." January 28, 1986.
"Radio Address to the Nation on Flag Day and Father's Day." June 14, 1986.
"Address to the Nation on the Campaign against Drug Abuse." September 14, 1986.
"Remarks and a Question-and-Answer Session with the Students and Faculty at Moscow State University." May 31, 1988.
"Farewell Address to the Nation." January 11, 1989.
"Reagan's Letter Announcing His Alzheimer's Diagnosis." November 5, 1994.

Movies

Bell, Robin, dir. *Positive Force: More Than a Witness; 30 Years of Punk Politics in Action*. New York: PM Press, 2015.
Bishop, Michael, and Scott Jacoby, dirs. *Rage: 20 Years of Punk Rock West Coast Style*. Classified Films, 2000.
Bushnell, Bo, and Bryan Ray Turcotte, dirs. *The Art of Punk*. Los Angeles: Kill Your Idols/Western Empire, 2013.
Crain, Bryan, dir. *Oil Capital Underground: The Genesis and Evolution of Punk Rock in Tulsa—Late 70s to Mid 90s*. 2018.
Crawford, Scott, dir. *Salad Days: A Decade of Punk in Washington, DC (1980-1990)*. Washington, DC: New Rose Films, 2015.
Dynner, Susan, dir. *Punk's Not Dead*. Los Angeles: Aberration Films, 2008.
Losurdo, Joe, and Christina Tillman, dirs. *You Weren't There: A History of Chicago Punk, 1977-1984*. Chicago: Regressive Films, 2007.
Markey, David, dir. *1991: The Year Punk Broke*. We Got Power Films, 1992.
———, dir. *Slog*. Los Angeles: We Got Power Films, 1982.
Mills, Jonathan W. C., dir. *Clockwork Orange County: The Rise of West Coast Punk Rock!* Beverly Hills, CA: Endurance Pictures, 2012.
Pierschel, Marc, and Michael Kirchner, dirs. *Edge*. Edge Syndicate, 2009.
Rachman, Paul, dir. *American Hardcore*. Culver City, CA: Sony Pictures Classics, 2006.
Redford, Corbett, dir. *Turn It Around: The Story of East Bay Punk*. New York: Stingray Qello Concerts, 2017.
Schneider, James June, and Paul Bishow, dirs. *Punk the Capital: Building a Sound Movement*. Warren, NJ: Passion River Films, 2012.
Spheeris, Penelope, dir. *Suburbia*. Atlanta: New World Pictures, 1984.
———, dir. *The Decline of Western Civilization*. Los Angeles: Media Home Entertainment, 1981.
Stone, Drew, dir. *All Ages: The Boston Hardcore Film*. Boston: Gallery East, 2012.
———, dir. *The New York Hardcore Chronicles Film*. New York: Stone Films, 2017.
Tozzi, Steve, dir. *Riot on the Dance Floor: The Story of Randy Now and City Gardens*. Playfort Productions, 2014.

Index

Italic page numbers refer to illustrations.

abortion, 76, 80, 94, 100
Abused, 72, 121
Accelerators, 32, 33
Acidez, 175
Adolescents, 15, 23, 55
Adrenalin OD, 16, 57–58, 122
Afflicted, 131
Afghanistan, 109
African Americans: in Bad Brains, 12; and police violence, 133, 134–35, 137; and Ronald Reagan's civil rights record, 147–48, 158, 163, 166, 167; in Ugly Americans, 85; in Whipping Boy, 38. *See also* race and racism
African National Congress, 155
Agent 86, 50
Agent Orange, 15, 23, 55, 73
Agnostic Front, 16, 68, 121
AIDS crisis, 83, 85, 88
AK-47 (band), 137–38, 166
Allen, Richard, 95
Alley Cats, 129
Allman, Karen (K Nurse), 38
Alternative Tentacles, 15, *102*, *104*, 124–25, 150
Ambrosch, Gerfried, 6, 180
American Civil Liberties Union (ACLU), 51, 77, 83, 160
American Hardcore (documentary), 18, 48
American Nazi Party, 151, 157, 160
America's Hardcore, 128
Angley, Ernest, 91–92
Angola, 119
Angry Red Planet, 43–44
Angry Samoans, 84–85, 86, 87

Annual Convention of the National Religious Broadcasters, 81
Anti-Climex, 98
Anti-Dogmatikss, 99
Anti Scrunti Faction (AS.F.), 144
A.P.F. Brigade (Anarchy, Peace, and Freedom Brigade), 99
A.P.P.L.E., 22
Arcatones, *103*
ARENA (National Republican Alliance), 117
Armed Citizens, 67
Articles of Faith, 17–18, 48, 158
Artificial Peace, 58, 121
Asocial, 98
Assassination Squad, 175
Assault & Battery, 121
Atwater, Lee, 163
Australia punk scene, 98
Authorities, 145
Autodefensa, 99
Avengers, 13
Azerrad, Michael, 125, 168

Bad Brains, 8, 11–12, 13, 14, 15, 17, 158
Bad Religion, 47–48, 62, 74, 97–100, 122, 172, 177–78
Baier, Bret, 174
Bakker, Jim, 91–94
Bakker, Tammy Faye, 92–94
Bale, Jeff, 29, 150, 153
Bates, Toby Glenn, 147
Battalion of Saints, 97
Battle of People's Park, 49
Battle Pussy, 177
Beach Boys, 26, 35, 60

227

Beastie Boys, 16
Bedlam, 69, 89
Beefeater, 31
Beer City Records, 89
Beers, John, 63, 165
Belching Penguin (BP), 57, 112
Belew, Kathleen, 160
Belgium punk scene, 34
Bell, Terrel, 59–60
Bergen-Belsen concentration camp, 21–22
Berkeley 924 Gilman Street club, 49
Biafra, Jello: and Alternative Tentacles, 15, 124; bid for San Francisco mayor, 12; on Christian Right, 78, 79–80; on El Salvador, 117; on homosexuality, 86; lyrics of, 12; on military draft, 110; on Nazism, 160–61; on nuclear war, 124; on Barack Obama, 173; on Ronald Reagan, 3, 19; on Reaganomics, 31; and Rock Against Reagan shows, 16; on Donald Trump, 169, 177, 178, 179; vocal style of, 41
Big Boys, 16
Biko, Steve, 155
Black Flag: *Damaged*, 138; on depression, 56; and Elks Lodge Riot, 129; as foundational for punk scene, 13; *Jealous Again*, 12, 138–39; *Let Them Eat Jellybeans!*, 15; on police, 134, 138–39, 142, 144; on race, 12, 159–60, 161; on schools, 62; tour, 12–13; on west coast, 8
Black Lives Matter, 163–64
Black Market Baby, 99–100
Blush, Steven, 29, 132, 134–35
Bond, Ronnie "U-Ron," 136
Bondage, U-Ron, 16
Bondi, Vic, 17–18, 48, 158–59
Bonds, Gary U. S., 60
Boon, D., 4, 15
Bored Youth, 18
Bork, Robert, 158
Boston punk scene, 17, 141–42
Brady, James, 24

Brazil punk scene, 34, 99
Brecht, Kurt, 111–12
Brezhnev, Leonid, 121
Brown, Jerry, 79
Brown, Richard, 157–58
Brown v. Board of Education (1954), 152
Bryant, Anita, 78
BSY (Bored Suburban Youths), 57
Buchan, Wattie, 99
Buchanan, Pat, 88
Bum Kon, 112
Bush, George H. W., 170–71
Bush, George W., 41, 171–73, 180
Butthole Surfers, 16
Butylated Hydroxy Toluene (BHT), 40

California punk scene, 12, 15, 20, 54, 55, 56, 58, 62, 138–40, 142
Canada punk scene, 18–19, 34, 98, 175, 176
Candy Warpop, 175, 176
Cannon, Lou, 10, 84, 88
Capitalist Casualties, 69
Capitol Punishment, 116, 149
Cappo, Ray, 72
Capretta, James, 169
Carter, Hodding, 155
Carter, Jimmy: on crisis of confidence, 46; defense spending, 121; education policy, 59; and election of 1976, 36–37; on El Salvador, 115; environmental policies, 65, 66; Billy Milano on, 89; pardoning of draft evaders, 109; Ronald Reagan's defeat of, 10, 109, 152; on Selective Service System, 109; support in South for, 62
Catholics: punk rock lyrics on, 95–97, 98; and Ronald Reagan, 94–97, 100
Cause for Alarm, 32
CBMT (Complicated Bone Marrow Transplant), 118
Central America, 115–17, 119
Challenger space shuttle, 44–46
Chaney, James, 147
Channel 3, 95–96

Chaotic Dischord, 99
Chekov, Pavel, 177
Chemical Waste, 64
Chemotherapy, 96–97
Chicago punk scene, 17–18, 86
Chico, 32
Christian Broadcasting Network Satellite Service, 89–90
Christian Right: agenda of, 77; and AIDS crisis, 88, 89; and George W. Bush, 171; and Catholics, 94–97, 100; emergence of, 77; and fascism, 78, 79, 99–100; on homosexuality, 80, 92, 93, 100; James Davison Hunter on, 100; on Jewish people, 82; monetary contributions to, 79; Moral Majority and, 17, 77, 80–81; notable figures of, 75; political activism of, 76–77, 78, 81, 83; punk rock lyrics on, 7, 16–17, 18, 23, 25, 77–80, 81, 82, 89–94, 100; and Ronald Reagan, 25, 75–77, 78, 79–80, 81, 83, 84, 88; on secular humanism, 81; and televangelism, 89–94; and Donald Trump, 169
Christian Voice, 77
Christ on a Crutch, 123
Christ on Parade, 112
Chronic Sick, 20, 164–65
C.I.A., 117–18, 119
C.I.A. Records, 16, 136
Circle Jerks, 15, 62, 81, 82
Circle One, 114, 139–40, 144
civil rights movement, 147, 148, 158
Clark, William, 95
Clash, 108
Clean Air Act, 65
Clinton, Bill, 170–71, 173
Clitboys, 156
Cliterati, 175
Clockwork Orange County (documentary), 86
Cobain, Kurt, 66
Coe, Kevin, 41
Coffin Break, 170
Cohen, Steve, 69–70

Colcor, 62
Cold War, 1, 107–8, 115, 126, 142
Commission on Pornography, 49–50
Communications, 102
communism, 32, 76, 94, 107, 111, 125
Comprehensive Environmental Response, Compensation, and Liability Act, 66
Confederate flags, 62, 146
Conflict (band), 38
Confront (band), 73
consumerism, 5, 30, 34, 47–48, 55, 72, 91
Controllers, 90
Cook, Blaine, 29
Cool, Tré, 40, 118
Cooper, Alice, 60
Coors, Adolph, 119
Coors, Joseph, 119
Coors Brewing Company, 119
Corrosion of Conformity, 62, 69, 149, 154
Corrupted Morals, 49–50
Cotton, Tom, 169
Council for National Policy, 119
Crash Course, 43
Creedence Clearwater Revival, 110
Criminal Justice, 99
Crisis Man, 174
Cro-Mags, 16
Cronkite, Walter, 65
Crooks, Thomas Matthew, 168
Crowley, Kevin, 72
Crucifix, 98
Crucifucks, 25–26, 27, 35, 129, 131–32, 133
Crutch, 177
Cuba, 115, 116
Cuban Missile Crisis, 120
Cuckoo's Nest (Costa Mesa, CA), 134
culture wars, 100
Cunningham, David, 152

Dad and the Boys, 107
The Damnit Jims, 175

Danforth, John, 2
Darby Crash, 70
Dare to Defy, 163
Dart, Doc, 25–26
Dayglo Abortions, 18, 34, 98
Dead Kennedys: and John Beers, 63; on Christian Right, 77–80, 81, 82; on environmentalism, 69; and Klaus Flouride, 38; as foundational for punk scene, 13; *Fresh Fruit for Rotting Vegetables*, 12; *Give Me Convenience or Give Me Death*, 86; *In God We Trust, Inc.*, 15, 78–80, 81, 103, 134; and *Let Them Eat Jellybeans!*, 15; on military draft, 110; on Nazism, 21, 160–61, 162; on police, 144; Ronald Reagan in lyrics of, 12, 19; on Reaganomics, 30–31; and Rock against Reagan tour, 35; symbol of, 79–80; Margaret Thatcher in lyrics of, 3
Dead Reagans, 18
Death Sentence, 98
Death to W, 172
Deaver, Michael, 171
Decline, 124
The Decline of Western Civilization (documentary), 54, 139
The Deer Hunter (film), 114
Defectors, 83
Demented Youth, 26–27
Denmark punk scene, 34
Department of Energy, 65
Descendents, 15, 58–59, 87
Detention, 117
D.I., 23, 54, 115, 124, 174
Dickies, 87
Dicks: in Austin, 16, 132; on homosexuality, 86–87; on Ku Klux Klan, 154; on military draft, 110–11; on police, 132–34, 166; on Ronald Reagan's foreign policy, 111; Rock against Reagan tour and, 35
Dictor, Dave: in Austin, 132; on Christian Right, 77; on death, 108; and M.D.C., 3, 16, 108, 132, 135,
179–80; on Nazism, 162; on race, 158–59, 166; on Ronald Reagan, 3, 16; and Rock Against Reagan shows, 16; and R Radical Records, 16; on Donald Trump, 179–80
Diddly Squat, 124
Dirty Rotten Imbeciles (D.R.I.), 16, 31, 33, 35, 92, 111–12
Disability, 128–29
Discharge, 99
Dischord Records, 14, 29, 31, 58, 71, 82, 142, 143
Discogs, 88
D.O.A., 18–19, 34, 98, 105, 117, 176, 180
Doctor Dreams Records, 48
Dodd, John, 151
Dog Killer, 32–33
Dolan, Terry, 78
Dom Intelligens Befriade, 175
Doomsday Clock, 120
Dow Chemical, 68
D.R.I. (Dirty Rotten Imbeciles), 16, 31, 33, 35, 92
Dr. Know, 116
Duarte, José Napoleon, 116–17
Dugger, Ronnie, 119, 157
Duncombe, Stephen, 148
Dunn, Charles W., 147
Dunn, Kevin, 8

Earth Day, 64–65
Econochrist, 48
Effigies, 17
Eisenhower, Dwight D., 41
ELF, 83
Elks Lodge Riot, 129–30
El Salvador: punk rock lyrics on, 108, 113–20; and Reagan Doctrine, 108, 113, 115–17, 119
Emmet, Oman, 31
Ensminger, David, 39
Entropy, 112
Environmental Protection Agency, 65, 68, 70
Epitaph Records, 47

Equal Rights Amendment, 78
Essary, Glen, 123
evangelicalism, 75
evolution, 81

Fair Housing Act, 149, 164
Fall Children, 174–75, 176
False Prophets, 58, 97
Falwell, Jerry: on AIDS crisis, 83, 88; and Jim Bakker, 93; and Christian Right, 75, 77–78, 81, 83; "I Love America" rallies of, 80; as Moral Majority founder, 78, 80, 93, 94; political activism of, 80, 83; punk rock lyrics on, 78, 82, 83, 91, 93–94, 98; on Ronald Reagan, 76, 80, 93
family values, 76, 94
Fartz, 28–29, 97, 122, 153, 154, 172
fascism: and Christian Right, 78, 79, 99–100; and police, 130, 131; and Reaganism, 19, 20, 21, 22, 23, 40, 41, 79, 150, 162; and Donald Trump, 162, 177, 180
Fatal Existence, 116
Fatal Vision, 154
Fat Mike, 172
Faulkner, Tom, 95
Fear and Loathing, 98
Fearless Iranians from Hell, 43
Final Conflict, 128
Finland punk scene, 34
First Amendment, 75, 81
First Blood (film), 114
5.0.5.1., 116–17
5 Balls of Power, 150
Fix, 18
Flea, 54
Fleck, Tim (Tim Phlegm), 137–38
Flipper, 4, 66–67, 68
Flouride, Klaus, 38
Flower, Wayne, 69
Floyd, Gary, 110–11, 132–34, 154, 166
Floyd, George, 163
folk music, 11
Foner, Eric, 41

Ford, Gerald, 36, 59
Foster, Jodie, 24–25
Free South Africa Movement, 155
Freeze, 17, 98, 161–62
Frontier Records, 15
F.U.'s, 17, 161–62

Gang Green, 17
Gay Cowboys in Bondage, 87
gay rights, 76–78, 83–84, 88, 89, 93, 94, 136
Generation X (generation), 8
Genesis, 108
Germs, 13, 90
Gibbs, Lois, 67
Gibbs, Melissa, 67
Gibbs, Michael, 67
Giftigt Avfall, 176
Gilliam, Dorothy, 152
Ginn, Greg, 15, 138–39, 159
Giuliani, Rudy, 176–77
Glasser, Ira, 51
Glover, Milton, 137, 166
Go Gos, 129
Goldwater, Barry, 119–20
Goodman, Andrew, 147
Gorbachev, Mikhail, 1
Gorsuch, Anne, 68
Government Issue (G.I.), 14, 29, 56, 91, 143–44
Graffin, Greg, 47, 74, 178
Graham, Billy, 91–92
Grandin, Greg, 170
Graven Image, 122
Green Day, 40, 118, 180
Grenada, 111–12, 113, 119
grunge music, 170
Guatemala, 119
Guleff, Sasha, 174
Gurewitz, Brett, 47, 172

Hadden, Jeffrey, 75, 90, 94
Haenfler, Ross, 71–72
Hahn, Jessica, 92
Haig, Alexander, 95, 116

Index   231

Hammer, Armand, 67
Hampton, Carl, 136
Harsh Reality, 123
Hart, Grant, 42
Hartman, Andrew, 76–77
Hated Principals, 128
Heart Attack, 16, 67–68
Heclo, Hugh, 53, 108
Helms, Jesse, 78, 151
Hennsler, Barry, 164
Heston, Greg, 62
Hill, Jody, 140
Hinckley, John, Jr., 6, 24–25, 168
Hispanic Americans, 47
Hitler, Adolf: and George W. Bush, 172; in punk rock album artwork, 124, 172; and Ronald Reagan, 6, 20, 21, 22, 23–24, 28, 34, 160; and Donald Trump, 175, 179, 180
Hoffman, Stanley, 37
Holden, Constance, 65
Homophobic Records, 84
Homo Picnic, 87
homosexuality: Christian Right on, 80, 92, 93, 100; punk rock lyrics on, 83–89, 94, 164. *See also* gay rights
Honor Roll, 122
Hooker Chemical Company, 66, 67, 68
Hooligan, Danny, 85
Horovitz, Adam, 16
House Un-American Activities Committee, 45–46
Houston, Penelope, 13
Howe, Julia Ward, 29
Hudson, Rock, 88
Hufstedler, Shirley, 59
Human Therapy, 48
Hunter, James Davison, 100
Hurchalla, George, 7, 120, 128–29
Hüsker Dü, 42, 63
Hypnotics, 21

(Impatient) Youth, 98
individualism, 55
Insane (band), 116

International Association of Police Chiefs, 145
Iran-Contra Affair, 3, 49, 117–19, 170
Iranian hostage crisis, 107, 117–18
Iraq, 172
Isler, Don, 107
Ism (band), 25
Ismach, Josef, 25
Isotope Soap, 175–76
Italy punk scene, 34

Jackson, Andrew, 169
Jackson, Kenneth, 57
Jack Tragic and The Unfortunates, 88, 89
Jefferson, Alphine, 148
Jello Biafra and the Guantanamo School of Medicine, 173, 177, 179
Jerry's Kids, 17, 113–14
JFA (Jodie Foster's Army), 24–25, 63
John Paul II (pope), 27
Johnson, B. K., 137
Johnson, Haynes, 90–91, 115–16
Jones, Jim, 97
Jones, Thomas K., 123
Jug Head (Heavy Mental), 58

Karne Krua, 99
Kashan, Lauren, 177
Keller, Bill, 171
Kelly, Jack "Choke," 141
Kennedy, John F., 25
Kim Jong Un, 176
King, Coretta Scott, 151
King, Martin Luther, Jr., 151, 153, 155
Klowden, David, 117
Knowledge, 171
Kohl, Helmut, 21
Krauthammer, Charles, 107–8
Ku Klux Klan: as neo-Nazi organization, 160; and punk rock album art, 112, 134–35; punk rock lyrics on, 23, 39, 40, 133, 150, 151–56, 177; and Ronald Reagan, 146, 147, 151–52, 154, 155–56, 157, 159; and Donald Trump, 169, 180; and Unite the Right rally, 165

Lagdameo, Eric, 143
LaHaye, Tim, 81
Landlords, 61, 63, 165, 166
Last (band), 129–30
LaVoie, Mark, 36
Lebanon, and Reagan Doctrine, 113, 114–15, 118, 119, 144
Left (band), 89
Lekachman, Robert, 32–33, 94, 125
Leland, Mickey, 167
Lennon, John, 27
Lennonburger, 29–30
Lewd (band), 57
LGM-118 Peacekeeper missile, 92
Liberty University, 93
Libya, 26, 119
Lichtt, Darrel, 58
Liebman, Robert C., 77
Limbaugh, Rush, 174
Lincoln, Abraham, 25
Liquids, 177
Litwin, Peter, 170
Livermore, Larry, 40
Loesser, Frank, 98
Lombardo, Tony, 58–59
Lookout Records, 40
The Lookouts!, 40, 118
Lose, Bruce, 66–67
Los Olvidados, 90–91
Lost Generation, 154
Louis XVI (king), 15
Love Canal, 66–67
Love Canal Homeowners Association, 67
Love Canal Parents Movement, 67
Lowy, Richard, 148
Lucks, Daniel: on Ronald Reagan's civil rights policy, 159, 167; on Ronald Reagan's racism, 146, 147, 153, 155, 157, 163, 165; on Rehnquist, 158; on Trump, 169
Lyle, Eirck, 4

Macias, John, 114, 139–40
MacKaye, Ian: and Dischord, 14, 144; on harassment from jocks, 86; on police, 144; on race, 158–59, 164; on religion, 98; and straight edge movement, 71–72
MacLean, Jim, 119
Macolino, Greg (Greg Gory), 164–65
Maloney, Sean L., 89
Manson, Charles, 14
Marching Plague, 122
Marie Antoinette (queen), 15
Markey, Dave, 170
Martin Luther King Jr. Day, 151, 153
Marxism, 32, 98, 111, 116, 118, 132, 151, 157
Maskell, Shayna, 11, 14
Mattson, Kevin, 4–5, 13, 42, 136
McAndrews, Lawrence, 96–97
McClain, Jon, 85
McConnell, Mitch, 176
McDonald, Jeff, 62
McDonald, Steve, 62
McDonald's, 34
McGirr, Lisa, 55
M.D.C. (Millions of Damn Christians), 77
M.D.C. (Millions of Dead Christians), 134
M.D.C. (Millions of Dead Cops): and Battle Pussy, 177; and Dave Dictor, 3, 16, 108, 132, 135, 179–80; "John Wayne Was a Nazi," 16; *Millions of Dead Cops*, 104, 134–35; on Nazism, 162; on Nicaragua, 118–19; on police, 134–35, 139, 166; on Ronald Reagan, 19; and Rock against Reagan tour, 35; on Trump, 179
M.D.C. (Millions of Delusional Citizens), 134
M.D.C. (Multi-Death Corporation), 134
Meatmen, 18
Mecht Mensch, 44–45
Meese, Edwin, 49–50, 156, 169
Meese Report, 50
Middle Class, 13, 55, 90
Midwest punk scene, 17–18, 57, 58, 61–64

Mike, Fat, 172
Milano, Billy, 88–89
military draft, 19, 20, 29, 108, 109–13, 117, 120
Military Manpower Task Force, 109
military strength, 76
Minor Threat: Government Issue compared to, 29; *In My Eyes*, 14; *Minor Disturbance*, 13; *Minor Threat*, 14; on race, 158–60; on religion, 98; and straight edge movement, 71–72
Minutemen, 4, 15
Miret, Roger, 68, 121
Missing in Action (film), 114
Mission for Christ, 26
M.O.D. (Methods of Destruction), 88–89
Modern Warfare, 83
Mondale, Walter, 41, 106
Money Dogs, 38
Moral Majority (band), 81; and Angry Samoans, 84; and Christian Right, 17, 77, 80–81; Jerry Falwell as founder of, 78, 80, 93, 94; on homosexuality, 83; impact of, 80–81, 100; as political action committee, 80; pro-family and pro-America platform of, 77; punk rock lyrics on, 39, 77, 78, 81, 82–83, 93, 95, 98, 100
Moral Majority Dance Band, 83
Morgan, Rick, 49–50
Morons, 58
Morris, Chris, 130
Morris, Keith, 81–82, 129, 138
Mould, Bob, 42
Mr. Epp and the Calculations, 83
MRR (*Maximumrocknroll*): on Angry Red Planet, 43; on Articles of Faith, 17; on Channel 3, 95; on Christ on a Crutch, 123; on Conflict, 38; on Corrupted Morals, 49; on Dicks, 87; on Dirty Rotten Imbeciles, 31; on Fartz, 28, 153; on hardcore punk, 13; on Landlords, 63, 165; on Ian MacKaye, 158, 164; on Money Dogs, 38; on Moral Majority Dance Band, 83; on

Negative Element, 95; on *No Core*, 62; on Ronald Reagan's death, 3–5; on 7 Seconds, 150; on Spastic Rats, 154; spring 1983 issue of, 35; on SS Decontrol, 72; on Stark Raving Mad, 40–41; *Turn It Around!* compilation of, 119; on Ugly Americans, 85; on Unified Field, 43
MTV, 108, 170–71
Muir, Mike, 27, 168
Murphy's Law, 16
Musical Suicide, 122
Mussolini, Benito, 124
Mutha Records, 118
Mystic Records, 145

Naked Hippy, 87
Naked Raygun, 17, 45–46, 51, 118, 120, 178–79, 184
National Catholic Education Association, 95
National Commission on Excellence in Education, 59–60
National Environmental Policy Act, 65
National Security Council, 114
National Socialist Party of America (NSPA), 160
Nazi Bitch and the Jews, 129, 131, 132
Nazism: and Adolph Coors, 119; and military draft, 109; and police, 130, 138; punk rock lyrics on, 16, 19, 21–24, 28, 40, 97, 154, 160–63; and Ronald Reagan, 19, 21–24, 28, 29–30, 115, 163; and Trump, 174–75; and Unite the Right rally, 165
Necros, 14, 18, 61–62, 128, 131, 148–49, 164
Negative Approach, 18
Negative Element, 95, 97
Negative FX, 121, 124, 141
Negative Trend, 13, 90
Nelson, Gaylord, 65
Nelson, Jeff, 14
Nena, 108
Neon Christ, 112

Neshoba County, MS, 146–47, 154
Netherlands punk scene, 34
New Alliance Records, 15
New Deal, 30
New Right, 55, 146
Newton, Wayne, 26
New York punk scene, 16–17, 67–68
Nicaragua, 108, 113, 117–18, 119, 175
Nicholas, Julius, 160
Nietzsche, Friedrich, 78
Nightmare on Sesame Street, 156
1991 (documentary), 170
Nirvana, 66, 170
Nixon, Richard, 59, 163
No Direction, 32
NOFX, 20, 131, 172
No Labels, 62, 154
Nolte, Joe, 129–30
None of the Above (N.O.T.A.), 144
Non-U Records, 17
Noonan, Peggy, 169
No Rock Stars, 61, 62–63
Norris, Chuck, 114
North, Oliver, 49, 117–18
Norton, Greg, 42
Noxious, Bob, 161
nuclear war: limited, 124; punk rock lyrics on, 108, 110, 120–26
Nuns, 13
N.W.A, 132

Obama, Barack, 46, 168, 173, 175, 178
Occidental Petroleum Corporation, 67
Ogg, Alex, 12
O'Hara, Craig, 7
Oi Polloi, 175
O'Neill, Tip, 52
Operation Urgent Fury, 111
Orwell, George, 56
Overkill, 63
Oz (club), 17
Ozzi, Dan, 173

Paez, Fred, 136
Pajama Slave Dancers, 87

Palestinian Liberation Organization (P.L.O.), 114
Parrot, Buxf, 134
Partnership for a Drug-Free America, 73
Past (band), 175
Pate, Amy, 175
Patriots, 42–43, 54
Patton, Raymond, 87
Peacekeepers, 121
Pedersen, Chris, 54
Pedestrian Abuse, 64
People's Party, 136
Perlstein, Rick, 13, 33, 55, 151
Pettibon, Raymond, 139
Pezzati, Jeff, 45, 120, 178–79
Pig Children, 38–39, 40
Planned Parenthood, 77
Plugz, 129
pluralism, 100
Poison Idea, 97–98
police: and Elks Lodge Riot, 129–30, 138; and Ku Klux Klan, 133, 134–35, 154; militarization of, 128, 129, 132; and mistreatment of punks, 144; and public perception campaigns, 137; punk rock lyrics on, 128–29, 130, 131–40, 141, 142, 143–45, 166, 179; and racism, 133, 134–35, 136, 141, 150, 166; Reagan's support of, 127
Pop-O-Pies, 97, 131
Porkeria T., 98
pornography, 8, 50, 76, 77, 80, 81, 100
Posh Boy Records, 15, 37
Potter, Gary, 100
prayer in schools, 76, 78, 79
Presley, Elvis, 98
Pressler, Lyle, 71
Prevaricators, 93–94
Prince, 108
Proletariat (band), 17, 98, 157–58
Protect America's Children campaign, 78
P.T.L. Klub, 92
punk (term), 7

punk rock lyrics: absurdism of, 26, 27, 30; on American Dream, 46–50; anger in, 108; as anti-authority, 130; boredomin, 56, 57; on George H. W. Bush, 170; on George W. Bush, 171–72, 180; on Catholics, 95–97, 98; on Christian Right, 7, 16–17, 18, 23, 25, 77–80, 81, 82, 89–94, 100; confrontational nature of, 8; as countermovement, 6; as cultural commentary, 8, 180–81; depictions of Ronald Reagan in, 6, 7; disaffection in, 5–6, 18, 19, 53, 57, 61, 73–74, 108; on end of times, 40; on environmental abuse, 53, 64–70, 112; on estrangement, 53; feelings on Reagan in, 3; on freedom, 41–44; "God is dead" in, 78; and grunge, 170–71; on John Hinckley Jr., 6; and homophobia, 63; on homosexuality, 83–89, 94, 164; on Ku Klux Klan, 23, 39, 40, 133, 150, 151–56, 177; on law enforcement, 40; as means of sharing ideas, 6; on military draft, 19, 20, 29, 108, 109–13, 117, 120; on Moral Majority, 39, 77, 78, 81, 82–83, 93, 95, 98, 100; on MTV, 171; on Nazism, 16, 19, 21–24, 28, 40, 97, 154, 160–63; on nuclear war, 108, 110, 120–26; on police, 128–29, 130, 131–40, 141, 142, 143–45, 166, 179; political charge of, 110, 136; pop punk, 170; pugnaciousness of, 12; queercore, 144; on racism, 12, 23, 39, 55, 85, 86, 147–50, 152, 153, 154, 157–60, 163–67, 173; on Reagan Doctrine, 39, 108, 113–20; on Reaganism, 4–5, 6, 7, 8, 11, 14, 15, 16, 23–24, 30, 32, 53, 60–61, 63, 66, 89; on Reaganomics, 30–33; on Reagan, 12, 14, 15, 19–21, 22, 23–30, 33–34, 36, 38, 39, 41, 43–44, 49, 50–51, 53, 55, 60–61, 66, 77, 78, 79, 82, 92, 99, 100, 107, 113, 118, 119, 141, 145, 157, 170, 171, 174, 175, 176, 178, 180, 185–93; on religion, 97–100; satiric approach to Reagan, 28–30; on schools, 53, 59–64, 66, 70; sociopolitical nature of, 11; on suburbs, 53, 54–59, 61, 66, 70; on televangelism, 89–94; on Margaret Thatcher, 3; on threat of war, 6–7, 19–20, 29, 30, 39, 44, 107, 112, 115, 120–23; on threats to Reagan's life, 24–28, 39; on Trump, 174–80, 181; on United States, 35, 36, 37–46, 47, 48–50, 53, 77; urgency and defiance in, 7–8, 120; on Vietnam War, 113–14; on World War III, 108

punk rock music: album artwork of, 14, 17, 18, 22, 23, 29, 79, 98, 99, *101*, *102*, *103*, *104*, 121, 134, 135, 139, 153, 154, 172, 175, 176; anti-Americanism of, 37; characteristics of, 8, 12, 19; and crossover thrash, 16; Elks Lodge Riot, 129–30; and folk music, 11; hardcore, 3, 7, 11–19, 42–43, 58, 70, 120, 153, 158, 160–62, 176; honesty and forthrightness in, 6; hypermasculinity of, 70; influence of, 11; as national movement, 13, 36; and Nazi rhetoric, 21; oppositional orientation of, 7, 8, 11, 70, 78, 110, 153, 168, 172, 174, 175, 181; and parody, 42; as protest music, 8, 21, 26, 39; Reagan as inspiration for, 13–14, 17, 18; rebirth of, 180–81; and straight edge movement, 70–73, 158; stylistic differences within, 8

punk scene: in Australia, 98; in Belgium, 34; in Boston, 17, 141–42; in California, 12, 15, 20, 54, 55, 56, 58, 62, 138–40, 142; in Canada, 18–19, 34, 98, 175, 176; in Chicago, 17–18, 86; clothing, 5, 14; in Denmark, 34; documentaries on, 54, 59, 86, 139, 170; drug use in, 70–73; in Finland, 34; foundations of, 13; hairstyles of, 14; and independent record labels, 14, 15; in Italy, 34; and law enforcement, 6, 7; in Midwest, 17–18, 57, 58, 61–64; in Netherlands, 34; in

New York, 16–17, 67–68; on Reagan Revolution, 2, 5, 7, 8, 9, 11, 18, 21, 23, 32, 99, 110–11, 125–26, 147, 164, 169; on Reagan's death, 3–5; show fliers of, 6, 63, 139; skate, 91; and skinheads, 160; in South, 62–63; in Spain, 34, 98–99; street art of, 4; in Sweden, 34, 35, 98, 175; in Texas, 15–16, 58, 132–38, 139, 142; in United Kingdom, 99, 160; in Washington, DC, 12–13, 14, 15, 17, 56, 58, 142–44; in West Germany, 34; and white middle-class privilege, 6, 7, 12
Punkvoter.com, 172
Pushead, 14, 161, 165
Putin, Vladimir, 176

Queens' Heart Attack, 97
Queer Pills, 84

race and racism: Black Flag on, 12, 159–60, 161; and n-word use, 163–67; and Barack Obama, 173; and police, 133, 134–35, 136, 141, 150, 166; punk rock lyrics on, 12, 23, 39, 55, 85, 86, 147–50, 152, 153, 154, 157–60, 163–67, 173; and Reagan's policies, 146–48, 153, 156–58, 163, 166, 167; and reverse discrimination, 159; and Jeff Sessions, 169; John Wayne on, 162; and White minority, 156–60; yuppie racism, 148. *See also* African Americans; Ku Klux Klan
Rambo (film), 114
Ramone, Joey, 22, 60, 154
Ramone, Johnny, 22
Ramones, 22–23, 36, 60, *101*, 154, 184
Rapport, Evan, 55
Ratner-Rosenhagen, Jennifer, 9
Reagan, Jack, 94–95
Reagan, Nancy, 18, 30, 70–73, 91, 112, 156–57
Reagan, Ron, 113
Reagan, Ronald Wilson: acting career, 22; on affirmative action, 152, 154,

157, 159; on AIDS crisis, 88, 89; Alzheimer's diagnosis, 1, 4; on American Dream, 46–50; approval ratings, 24, 52; assassination attempt, 6, 19, 24–28, 168; backlash on Soviet Union policy, 106–7; in Bitburg, Germany, 21–22, 34; and George W. Bush, 171, 173; as California governor, 62, 64, 76, 113, 127, 138, 145, 149, 162; Cancer Panel, 67; and Catholicism, 94–97, 100; on *Challenger* space shuttle, 44; and Christian Right, 25, 75–77, 78, 79–80, 81, 83, 84, 88; civil rights record, 147–48, 149, 158, 159, 163; and Cold War, 1, 42, 107–8; courage-oriented narratives, 44–46; death of, 1, 3–4; defense investments, 120–21, 125; on drug use, 70–73; economic policies, 30–33, 51, 65–66, 147; on education, 59–60, 62, 64; and election of 1980, 10–11, 12, 13–14, 18, 20, 23, 31, 36–37, 65, 109, 146–47, 152, 154, 155, 156, 159; and election of 1984, 16, 23, 40, 51, 52, 118, 124, 152, 155, 159; on end of days, 74; environmental policies, 64–70; on evil empire, 172; farewell address to nation, 10, 52; first inaugural address, 10–11, 46; Flag Day address, 45; foreign policy, 39, 107–8, 111–12, 114–16, 119–20, 125; on freedom, 41–44, 45, 47; funeral service, 1–2, 33; on gay rights, 83–84; and Billy Graham, 91; and Hitler, 6, 20, 21, 22, 23–24, 28, 34, 160; ideology, 174; illusory mandate, 10; inauguration, 15, 17, 18, 20; and Iran-Contra scandal, 3, 49, 117–18, 119, 170; judicial appointments, 95, 158; and Ku Klux Klan, 146, 147, 151–52, 154, 155–56, 157, 159; Labor Day address, 46; and "land of liberty" narrative, 39; on law enforcement, 127–28, 130, 132, 141, 144, 145; as leadership model, 2; legacy, 2, 4,

Reagan, Ronald Wilson (cont.)
52–53, 174; "Let's make America great again" slogan, 37, 40, 169; on military draft, 109, 112–13; moralism, 70, 72, 75–77; and Moral Majority, 17; on "Morning in America," 5; and Nazism, 19, 21–24, 28, 29–30, 115, 163; on nuclear war, 120, 123, 124; on America's future, 1, 2, 10–11; policies, 4, 35, 53; popularity, 24, 25; popular vote margin, 10; and punk rock album artwork, 17, 18, 22, 23, 29, 49, 99, 121, 153, 154, 172, 175; punk rock lyrics on, 12, 14, 15, 19–21, 22, 23–30, 33–34, 36, 38, 39, 41, 43–44, 49, 50–51, 53, 55, 60–61, 66, 77, 78, 79, 82, 92, 99, 100, 107, 113, 118, 119, 141, 145, 157, 170, 171, 174, 175, 176, 178, 180, 185–93; on punk rock show fliers, 63; punks' response to death of, 2–3, 4; radio address on policy initiatives, 106–7; Religious Roundtable's National Affairs Briefing Conference address, 75–76; on school desegregation, 152–53, 154; and Jeff Sessions, 169; and "shining city upon a hill," 48, 52, 75–76; on South African regime, 155; "States' Rights" speech, 146–47; and suburbs, 55–56; "To Restore America" speech, 36; and Trump, 169, 174; and John Wayne, 162

Reagan Doctrine, 39, 107–8, 113–20

Reagan Era Rejects, 16

Reaganism: failed promises of, 47; and fascism, 19, 20, 21, 22, 23, 40, 41, 79, 150, 162; hypocritical aspects of, 30, 53; militarism of, 19; punk rock lyrics on, 4–5, 6, 7, 8, 11, 14, 15, 16, 23–24, 30, 32, 53, 60–61, 63, 66, 89; and wealth, 68

Reaganomics, 30–33

Reagan Revolution: and George H. W. Bush, 170; and Catholics, 95, 97; conservativism of, 72; and Coors Brewing Company, 119; environmentalist counterattack against, 69; and exceptionalist agenda, 37; and far-right-wing conservatism, 160; fiscal policies, 100; and Jesse Helms, 151; initiation of, 10; punk scene's reaction to, 2, 5, 7, 8, 9, 11, 18, 21, 23, 32, 99, 110–11, 125–26, 147, 164, 169; Ronald Reagan's farewell address on, 52

Reagan Youth, 17, 23, 35, 69, 172, 177

Real Evangelism Bible Conferences, 82

Really Red, 15–16, 58, 81, 98, 122, 136, 138, 166

Red C, 142–43, 144

Redd Kross, 61, 62

Red Hot Chili Peppers, 54

Red Krayola, 122

Redwood National Park, 65

Regan, Donald, 41

Rehnquist, William, 158

religion: punk rock lyrics on, 97–100. *See also* Catholics; Christian Right; Moral Majority

Religious Roundtable, 75–76, 77

Replacements, 63

Republican Party: and, 23; and racism, 146–47, 157; Ronald Reagan's role in, 36, 146–47, 155; Southern strategy of, 146, 163; Trump's role in, 174

reverse discrimination, 159

Reyes, Ron (Chavo Pederast), 12, 56, 62, 139, 159

Rich, Frank, 174

Rich, Robert (Dalton Trumbo), 45–46

Richard, Paul, 122

Riefenstahl, Leni, 175–76

Rights of the Accused, 64, 97

right-wing moralism, 53

Roberts, Oral, 94

Robertson, Pat, 75, 89–90

Robison, James, 75

Rock against Reagan, 28, 35, 172

Role, Ron, 33

Rollins, Henry, 12, 14–15, 56, 66, 86, 138, 142

Romero, Oscar, 115
Ronald Reagan Presidential Library, 1, 2
Roosevelt, Franklin Delano, 41
Roosevelt, Theodore "Teddy," 65
Rower, Casey, 23–24
Rowse, Arthur, 31, 53
R Radical Records, 16
Ruland, Jim, 172, 178

Saccharine Trust, 15
Sacred Denial, 83
Sadat, Anwar, 27
Saigon (band), 44
Saunders, Mike, 84–85
Scalia, Antonin, 95
Schaller, Michael, 125
Scheer, Robert, 123, 124
Schlafly, Phyllis, 78
Schmaljohn, Pat, 69
Schwerner, Michael, 147
Scopes trial, 81
Scotland's Exploited, 99
Scream, 143
Screen Actors Guild, 45
Seconds, Kevin, 39, 73, 150, 152
secular humanism, 81
Seeger, Pete, 45–46
Selective Service System, 109, 110, 112–13
Sensitives, 176
Sessions, Jeff, 168–69
7 Seconds, 39–40, 72–73, 87–88, 150, 152–54
Sewer Trout, 118–19
Sex Mutants, 115
SFH (Shit from Hell), 175, 176
Sharptooth, 176–77
Shatter, Will, 4
Shattered Faith, 15, 20–21, 37–38
Shithead, Joey, 19, 34, 176
Shupe, Anson, 75, 94
Silent Age, 90, 113
Sin, 34, 64, 170
Sinister, Simon Bob, 85

skate punk scene, 91
skinheads, 160
slam dancing, 128
Sluts, 109
Smith, Bailey, 82
Smith, Kendon, 155
Smith, Winston, 79
Snobbslakt, 175
Social Distortion, 15, 23, 55
Social Divorce, 177
Social Policy (magazine), 31
Social Unrest, 50, 98
Society System Decontrol, 141–42
Sockeye, 87
Sonic Youth, 170
Sötlimpa, 175
South Africa, 155
Southern Baptist Convention, 82
Southern punk scene, 62–63
Soviet Union: and Afghanistan, 109; and Central America, 115; military superiority of, 36; and Ronald Reagan, 2, 106–8, 120, 124, 125
Spain punk scene, 34, 98–99
Spastic Rats, 154
Speakes, Larry, 152
Spheeris, Penelope, 12, 54, 56, 59
Spike, Kid, 90
Spring, David "Springa," 142
Squip, Tomas, 31
SS Decontrol, 72, 141, 141–42
SST Records, 15, 63
Stabb, John, 29, 56, 91, 143–44
Stahl, Peter, 143
Stains, 134, 162
Stark Raving Mad, 40–41, 150, 166
"Star Spangled Banner," 40
State of Alert (SOA), 12, 14, 142, 143, 144
State of Confusion, 69
Statue of Liberty, 42, 43, 46
Steel, Danielle, 171
Stevenson, Bill, 87
Stewart, Potter, 8
Straw Dogs, 175

Strejcek, Nathan, 82
Strike Under, 17
Subculture, 96
Suburban Death Trip, 121–22
Suburban Filth, 99
Suburban Mutilation, 57
Suburbia (documentary), 54, 56, 59
Subverts, 17
Suicidal Tendencies (ST), 3, 6, 27, 128, 144, 168, 177
Superfund program, 66, 68
Surrogate Brains, 93, 154–55
Sweden punk scene, 34, 35, 98, 175

Taxi Driver (film), 24
Teenage PhDs, 56–57
Teen Idles, 13, 14
televangelism, 89–94
Texas punk scene, 15–16, 58, 132–38, 139, 142
Thatcher, Margaret, 2, 3, 19, 99, 124, 175
Thedic, Pat, 58
The Sarcastic Assholes (TSA), 149
Thompson, Stacy, 169–70
Thorn, Mike, 3–4
Tigre, Tony, 87
Tongue Avulsion, 26
Torres, José Campos, 136–37
Total Chaos, 175
Touch and Go Records, 18
Toxic Reasons, 18, 124, 125, 144
traditional family values, 76, 77
Tragic, Jack, 88, 89
Traina, Nick, 171
Tremblay, Maxwell, 148
Troy, Gil, 10
Troyer, Casey, 115
Trudeau, Pierre, 19
Truman, Harry, 41, 52
Trumbo, Dalton (Robert Rich), 45–46
Trump, Donald, 4, 162, 168–69, 171, 174–81
T.S.O.L. (True Sounds of Liberty), 15, 23, 54, 55, 122

Tunches, Jeff (Spunge Oid), 41, 166
Turner, Nat, 155
Turner, Randy "Biscuit," 16
Tutu, Desmond, 155, 163

UC-Berkeley, 49
Ugly Americans, 85
Ultra Violence, 67
Unaware, 149
Uncommon Valor (film), 114
Undead, 16
Unified Field, 43
Uniform Choice, 72, 97, 121
United Kingdom punk scene, 99, 160
United Mutation, 157
United Nations, 111, 114
United States: and American Dream, 46–50; and exceptionalism, 37, 42, 44, 48; as "home of the brave," 44–46; as "land of the free," 41–44; punk rock lyrics on, 35, 36, 37–46, 47, 48–50, 53, 77
Unite the Right rally (2017), 165
Unseen Force, 98
Up-Tight, 154
Urban Waste, 16, 128, 144
US Bombs, 172
Useless, 16
US State Department, 114, 115, 116
US Supreme Court, 8, 95, 153, 158, 160

Valdez, Raul, 134
Vandals, 23, 54, 55
Vatican Commandos, 154
Vicious, Sid, 70
Vicious Circle, 128
Vietnam Syndrome, 113, 114
Vietnam War, 107, 109, 110, 113–14, 117, 120; veterans of, 35, 113–14
Vig, Butch, 44
Violent Apathy, 18
Violent Image, 149–50
Void, 55, 58, 164–65
Voss, Mike, 91

Walker, Alice, 166
Wallace, George, 157
Warboy, 43
Wartorn, 172
Washington, DC: as national and local space, 14; punk scene in, 12–13, 14, 15, 17, 56, 58, 142–44; and Rock against Reagan tour, 35
Washington, George, 51
Wasted Youth (Los Angeles quartet), 13–14, 19, 20, 79, *101*, 134
Watt, James, 26, 35, 60
Watt, Mike, 15
Wayne, John, 162, 179
Weavers, 45
Weinberger, Casper, 123
Weirdos, 13, 108
Weird Science (film), 49
Westerberg, Paul, 63
West Germany punk scene, 34
Whipping Boy, 38–39
White power movement, 160, 163, 164
White Suburban Youth, 57
White supremacy, 151, 155, 157, 159, 162, 164, 165, 178
White Trash, 82
Wiedlin, Jane, 129

Wiesel, Elie, 21–22
Wild and Scenic Rivers system, 65
Wilentz, Sean, 88
Wilkinson, Bill, 152
Williams, Daniel, 76, 80–81
Wipers, 37
Witcher, Marcus, 174
Women's Action for Nuclear Disarmament, 123
World War III, 108

X (band), 129
X, Malcolm, 155

Yohannan, Tim, 38, 96, 161
Young, 16
Youth Attack, *105*
Youth Brigade (LA), 82
Youth Brigade (Washington, DC), 14, 81, 82
Youth International Party (Yippies), 35
Youth of Today, 72, 154
Youth Patrol, 18

Zeapplin, Lead, 58
Zeroes, 129
Zingarelli, Annelle, 132

www.ingramcontent.com/pod-product-compliance
Lightning Source LLC
Chambersburg PA
CBHW030539230426
43665CB00010B/956